Foreign Earned Income Exclusion

AVOIDING IRS AUDITS OF FORM 2555

Clinton J. Donnelly

Original and modified cover art by NaCDS and CoverDesignStudio.com

Send comments and inquiries to info@donnellytaxlaw.com, mailing address:
Clinton J. Donnelly
337 Garden Oaks Blvd #95616
Houston, TX 77018 USA

Foreign Earned Income: Avoiding IRS Audits of Form 2555
Clinton J. Donnelly. —1st ed.
ISBN 978-0-9986725-0-2

Contents

Dedicated to my wife and muse, Linda.

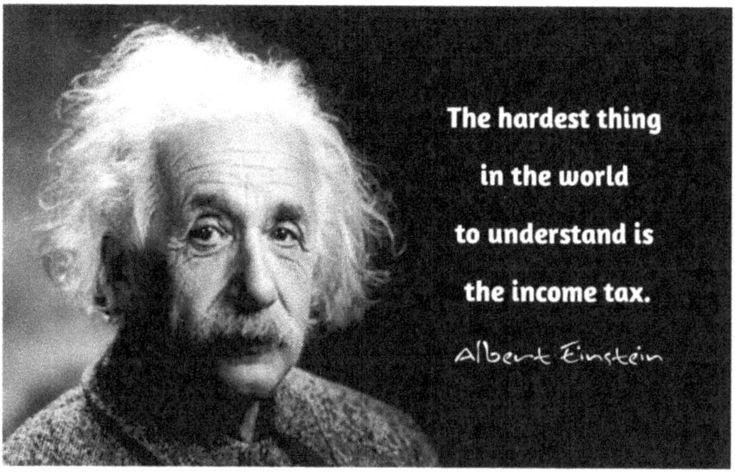
The hardest thing
in the world
to understand is
the income tax.
Albert Einstein

CHAPTER 1

A Giant Tax Break

The Foreign Earned Income Exclusion

The Foreign Earned Income Exclusion (FEIE), reported on IRS form 2555, is one of the most significant tax breaks that a US citizen living abroad can get. It allows you to exempt or exclude from taxation up to $102,100 of income.[1] For most people, that works out to a tremendous savings, up to $21,000. In fact, FEIE is one of the best tax breaks available.

Furthermore, if you live abroad and your employer provides either an allowance for housing or pays for housing directly, a housing exclusion may apply. If so, you can also exclude a portion of those costs from your taxes as well. Self-employed people can get the same break through a housing deduction (as opposed to an exclusion).

The tax break is a good incentive to work abroad, during which time you do not normally pay state income tax on your foreign income or Obamacare taxes. When you file for these tax breaks, it is essential to fill out the forms correctly to reduce the chances of being audited by the IRS.

While other books on the market merely state the rules for FEIE, this book is unique because it explains how to reduce your risk of failing an IRS audit of the form. This book includes summaries of over 300 court

[1] The amount that can be excluded is set each year by the IRS. Here are the recent limits: $92,900 (2011), $95,100 (2012), $97,600 (2013), $99,200 (2014), $100,800 (2015), $101,300 (2016), $102,100 (2017).

cases of real people with unique situations, perhaps like yours, and how the courts applied the law. The money you save properly using FEIE and avoiding audits should greatly exceed the cost of this book.

While the concept of exclusion is easy to understand, determining whether you qualify for exclusion can be complicated, and the more you dig into the details, the more complicated it gets.

Are you qualified?

FEIE is a tremendous program for qualified individuals. To be deemed "qualified," you must meet certain criteria:

- You must have foreign earned income—income earned in a foreign country.
- You must have your tax home in a foreign country.
- You must be eligible for the exclusion.

First, you must have foreign earned income (IRC 911(b)). [2] This is income that results from your own labor, whether in wages as an employee or, if self-employed, as personal services. Foreign earned income is not passive income like investment income, interest, or dividends.

Next, your home for the year must be in a foreign country (Regs 1.911-2(a)).[3] This is the most common point that auditors will contest to disqualify a person from FEIE. To demonstrate that your tax home for the year is in a foreign country, you must satisfy one of two tests: The Bona Fide Residence Test or The Physical Presence Test. This topic will be explored in several chapters in the book.

The final criterion for qualification for FEIE is that you be eligible for exclusion (Regs 1.911-7(a)). To be eligible, you must be filing your taxes in a timely manner, you must not have previously revoked your right to use the exclusion, and you must not be precluded by treaty benefits. Most importantly, you must file or amend your return to use the exclusion before the IRS initiates an inquiry or audit of your return.

[2] The abbreviation IRC 911 means the Internal Revenue Code, which is reproduced in the Internal Revenue Code chapter.

[3] The abbreviation Regs 1.911 refers to the Internal Revenue Regulations section 1.911 which is reproduced in the Internal Revenue Regulations chapter.

What is the purpose of FEIE?

The purpose of FEIE is to promote the expansion of US businesses overseas. The assumption is that foreign expansion is good for the US economy, which benefits from increased exports and repatriation of profits.

The US taxation system was established in 1913. It is based on a principle of *worldwide taxation* of the income of US citizens and legal permanent residents or Green Card holders. This means someone born in the US who grew up abroad may still have an obligation to file and pay income taxes even if they have never returned to the US since birth.

Each country is free to establish its own income taxation scheme. Most countries practice some variation of a *territorial taxation system*, meaning that a taxpayer only pays taxes to the country when his or her home (abode) is in that country. If a person leaves that country for an indefinite period, that person can pay reduced or no taxes there.

The FEIE is now about 90 years old and it is not likely to disappear. Congress has re-examined the rationale for keeping the FEIE many times and has not removed it. In fact, other benefits for foreign workers have been added over time, such as the foreign tax credit and double taxation treaties. They have even made claiming the FEIE easier in several ways. For example, the physical presence test was reduced from 550 days in 18 months to 330 days in 12 months.

Worldwide taxation puts US citizens and legal residents at an income disadvantage compared to expats from other countries. Consider the example of a multinational energy company, which needs to send a worker to Indonesia for three years. Imagine that the company is considering sending either a British or a worker from the US. Because the United Kingdom practices territorial taxation, the British worker, if hired, would enjoy an increase in take home pay because he or she would not pay UK income tax anymore. The US worker, however, would receive no such benefit. Both workers incur the extra expense of moving their home abroad, but the worker from the US gets no financial relief from the government tax system for the sacrifice. If the employer gives the US worker a temporary pay increase as an incentive, the US worker becomes a more expensive option to the employer.

A tax court case in 1926 lost by the taxpayer highlighted this disadvantage for US citizens working abroad. Congress responded by amending the tax code by adding the FEIE to provide relief to US workers for the competitive disadvantage caused by the worldwide taxation of its citizens.

Goals of this book

Remember that the primary purpose of the IRS and any tax system is to bring in money for a government. At the time of this writing, the US government is a staggering $20 trillion in debt, and the government needs big money fast. A mountain of high-speed computers is scouring through tax returns to catch mistakes, and these very computers will eventually analyze your returns. IRS Revenue Officers (auditors) are on a monthly quota to bring in additional tax collections. If Revenue Officers can deny your claim of exclusion, they can quickly bring in up to $25,000, depending on how much you excluded, plus the 20% accuracy penalty and interest. They can also typically discredit your exclusion over multiple years, making the fines even higher.

The goals of this book are threefold: to help you prepare FEIE form 2555 without committing the common errors that alert IRS computers; to explain in detail how the exclusions work; and to equip you with primary sources of information such as the Internal Revenue Code, the Internal Revenue Regulations court opinions on 301 cases related to exclusions to help you make filing decisions.

CHAPTER 2

Expect to be Audited

Expect to be audited by the IRS

Be aware that the IRS is auditing foreign returns at a rate 19 times higher than domestic filers.[4] Your likelihood of being audited is roughly 5% each year. If you live abroad for twenty years, it is highly likely that you will get audited, either through an inquiry letter from the IRS—an "automated audit"—or a direct contact with a Revenue Officer (which is more serious). The premise of this book is that the best way to avoid audits is to be careful about how you complete form 2555.

Taxes are about obeying laws

Are taxes about accounting or laws? The short answer is taxes are about complying with laws. Some of those laws require applying generally accepted accounting principles (accounting rules). While filing taxes can involve complex accounting rules, especially for companies, tax software and tax reporting documents (W-2 and 1099s) simplify the accounting aspects for individual domestic filers. However, foreign filers must file *information returns* in addition to *tax returns*, and information returns are legally complex. The penalties for failing to file

---

[4] Internal Revenue Service, "IRS 2015 Data Book (2016) <www.irs.gov/pub/irs-soi/15databk.pdf> accessed 18 Oct. 2016.

or falsely filing information returns dwarf the penalties applied to tax returns, so filing the information return correctly is crucial.

When you sign your tax and information returns, you are agreeing to the following statement: "Under penalties of perjury, I declare that I have examined this return and accompanying schedules and statements, and to the best of my knowledge and belief, they are true, correct, and complete."[5] The penalty for perjury is up to five years in prison. Filing a fraudulent tax return carries a penalty of up to $250,000, five years in prison, and an additional 75% penalty on taxes owed. Filing information returns and tax returns is, therefore, not a responsibility to be taken lightly.

The FEIE lets people exclude the first $102,100[6] from taxation, equaling about $21,000. If the IRS determines in an audit that you were not eligible for FEIE, then you will owe that tax (up to $21,000), plus a 20% accuracy related penalty ($4,200) and interest on both. It is important to be certain you are eligible for the exclusion before filing, and this book will help you to do that.

What do the tax code and regulations say about FEIE?

Information from the legal sources on FEIE will allow you to become more familiar and confident with this process. I am providing you with access to the primary sources of the law on this topic, namely the complete texts of the Internal Revenue Code and the Internal Revenue Regulations regarding FEIE. In addition, I have provided a topical arrangement of tax court cases related to foreign earned income exclusion so that you can learn from other peoples' experience.

Most peoples' understanding of FEIE comes from reading IRS publication 54, the instructions for form 2555, and information on the IRS website. While this information is useful, it is very important to know that the courts do not consider either these publications or any opinions of an IRS employee as forms of substantive law. It follows that

---

[5] IRS form 1040, p. 2.

[6] This limit changes year to year. Always check the current limit for your tax year

you should not rely on your reading of these documents to decide whether to take exclusion or not. The Code, Regulations, and rulings are substantive; therefore, they are more important than forms and instructions. You are responsible for complying with the law, not necessarily with what is written in the instructions for the form. If you are not comfortable with this responsibility, you should get experienced help.

No more hiding

Until recently, some people hid their financial affairs while living abroad. They did not report their income or file taxes and may have lived in locations considered tax havens to enable hiding. These days are effectively over. The IMF and OECD have slowly increased international cooperation to increase transparency and tax justice.

In 1988, the OECD created the Convention on Mutual Administrative Assistance in Tax Matters. Twenty years later, in 2009, in response to the 2008 global financial crisis, the G20 meeting of finance ministers and central bank governors called on all countries to sign the Convention and cooperate.[7] In 2016, they reiterated their call.[8] Presently, 108 countries have signed, including all 34 OECD countries, the EU, the G20 countries and many developing countries. Some smaller countries in need of financial assistance may be pressured by the IMF and OECD to sign the Convention. To see the complete list of the Convention signees, see the later chapter listing the Convention members.

The Convention calls on member countries to provide administrative assistance to other countries, stating that "such administrative assistance shall comprise: exchange of information, including simultaneous tax examinations and participation in tax examinations abroad; assistance in recovery, including measures of conservancy; and service of

---

[7] G20 Research Group, "G20 Leaders Statement: The Pittsburgh Summit" (2009) <www.g20.utoronto.ca/2009/2009communique0925.html#system> 28 Jan. 2017.

[8] G20 Research Group, "G20 Leaders Statement: The Hangzhou Summit" (2016) <www.g20.utoronto.ca/2016/160905-communique.html> 28 Jan. 2017.

documents."[9] In layman's terms, "tax examinations" are audits; "measures of conservancy" is seizing assets in foreign countries; "service of documents" is legal actions like liens and civil lawsuits, and "assistance in recovery" is exchanging information about someone alleged to be evading the payment of foreign taxes.

The US Foreign Account Tax Compliance Act (FATCA) laws represent a unilateral action to force all banks in the world to disclose bank account information about US citizens and legal residents to the IRS. In 2016, banks started to disclose this information. FATCA is unique to the US because it leveraged the de facto "reserve currency" status of the US dollar to compel banks to comply. In fact, the US is likely the only country that could have enforced a unilateral law on the rest of the world.

Other countries saw the benefit of having foreign bank information and the "automatic exchange of information" sections of the Convention have been elaborated for exchanging bank information between participating countries. Some have nicknamed the law "GATCA" because it is like a "global FATCA" for other countries. The OECD has developed Common Reporting Standard (CRS) for exchanging this information, to be applied starting in November 2017. The US, however, has not agreed to the common reporting standards, so at this time, the US is not sharing US bank account information owned by foreigners with foreign countries. We can expect this to change in the future.

This new spirit of cooperation is in sharp contrast to the lack of cooperation in the pre-globalization tax haven days. Many countries, including the US, include mechanisms for mutual enforcement in bilateral tax treaties with other countries; in other words, this is a standard feature of international tax treaties today.

---

[9] Convention on Mutual Administrative Assistance in Tax Matters, amended, chapter 1, article 1 <www.oecd.org/ctp/exchange-of-tax-information/ENG-Amended-Convention.pdf>

The IRS is targeting foreign filers & non-filers

The IRS has been organizing for the aggressive pursuit of both foreign tax filers and non-filers. Statistics suggest that 85% of US taxpayers abroad are not filing tax returns.[10] Of the 15% who are filing, over half claim FEIE.[11]

Following the US tax code and paying taxes is voluntary. It is your responsibility to file in order to receive the benefit of FEIE and any other tax credits and deductions. You have three years—with late filing penalties—to submit or amend a tax return. After that, no tax filing can be made. The IRS has three years to find a problem with your filing. If you do not file a tax return, then the statute of limitations doesn't apply, and you are indefinitely vulnerable. The IRS can go back as far as they want to charge you for both back taxes and tax evasion. Therefore, it is very important to file a tax return every year, even if you owe $0 in taxes. Filing taxes starts the statute of limitation clock, and this can protect you.

A very common misconception held by foreign filers is the belief that, since the FEIE would exclude all your income and you would owe $0 in taxes, you do not have to file. The reality is that you do not get the exclusion *unless* you file.

For many decades now, US taxpayers abroad have been responsible for filing foreign information returns. These returns are different from tax returns because there is no tax owed. The information returns declare information about foreign owned or controlled assets. The most commonly known information return is called the Foreign Bank Account Report (FBAR) and is reported on form FinCen-114. This form is required if the total of your foreign financial bank accounts is $10,000 or more during the year. Recall that you are required simply to report the accounts; there is no tax. The penalties for not filing an information

---

10 Internal Revenue Service, "IRS 2015 Data Book" (2016) <hwww.irs.gov/pub/irs-soi/15databk.pdf> accessed 18 Oct. 2016.

11 US Government Accountability Office, "Tax Policy: Economic Benefits of Income Exclusion for U.S. Citizens Working Abroad are Uncertain" (2014) GAO-14-387.

return can quickly exceed $100,000. The IRS is targeting those not reporting.

Similar to the FBAR is form 8938 for reporting foreign assets, which includes everything reported on the FBAR plus all other foreign assets and investment contracts with foreigners. The penalty for not filing form 8938 when required starts at $10,000 when the IRS mails you an inquiry letter. The fine grows to $50,000 if you do not respond to the letter within six months, after which time the IRS can order that your US passport be revoked. In addition, the IRS can assess a 50% penalty of the value of unreported assets per each year. If you have not been filing, then the statute of limitation clock has not been started, and the IRS can assess penalties that could reach five times the value of the asset! This is enormous.

When are information returns required?

There are more foreign information forms the IRS wants filed each year. If you own or control directly or indirectly through others 10% or more of a foreign company, you must file a return. If you are a partner in a foreign partnership, you must file a return. If you own or benefit from a foreign trust or foundation, you must file a return. Furthermore, if you purchased foreign insurance, you owe a quarterly excise tax on the insurance premiums, and any transfers of assets to foreign person or businesses need to be rcported.

The penalty for not filing all necessary foreign information returns is similar to the penalty for not filing form 8938. There is an immediate $10,000 penalty when you receive the IRS inquiry letter and it grows to $50,000 if not responded to in six months. Because the IRS only communicates by letter to your last address in their files, it is relatively easy to end up owing the IRS $50,000 without even knowing about it.

In addition, there are penalties per year varying from 40-50% of the value of the assets, meaning that multiple years can be penalized if not reported. Total penalties could exceed five times the value of the assets. An important court case is that of Charles Zwerner, who held more or less $800,000 in an offshore bank account, unreported. After appeals, the final decision was that Zwerner was fined $3.4 million dollars, over four times the account balance!

If you need to file an information return, understand that it is more complex than a tax return. While tax returns are about accounting issues, information returns involve legal issues. Unless you have a strong legal background, I do not advise that you handle information returns yourself. It is best to hire an Enrolled Agent or tax lawyer who has significant experience in foreign information returns. Your advisor can also advise you to participate in one of several "tax amnesty" voluntary disclosure programs to protect you against past incorrect filings.

CHAPTER 3

Form Part I

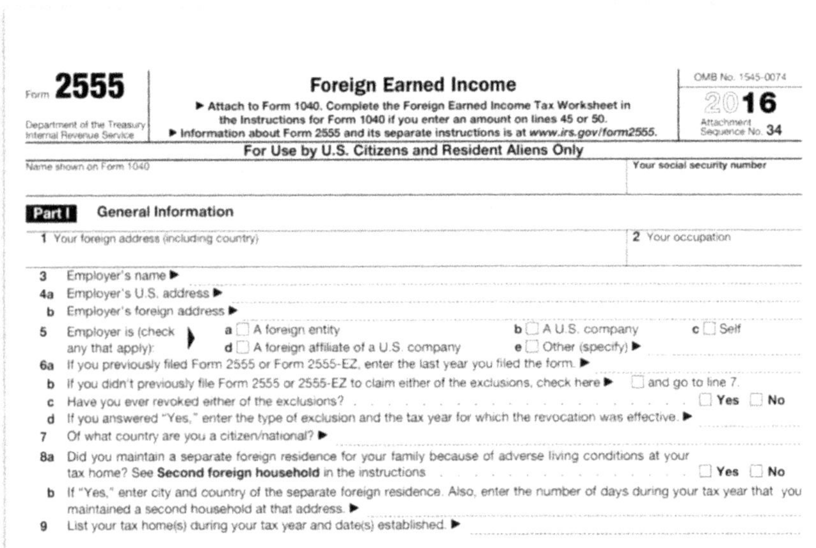

Form **2555**

Department of the Treasury
Internal Revenue Service

Foreign Earned Income

▶ Attach to Form 1040. Complete the Foreign Earned Income Tax Worksheet in the Instructions for Form 1040 if you enter an amount on lines 45 or 50.
▶ Information about Form 2555 and its separate instructions is at *www.irs.gov/form2555.*

OMB No. 1545-0074
2016
Attachment Sequence No. 34

For Use by U.S. Citizens and Resident Aliens Only

Name shown on Form 1040 | **Your social security number**

Part I **General Information**

1 Your foreign address (including country) | 2 Your occupation

3 Employer's name ▶
4a Employer's U.S. address ▶
b Employer's foreign address ▶
5 Employer is (check any that apply): a ☐ A foreign entity b ☐ A U.S. company c ☐ Self d ☐ A foreign affiliate of a U.S. company e ☐ Other (specify) ▶
6a If you previously filed Form 2555 or Form 2555-EZ, enter the last year you filed the form. ▶
b If you didn't previously file Form 2555 or 2555-EZ to claim either of the exclusions, check here ▶ ☐ and go to line 7.
c Have you ever revoked either of the exclusions? . . . ☐ **Yes** ☐ **No**
d If you answered "Yes," enter the type of exclusion and the tax year for which the revocation was effective. ▶
7 Of what country are you a citizen/national? ▶
8a Did you maintain a separate foreign residence for your family because of adverse living conditions at your tax home? See **Second foreign household** in the instructions . . . ☐ **Yes** ☐ **No**
b If "Yes," enter city and country of the separate foreign residence. Also, enter the number of days during your tax year that you maintained a second household at that address. ▶
9 List your tax home(s) during your tax year and date(s) established. ▶

Are you a qualified individual?

Part I of form 2555 is innocently entitled "General Information," but it is very significant because this section is one of the three key tests determining whether you qualify for exclusion. Most people find these questions somewhat random. Some people are suspicious about disclosing too much information or too little information, but the answer to each question has the potential to trigger an audit and cause the loss of exclusion.

Your foreign address

Which address should you put on line 1?

There are five audit risk reduction ideas for completing the foreign address:

1. Do not use a US address; it undermines your claim to a tax home in a foreign country. The address you use on form 2555 can be different from the address you use on form 1040. The address for form 1040 should be a US address where you can always be reached—maybe the home of a relative or a mail forwarding address.

2. In contrast, the address for form 2555 line 1 *must be a foreign address where you lived during the tax year.* No mail will be sent to this address.

   Your recordkeeping must prove that you actually live at the address. The best proofs include your name, the address, and a date during the tax year. Examples include a lease agreement, receipts of lease payments, and a utility bill (not telephone). The more evidence, the better. Photos are okay, but legal documents and invoices from utilities are best. Keep this evidence for at least six years if not indefinitely.

3. If you lived at multiple foreign addresses during the year, how do you fill out line 1? You need to provide all the addresses. Write "See Statement 1,"[12] then attach a statement

---

[12] There may be other statements, so it doesn't have to specifically be "1". Follow the format. Your tax software may provide a means for doing this.

to the return entitled "Statement 1" listing the addresses of each residence during the year. Again, keep records of legal proof that you lived there.

4. What if you lived in hotels or hostels? This is not a problem. Many people, especially single people or high-tech nomads, live in rented quarters permanently. However, one of the requirements of a qualified individual is that your tax home is in a foreign country. So, your address needs to project some permanence as evidence of living there. Renting for short periods, by the night or by the week, does not suggest that you have moved your tax home. Again, keep your receipts.

   It would be better to obtain a monthly lease agreement allowing for multiple months of leasing. Of course, you will need proof that you stayed for months, such as payment receipts (More on this in the discussion of line 9 on tax home.) If you frequently change locations because you are an itinerant or nomadic worker, your home is where your work location is.

5. If you fly home to the US every few weekends, this conduct suggests that you are keeping ties in the US and that you are maintaining a tax home in the US. This common mistake will undermine your claim to a foreign tax home and your eligibility for exclusion, and can end up costing you more than just airfare!

Your occupation

To qualify for the exclusion, you need to be performing what the IRS calls "personal services." There are three audit related risks related to occupation:

The occupation you name must support the perception that you are doing personal services. Here are four examples of what **not** to write as occupation:

1. Claiming that you are "retired" does not suggest that you are performing personal services. This is a tempting response for people who have retired from their job in the US and are doing some form of labor abroad.

2. Claiming that your occupation is "visitor" does not suggest that you are performing personal services. This may be what you told foreign immigration officials out of fear that the IRS would somehow cross check to see what you claimed you were doing. Do not have this worry.

3. Finally, claiming that you are "self-employed" does not support your claim of performing personal services. People engaged in generating passive income like investors can claim to be self-employed but it doesn't support your obligation to prove that you are engaged in personal services. Line 5 offers you the place to indicate that you are self-employed, but here, be more specific about the type of services you do.

4. Other examples of what not to say are owner, investor, financier, nomad or other professions that don't imply that personal services were being done by you.

The occupation you cite on Form 2555 line 2 must be the same as the occupation you put in the signature block area on Form 1040 page 2. Inconsistency in occupation may lead to an uncomfortable discussion with an auditor.

Further, you should keep proof in your permanent records that you actually were engaged in a certain profession and conducted personal services. Examples of evidence include pay slips from employers, any records from an employer with time stamps during the tax year or other employer recognition. If you are audited four years from now, how can you prove you were performing personal services in a foreign country? For self-employed persons, evidence can be client invoices with proof of payment.

Your employer's name

Who is your employer? The employer is the company that pays or paid you and your pay slips or other evidence of work should have this company's name on it.

1. If you worked for multiple employers during a year, enter "See Statement 1" and attach a separate page entitled "Statement 1" listing all the employers and their US and/or foreign address (lines 4a and 4b). If you do this, you can leave lines 4a and 4b blank because the addresses are on the statement.

2. If you were self-employed, write "self-employed" on line 3, leave line 4a blank, and put your own address on line 4b. If you are self-employed, you are subject to self-employment taxes.

Your employer's address

Be very careful about which address you put down as your employer's address. Multinational companies have many addresses. Which one should you enter in these lines? I recommend putting down the local address of the company employing you, not a national or divisional headquarters. Check to see what address is used on the check or pay slip and use this address because it agrees with your other proof of performing personal services.

There are three audit risks related to employer's address:

1. Entering a US address for your employer creates an audit point because US employers must issue a W-2 form each year to their employees. Does your tax return have a W-2 showing income from the employer? If you put a US address

and do not have a W-2, it suggests that you did not report all your income on your tax return. An auditor will detect this inconsistency.

2. If your employer was a US employer and has given you a 1099 form instead of a W-2, then the employer is treating you as an independent contractor, which is different than being an employer. You probably should not be listing this entity as an employer because it sees itself as your client.

3. If you are self-employed, be very careful to list only a foreign address as your address. Do not put a US address, not even your US mailing address, because this suggests that you are maintaining a US tax home.

The type of employer

This question touches on issues like those regarding employer address.

There are five audit risks related to type of employer:

1. If your employer issues you a W-2 or 1099 tax document reporting your income, then you should check the "US employer" box. There should also be a US address on line 4a.

2. If your income was from self-employment, check that box. Note that self-employed people are subject to self-employment tax.

3. A "foreign entity" is any company, partnership, trust, or non-profit that is incorporated under the laws of a foreign country.

4. The distinction between "foreign entity" and "foreign affiliate" needs to be clearly understood.

a. "Foreign affiliate" has a very specific meaning that is not clear on the form or the form instructions. Do not check this box unless you are certain it applies.

b. The meaning of foreign affiliate comes from Title II Social Security Act: "A foreign affiliate is any entity (not just a foreign corporation) in which an American employer owns at least a 10% interest in voting stock or profits. This ownership may be direct or through one or more entities."[13]

c. Be aware that checking "foreign affiliate" will lead to deeper questions about the nature of who your employer was during an audit. A US employer has the option to extend social security and Medicare benefits to US citizens and permanent residents. Of course, extending benefits means that the employer and the employee are responsible to pay social security and Medicare benefits. During an audit, an auditor would look for evidence that you, as the employee, paid these tax obligations. See the chapter on employment tax.

5. Multinational companies based in the US may choose to register themselves in a foreign country. Companies do this when they want to engage in business in the foreign company without giving up their international identity. They will usually establish a local office in a foreign country where people work. In tax treaty parlance, this is called a "permanent establishment." In this case, the business is both a foreign entity and a foreign affiliate, but I would check foreign entity, since only one box can be checked.

---

[13] IRS Form 2032 (2016)

Revoked exclusions

Revoked exclusions are, in my opinion, a senseless complexity designed to deprive foreign workers of flexibility and to entrap them in the complexity of the tax code. Let's dissect what it means to revoke exclusion.

Before you can revoke exclusion, you must first "elect" exclusion. The FEIE and the housing exclusion are elected by using them on form 2555 in a return. The first time you complete form 2555, you have effectively elected to exclude either your foreign income or housing or both, depending on how you completed the form. Once you make this election, it remains in effect for subsequent years until you revoke the election.

How is the election revoked? It is revoked by simply not claiming the exclusion on your return. The most likely scenario is when someone is working offshore for a while and determines that using the foreign tax credit (form 1116) will save him or her a couple thousand dollars more than using the exclusion during that year.

Here's the rub: when exclusion is revoked, you are prohibited from claiming the exclusion again for five years. This is what the form questions are aiming for.

There are three audit risks related to revoked exclusions:

1. Line 6a should always be the prior tax year, assuming you filed a form 2555. If you did not file from 2555 for the previous year, list the last year you filed. If you previously revoked your election, this year should be five tax years before the current tax year. A number five year or less is an audit point.

2. If there is a story why it is not the last tax year, I recommend entering "See Statement 1" and attaching an explanation of the answer. This approach frustrates the IRS computers, which are doing simple number checks. At the same time, you are being forthright.

3. If this is the first year you have filed a form 2555 in your life, you can leave 6a, 6c and 6d blank.

If you have filed form 2555 before but never used the housing exclusion, this is not the same as revoking the housing exclusion. Again, to revoke exclusion, you first would have had to invoke it. Be cautious, because any confusion here can attract audit questions.

What if you have used form 2555 to invoke the exclusion and the housing exclusion/deduction, but then in the next year, you do not need the housing exclusion? What should you do? If you fail to invoke the housing exclusion in a year, then you have "revoked" the housing exclusion and you must wait six years to use it again. I recommend completing the form to use the housing exclusion even if the excluded amount turns out to be $0; this prevents you from automatically revoking the housing exclusion and it takes nothing away from your income exclusion.

Of what country are you a citizen or national?

A citizen by definition has an implied right to be in a country without needing a visa. If you are a citizen of another country than the US, you should list that foreign country, particularly if it is connected to your foreign earned income or tax home in any manner.

This citizenship becomes useful later in the bona fide residence test and tax home test.

What about a second foreign household?

When we consider the question of a second foreign household, it begs the question of where is the *first* foreign household? The first foreign household is the residence where you as the earner of foreign income live. However, for some people, this location may be too dangerous, unhealthy or otherwise adverse for your spouse and dependents to live in.[14]

[14] 26 USC 911(c)(3)(B).

If your spouse and dependents live outside the US but not with you, that place is considered a second foreign household. In such a case, the expense of the first and the second households could be included in the calculation of the housing exclusion. If the first household is not dangerous, unhealthy, or adverse, then the costs of the second household are not includable in the housing exclusion.

CHAPTER 4

Where is your Tax Home?

The last question of Part 1 is perhaps the trickiest question to answer correctly during an audit. To qualify as someone who can claim the foreign earned income exclusion, your tax home must be in a foreign country and you must meet either the bona fide residence or physical presence tests. To understand what a "tax home" is, we must differentiate it from an "abode." Both terms have special meanings in tax law. During an audit, an auditor would likely quiz you on matters related to these two definitions. The easiest way for an IRS auditor to deny your exclusion is to determine that you didn't have a foreign tax home. This is a very subjective decision. Many of the court opinions in the chapter on court cases are denials of foreign tax home.

So, what is a tax home?

> *Your tax home is your main place of business, employment, or post of duty regardless of where you maintain your family home. If you do not have a regular or main place of business because of the nature of your work, then your tax home is the place where you regularly live. If you do not fit either of these categories, you are considered an itinerant and your tax home is wherever you work.*[15]

In contrast, the Tax Court and appellate courts have used the following definition of "abode" found in the Bujol decision:

[15] IRS form 8840; 26 Code 911(d)(3).

> *" 'Abode' has been variously defined as one's home, habitation, residence, domicile, or place of dwelling (Black's Law Dictionary 7, 5th ed. 1979). While an exact definition of 'abode' depends upon the context in which the word is used, it clearly does not mean one's principal place of business. Thus, "abode" has a domestic rather than vocational meaning, and stands in contrast to 'tax home' as defined for purposes of section" 162(a)(2) Bujol, 53 T.C.M. at 763.*[16]

An abode is also defined as

> *"the country in which he [or she] has the strongest economic, family, and personal ties... A taxpayer posted abroad will invariably have some connections with the foreign country in which he [or she] works, but if his [or her] ties to the United States are stronger, we have held that his [or her] "abode" remains in the United States."*[17]

Tax home, then, is the place of business, and abode is the location with the strongest ties. If your abode is in the US and you are working in a foreign country, then you are likely just on a travel assignment in a foreign country. Once you move your family, personal, and economic ties to a foreign country, then your foreign work site changes from a travel destination to a tax home.

A key characteristic of a tax home is whether it is temporary or indefinite. An individual is not considered to have a tax home in a foreign country at any time when their abode is in the US. Similarly, if your tax home is in a foreign country, temporary presence or maintenance of a dwelling in the US does not mean that your abode is in the US, even if your spouse and children use the dwelling.

Since moving an abode to a foreign country does not mean breaking all ties with the US, the challenge is proving that the foreign country is the "closer connection" from an economic, personal and family perspective.

The tax courts have made it clear that if your abode is in the US, you cannot have a foreign tax home. This is the most important issue for you when claiming FEIE. If the auditor feels that you do not have a tax home

---

[16] Office of Chief Counsel Memorandum AM2009-003 released 2/13/2009.

[17] Harrington v. Commissioner, 93 T.C. 297 p. 308 (1989)(holding that oilfield worker lacked "abode" in Angola). Evans, p. 9.

because your abode is not in a foreign country, the auditor will deny your exclusion and hit you with a stiff 20% penalty and back taxes. In tax court, it is your responsibility to prove that your abode is in a foreign country, all the while recognizing that the decision made by the court is subjective. You are wise to retain all evidence with your tax records.

Interestingly, the same topic arises when determining if an alien has acquired a closer connection to the US than to his or her home country. The IRS has developed a "closer connection" test with form 8840, which is also useful in determining abode. We will use this form to take a closer look at abode.

Disputing your claim that your abode and tax home are in a foreign country is usually the easiest way for an IRS Revenue Officer (auditor) to disqualify your exclusion based on a subjective decision.

Here are 27 audit risk points on the topic of whether your tax home and abode are in a foreign country. Expect a revenue officer to ask you these or similar questions:

1) *What type of visa do you have for entering the foreign country?*
   Does the visa give you a right to extended residence in the country for greater than a year or permanently? Using a visitor visa suggests a weak connection.

2) *Of what country or countries were you a citizen during the tax year?*
   Clearly, citizenship is a strong tie. If the US is your only citizenship, then you have an extra burden to prove a stronger connection elsewhere.

3) *What country or countries issued you a passport?*
   Some people can get a passport without having citizenship. For example, United Nations workers have a U.N. passport that they can travel on. Be careful if claiming to have other passports, because an auditor can ask to see the entry and exit visa stamps. Which passport do you use to enter and exit the tax home country? Using your US passport suggests greater reliance and thus a closer connection to the US.

4) *What are your passport numbers?*
New numbers are usually given when passports are re-issued, so always keep old passports to prove travel.

5) *Enter the number of days you were present in the United States during the last three years.*
This question relates to the bona fide residence test or physical presence tests.

6) *Did you apply for, or take other affirmative steps to apply for, lawful permanent resident status in the foreign country or have an application pending to change your status to that of a lawful permanent resident of that country?*
This question allows for applications to be in process. The act of applying is in itself an important proof of trying to establish a closer connection to a foreign country. Remember to obtain proof of applying. A letter from a foreign immigration lawyer affirming that an application is submitted is a good start.

7) *Where was your tax home on January 1st of the tax year?*

8) *After changing your tax home from its location on January 1st, where was your tax home for the remainder of the tax year?*
These questions touch on where your primary tax home was for the tax year. A reasonable follow up question is how much of your income you made in each tax home. This gets to the question of how much of the income is foreign earned income.

9) *Were you subject to tax as a resident under the internal laws of foreign countries for the period during which you maintained a tax home in each country?*
It may be difficult to prove you are subject to foreign income tax unless you actually file a tax return in the foreign

country.

10) *Have you filed or will you file tax returns for the tax year in the foreign countries?*
Filing income tax in a foreign country shows a strong connection even if the amount of tax paid is $0. In a counter-intuitive way, filing a foreign tax return could support your claim for exclusion. There are court cases where this was a determining factor.

11) *Where was your regular or principal permanent home located during the tax year?*
This question uses the terms "regular" and "principal" to again ascertain the location of your abode(s). If you had more than one permanent home available to you during the tax year, list the location of each and explain.

12) *Where was your family located?*
This is another way of asking where your abode was. Your tax proofs should include evidence that your family members were located at the abode in a foreign country. Examples of this evidence include passport entry/exit visa stamps, visa documents from a foreign country showing permission to be in a foreign country, and photos of boarding passes. There are court cases where this was a determining factor.

13) *Where was your automobile(s) located?*
If you expect to be indefinitely in a foreign location, you are more likely to sell your US car and own a car in a foreign country. A sales receipt of your car in the US is good evidence that you do not own a car there, and a purchase contract, insurance contract, and annual registration documents are good evidence that you own a car in a foreign country. These should be kept with your tax records. This question can be powerful in determining closer connection.

If you keep that old car in the US at your parent's house, it shows intent to maintain a tax home in the US. It could be an expensive car to keep if it costs you your exclusion! Similarly, owning or leasing a car long term in a foreign country is a forceful argument of an expectation of indefinite presence in a foreign country. In countries where you could easily rely on public transportation, metro, or taxis, ownership of a car might still make sense to prove your tax home. Consider buying a junk car and keeping it registered. Even if you never drive the car or lose some money on its future sale, it may be a bargain compared to losing exclusion.

14) *Where was your automobile(s) registered?*
Car registration shows your annual intent to be present in a foreign country. If you own your car in the name of a foreign company (common in certain countries for liability protection), you should retain evidence of ownership in the name of the company.

15) *Where were your personal belongings, furniture, etc., located?*
Clearly, shipping all your belongings to a foreign country to be with you is a powerful closer connection argument showing that you have committed yourself to a foreign country as your abode and tax home. Putting all your belongings in storage or your parent's basement suggests that your abode is more transient and is not as strong an argument for a foreign country as closer connection. Given the cost of a storage unit for an extended period and the risk of losing exclusion, it might be better to sell most of your goods on Craigslist than to hold on to them.

16) *Where was the bank(s) with which you conducted your routine personal banking activities located?*
This is a tricky question. Going to the bank to get money is a powerful indicator of where you are spending money. However, obtaining foreign bank accounts has become

increasingly difficult. Having a foreign bank account shows that you expect to be there indefinitely. That is good, especially if you can show regular transactions with a bank statement. Some expats keep all their money in the US and depend on ATM machines to withdraw money in foreign countries as their primary way of doing banking. Having and using foreign bank accounts is a strong closer connection argument. Not having them shows that you keep a close connection to the US economically. It is not necessary to dismantle your US assets and investments, but it is worth the time to get a foreign bank account to demonstrate your commitment to a foreign tax home and abode.

17) *Did you conduct business activities in a location other than your tax home? (Yes or No; If yes, where?)*
This is a tricky question because a tax home is where business activities occur. If you answer yes, consider carefully how the answer might undermine your claim of a foreign tax home. Note that it is possible to have multiple foreign tax homes during a year.

18) *Where was your driver's license issued? If you hold a second driver's license, where was it issued?*
Most countries will allow you to use your native driver's license for a couple months but then require you to register locally. If you fly a lot, you might find you can get away with not having to get a foreign driver's license, but this elusiveness may be expensive. It usually takes only a day or two to get a foreign license. This effort shows a strong closer connection. Likewise, letting your US driver's license expire indicates a strong closer connection to the foreign country.

19) *Where are you registered to vote?*
Of course, you cannot vote in a foreign country unless you are a citizen of that country, but you can register for absentee voting. Even if you don't think your vote counts for

much, registering for absentee voting shows your intent to be absent from your former tax home.

20) *When completing official documents, forms, etc., what country do you list as your residence?*
This is a great question if you have a copy of an official document to show as evidence. If you do not have or cannot obtain a copy of an official document or cannot remember what country you listed as your residence, it should not be used against you, but you should always think about this question when you do sign official documents.

21) *Have you ever completed a form W-8BEN or any other W-8 or W-9 form (relating to foreign status)?*
These are documents employees give to US employers regarding their tax status. W-8BEN is for non-US citizens and W-9 is for US citizens. US citizens working for US employers who would qualify for exclusion should consider giving their employers form 673 which claims an exemption from tax withholding because you are in a foreign country. Form 673 is a legal document showing evidence of your foreign tax home and is very helpful for showing closer connection.

22) *In what country or countries did you keep your personal, financial, and legal documents?*
If you plan to be indefinitely in a foreign country, you would naturally keep important documents and files with you. These days, people keep a lot of these files electronically, which is less compelling from a closer connection perspective. Of the *physical* documents you keep, where are they kept? Be prepared to answer this question if asked in an audit.

23) *From what country or countries did you derive the majority of your income?*
This is a bit of a trick question. A tax home is related to your

place of business, not where most of your income comes from. However, if you have passive investments, pensions, or investments in the US which more than finance your living, then the question could be raised that your alleged business is nothing but a hobby, especially if it is not bringing in large sums of income. Hobby income would not justify a tax home. If you are self-employed, are you bringing in a substantial income from self-employment? Further, can you show documents proving that income is coming from your work? Self-employed people have a higher burden of proof since there is always suspicion of fabricated evidence, whereas documents from an outside employer have more legitimacy.

24) *Did you have any income from US sources? (Yes or No; If yes, where?)*
Is the income passive? What is the history of it? Focus on where you performed personal services during the tax year, since these are what qualify you for FEIE. Questions about US income are trying to show that the US is your economic tax home.

25) *In what country or countries were your investments located?*
If you made investments of capital in the foreign country that is your claimed tax home and abode, this can be a strong argument for closer connection. Conversely, active investment activity like day trading and buying options suggests that you depend on the US for your economic well-being, which would argue against a foreign tax home. Consider leaving your funds in mutual funds, which do not require your active management.

26) *Did you qualify for any type of "national" health plan sponsored by a foreign government? (Yes or No; If yes, where?)*
If you qualify for a foreign national health plan, it represents a strong argument of closer connection and the intention to

reside indefinitely in a foreign country.

27) *Do you have any other information to substantiate your closer connection to a country other than the United States?*

•There are many other documents and actions that can help substantiate a closer connection. The ones listed above are important, but there are many others showing the intention to remain indefinitely in a foreign country and that you have become a part of the foreign country in economic, personal and family ways. Here are some ideas:

a) Activities that generate receipts or letters of involvement are critical. These receipts should have foreign addresses and be dated. For example, consider joining various organizations or institutions in a foreign country: a civic organization, the Rotary, a church, a chamber of commerce, a dues-paying club or other charitable organization.

b) Get a library card and check out a few books.

c) Get frequent shopper cards at the grocery, hardware store, wine store, etc. Workers on temporary assignment would not typically bother with these.

d) Send your children to school in the foreign country and keep the tuition receipts as evidence.

e) Fill your Facebook with photos of yourself in a foreign country.

f) If you are a regular photo taker, turn on the GPS tracking so that your photos have GPS meta data showing where you were and what you were doing.

g) Keep records of your boarding passes. Anyone using Global Entry for expedited passport checking should be aware that you do not get passport stamps. Global Entry keeps the data and they will not share it you—you will not get a printout of your entry and exit logs for the last year. The IRS, however, has access to this information through interagency information sharing. My recommendation is to always take a photo of your boarding pass. Make a habit of doing this and keeping the photos permanently.

Remember that discrediting your claim of a foreign tax home is the primary way an auditor is going to aim to disqualify you from exclusion. Be proactive in collecting evidence that shows both that you have a foreign tax home and have abandoned your abode in the US. If you own your home in the US, get a renter or be able to explain your treatment of it. Remember, this is a legal argument. Do not assume that an auditor will share your optimism about how the evidence supports your claim. An auditor's job is to disprove you, so collect plenty of solid evidence.

If an auditor denies your claim for FEIE, it is not the end of the world. You can appeal the auditor's determination to a supervisor or in Tax Court. These options require legal professionals and can be expensive, so it is better to spend money getting a car, driver's license and club memberships in the foreign country than to pay big bucks for US-based tax lawyers.

In summary, Part I of the form is critical; most people denied FEIE are denied because of inadequate answers in Part I. These seemingly innocuous questions must be carefully and correctly answered.

CHAPTER 5

Form Part II: The Bona Fide Residence Test

Part II **Taxpayers Qualifying Under Bona Fide Residence Test** (see instructions)

10 Date bona fide residence began ▶ and ended ▶

11 Kind of living quarters in foreign country ▶ **a** ☐ Purchased house **b** ☐ Rented house or apartment **c** ☐ Rented room **d** ☐ Quarters furnished by employer

12a Did any of your family live with you abroad during any part of the tax year? ☐ **Yes** ☐ **No**

b If "Yes," who and for what period? ▶

13a Have you submitted a statement to the authorities of the foreign country where you claim bona fide residence that you aren't a resident of that country? See instructions ☐ **Yes** ☐ **No**

b Are you required to pay income tax to the country where you claim bona fide residence? See instructions ☐ **Yes** ☐ **No**

If you answered "Yes" to 13a and "No" to 13b, you don't qualify as a bona fide resident. Don't complete the rest of this part.

14 If you were present in the United States or its possessions during the tax year, complete columns **(a)–(d)** below. **Don't** include the income from column **(d)** in Part IV, but report it on Form 1040.

(a) Date arrived in U.S.	**(b)** Date left U.S.	**(c)** Number of days in U.S. on business	**(d)** Income earned in U.S. on business (attach computation)	**(a)** Date arrived in U.S.	**(b)** Date left U.S.	**(c)** Number of days in U.S. on business	**(d)** Income earned in U.S. on business (attach computation)

15a List any contractual terms or other conditions relating to the length of your employment abroad ▶

b Enter the type of visa under which you entered the foreign country ▶

c Did your visa limit the length of your stay or employment in a foreign country? If "Yes," attach explanation ☐ **Yes** ☐ **No**

d Did you maintain a home in the United States while living abroad? ☐ **Yes** ☐ **No**

e If "Yes," enter address of your home, whether it was rented, the names of the occupants, and their relationship to you ▶

For Paperwork Reduction Act Notice, see the Form 1040 instructions. Cat. No. 11900P Form **2555** (2016)

To be an individual qualified for the FEIE, you must satisfy either the Bona Fide Residence Test or the Physical Presence Test. Failing one of these tests is the second most common reason for denying exclusion.

Typically, for the first and last year a person is working in a foreign country, the physical presence test is used. This test recognizes that you were in the States for part of the year. The Bona Fide Residence Test is used for the intervening years because it looks at a full calendar year.

When did your bona bide residence begin or end?

The word "bona fide" translates as "in good faith" in Latin. It means genuine or real. The questions in Part II of form 2555 primarily touch on key closer connection questions, which were covered in the prior chapter. Again, these questions are asked in an innocuous manner and can easily fool one into giving an answer that raises red flags with an auditor.

There are several ways to answer the above question. The best answer to the question "when did bona fide residency start?" is the date that you received temporary or permanent residency status from the foreign government. If you only rely on a visitor's visa to be in the country, then it undermines the claim of bona fide residency; visitors by definition do not have residency. Some people find it easier or cheaper to do a visa run to a neighboring country to renew a visitor's visa. If you can get even a temporary residency or extended permit that is at least a year long, this is very helpful. Applying for residency status can be a hassle, but the savings with FEIE should make it worth it.

If the residency has not ended, just write the word "continues" for the end date.

Your residency does not have to be in the same country for the whole year, and the country of residency does not have to be the country of employment.

What kind of quarters?

This is another "closer connection" question. There are four types of quarters:

- A purchased home shows a major investment and sign of economic connection.
- A rented apartment or home shows a weaker connection; try to get a rental period for a year or more.

- A rented room such as a hotel room, hostel or room in a house would need to reveal the terms of the rent.
- Quarters furnished by employer often do not address duration. Where is the abode for other family members? How long did you live in these quarters?

Did any family live with you?

This is another question aimed at investigating abode. There are two audit risks related to family dwelling place. If it can be shown that your family's abode is in the US, then you do not qualify for FEIE.

First, if your spouse and dependents' abode is in the US, then your abode is unlikely to be in a foreign country. Why aren't they living with or near you?

Secondly, is this a divorce or marital separation situation? You would have to demonstrate that you have established more important economic and personal ties separate from your spouse and dependents.

Statement of residency and paying taxes

In the Internal Revenue Code, residency and taxes are two criteria under which a bona fide residence test can be denied.

> *If—*
>
> *(A) an individual who has earned income from sources within a foreign country submits a statement to the authorities of that country that he is not a resident of that country, and*
>
> *(B) such individual is held not subject as a resident of that country to the income tax of that country by its authorities with respect to such earnings,*
>
> *then such individual shall not be considered a bona fide resident of that country for purposes of paragraph (1)(A).*[18]

[18] 26 US Code 911(d)(5).

Are you a resident of the foreign country you are living in? This question may seem strange, because we may not understand how claims of residency work.

There are two typical ways that residency claims on official paperwork can trigger IRS audit points:

When traveling, you may enter a country at an airport or border crossing and be required to complete a short form declaring your passport information, residency status, and reasons for entering the country. If you do not have bona fide residency in the country you are passing through, you are not likely to claim residence because you cannot prove it. You could be called upon to produce some sort of national identification card or permanent visa card. So instead, you end up claiming that you are a resident of the US. This is one reason why a person would claim US residency even while living abroad.

Of course, most people will not think of this, but when you indicate that you are a US resident, an auditor may then use this very point and to deny your FEIE.

The second way a person can trigger an audit point is by falsely claiming residency in a country other than the US to avoiding paying US income tax. Because of a large network of agreements for exchange of tax information, the IRS can discover if you make such a false claim, even though it may require a great deal of effort on the auditor's part.

The bottom line is this. You should apply for a non-visitor's visa at your earliest opportunity. Use a foreign lawyer to submit the paperwork so the foreign lawyer can give you a legitimate receipt or document proving you have made the effort. In countries where getting permanent residence is a drawn-out process, you usually will be given some sort of temporary status beyond a visitor's visa which should be sufficient for justifying your claim to bona fide residence.

Several court cases have been lost because the taxpayer made no effort to establish residency or to be involved in the community.

When were you in the US?

Once you have established foreign residency, it is reasonable for you to return to the US for brief periods whether for business or pleasure. However, the instructions state that you must be resident in the foreign country for an uninterrupted period that includes an entire tax year. Most people read that and think they can never leave the foreign country. A legally trained person, however, asks the logical question, "what does resident mean?" Resident means abode. Everyone leaves their "abode" when they go on vacation or business trips. These short journeys do not undermine the qualification of abode. However, if you go on an extended trip to the US, you need to be careful not to re-establish your abode back in the US by accident and lose your claim to exclusion. The tax courts have recognized that trips in the US of ten business days (two weeks) or less are considered *de minimus* trips that do not affect abode.

There are four audit risks related to travel to the US:

1) Stays over ten business days may expose you to an auditor's scrutiny. A simple trick to minimize this risk when you need to stay longer than ten days is to plan quick trips to Mexico or Canada for a weekend. This resets the ten-day clock. Stays over ten weekdays (two weeks) enter the caution zone.
    a) Is your family coming with you?
    b) Are you staying in your old home?
    c) What is the purpose of the visit?
    d) Did you stay in one place the whole time or multiple places?
    e) Was the trip required by business?
    f) Did you earn money by performing services in the US?

2) Be careful to be honest about the travel dates listed on this form. The IRS has access to the Department of Homeland Security passport data showing when you entered and exited the country and they can quickly check your dates. This information might soon be automatically checked by a computerized "under reporter" system, which catches unreported information on a return. The under-

reporter system issues letters demanding explanations, and these explanations are handled by revenue officers and trained personnel. It is much better to be honest and accurate and include an explanation than to be caught in a deception on your return. Dishonesty could expose you to charges of fraud and the risk of a $250,000 penalty and up to five years in prison.

3) The form also asks how many working days you had in the US on your visit. It is reasonable that a business trip back to the US would be accompanied by a few vacation days. This is not held against you. The key here is that a visit of over ten business days exceeds the *de minimus* rule and puts your claim of abode at risk. If you worked for two weeks then vacationed for an additional two weeks, this could be justified without losing your foreign abode status. I recommend keeping, with your tax records, evidence that you did vacation-type things like seeing relatives or visiting tourist sites. Preferably, this evidence should include time stamped receipts. Do not push your luck by doing this more than once a year.

4) The form also asks how much income was earned in the US on business. I would narrow the answer of this question to how much income was earned *because* you were in the US. For example, if your foreign employer pays you a regular monthly salary, that income would not be US income just because you were traveling there. On the other hand, if you are in the US on a paid speaking engagement or as an athlete or entertainer performing in the US, then the income is directly tied to your presence in the US; therefore, I would declare this income here.

Remember, income listed here as earned in the US cannot be counted toward the foreign income you are trying to exclude from taxation.

Other "closer connection" questions

There are two audit risks related to the additional closer connection questions

The first set of questions addresses the question of whether you are in a foreign country temporarily or indefinitely, and indefinite is the better option.

Proofs of indefinite stay in a foreign country include:

- Contractual terms related to the length of employment abroad
- The type of visa you have—preferably not a visitor's visa
- Whether the visa allows you to work in the foreign country and how long can you stay there

The second set of questions deals with forsaking your former abode in the US. It specifically asks if you maintained your home in the US. If you did, whom did you rent it to? If you rented it to a sibling or other relative, then you still have a strong connection. If you rented to people you are not related or connected to, then it suggests a more legitimate forsaking of abode. Be prepared to show a lease document and evidence of payments if audited.

In summary, if you uprooted your family and moved to a foreign country AND initiated the process to get the appropriate visa to authorize an indefinite or permanent stay in the country AND you do not visit the US for more than two weeks at a time, the Bona Fide Residence Test is pretty easy to satisfy.

CHAPTER 6

Form Part III: The Physical Presence Test

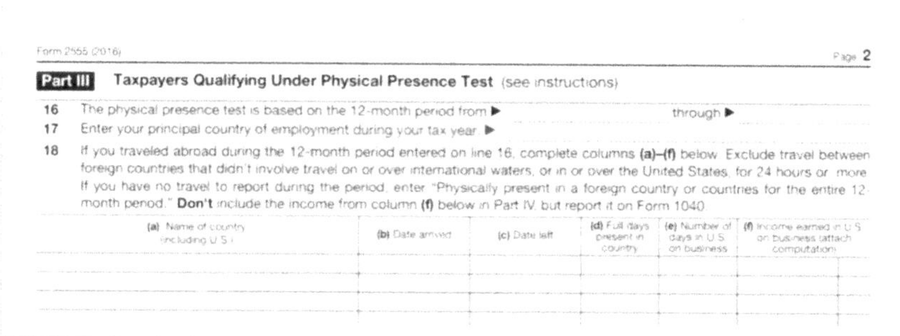

Form 2555 (2016) Page 2

Part III **Taxpayers Qualifying Under Physical Presence Test** (see instructions)

16 The physical presence test is based on the 12-month period from ▶ through ▶

17 Enter your principal country of employment during your tax year. ▶

18 If you traveled abroad during the 12-month period entered on line 16, complete columns **(a)–(f)** below. Exclude travel between foreign countries that didn't involve travel on or over international waters, or in or over the United States, for 24 hours or more. If you have no travel to report during the period, enter "Physically present in a foreign country or countries for the entire 12-month period." **Don't** include the income from column **(f)** below in Part IV, but report it on Form 1040.

(a) Name of country (including U.S.)	**(b)** Date arrived	**(c)** Date left	**(d)** Full days present in country	**(e)** Number of days in U.S. on business	**(f)** Income earned in U.S. on business (attach computation)

The second method to prove you were in a foreign country is the physical presence test. This test is used instead of the bona fide residence test described in the preceding chapter.

Most ex-patriots first learning about the FEIE have many questions about the Physical Presence Test. This is the test used for someone who just started working overseas during a tax year. Everyone becomes a junior lawyer trying to interpret the implications of these rules! This may be the first time an individual realizes that taxes are more about interpreting rules of law than rules of accounting, at least for the individual.

In this section, I will comment on what the Code and Regulations state and look at a couple definitions of terms. Then we will look at some examples to arrive at a better understanding of the rules. Unfortunately, every reader will have a unique situation, so these explanations may still leave some questions open; however, it is my desire to bring greater clarity to interpreting this law than is found on the IRS website or on blog sites.

As an Enrolled Agent, I sign my client's tax return as the preparer, placing my credibility and reputation on the line with each tax return. Getting advice from a person who is not going to sign your tax return means that person has no investment in the accuracy of their work. Sadly, too many people get tax filing advice over cocktail hour or on a blog post. You are held legally responsible for your own tax return; it is a legal document. Making incorrect or false claims on your return can expose you to significant penalties, and in the cases of intentional misrepresentation (fraud), up to five years in prison.

In my experience, the people most curious about the rules are also the ones at greatest risk of not qualifying; they tend to seek any angle to qualify for FEIE.

What do the Code and Regulations Say?

What does the Internal Revenue Code say? Now is the time to get empowered by reading what the actual laws say, found in the later chapters of this book. Read Internal Revenue Code section 911(d)(1)(B) and the Internal Revenue Regulations 1.911-2(d)-(h). There are some helpful examples and definitions of important terms. Note that the Code has greater weight than the Regulations.

Reading the law is only boring until you see your own life caught up in the descriptions; then it becomes much more real and interesting.

Read the synopses in the Cases and Ruling chapter. These are real people with unique situations perhaps like yours who went to court or were directly addressed by an IRS ruling or procedure. Most of these people skated close to the limits of the law. The IRS disagreed with them, so it took a judge to decide for or against. They are very interesting, especially if you look up the case and read the details.

What are the boundaries of a foreign country?

Most people concerned with the Physical Presence Test are people who went overseas to work but then traveled extensively. They are concerned that they will not qualify for 330 days test.

To begin this discussion, we must look at definitions. The first definition is "foreign country." Most of us think of the boundaries of a country as the land boundaries that we would see on a political map. However, look closely at the Regulation definition.

> *The term "foreign country" when used in a geographical sense includes any territory under the sovereignty of a government other than that of the United States. It includes the territorial waters of the foreign country (determined in accordance with the laws of the United States), the air space over the foreign country, and the seabed and subsoil of those submarine areas which are adjacent to the territorial waters of the foreign country and over which the foreign country has exclusive rights, in accordance with international law, with respect to the exploration and exploitation of natural resources.*[19]

What is this? There is an area outside the territorial waters that are still considered part of a country, exclusive areas for exploration and exploitation of natural resources? What international law are they talking about? They are referring to the United Nations Convention on the Law of the Seas (UNCLOS). UNCLOS redraws the world map like you have never seen before. Forget the world maps, which show the political land boundaries of countries.

The United Nations Convention on the Law of the Seas

Historically, most countries treated the first three miles off the coast as part of their territory. In the 1970s and 80s, some countries would go too close to other countries to drill for oil, explore for minerals, and to

---

[19] Revenue Regulations 1.911-2(h).

harvest fish. In reaction to this, countries expanded their territorial waters to 12 miles off the coast, but this still was not enough. At the same time, the U.N. began discussions to define the territorial limits. This convention was known as the U.N. Convention on the Law of the Seas (UNCLOS). The US was an active participant in the formulation of UNCLOS. The third version of UNCLOS was finalized in 1994 when it was ratified by the minimum of sixty countries

UNCLOS defines an area adjacent to territorial waters as the Exclusive Economic Zone of a country. This is an area where the country has exclusive rights over the economic activity, including exploration and exploitation of natural resources. This sounds like the "adjacent areas" in the Regulation definition of foreign country.

Interestingly, the US, although an active negotiator in UNCLOS, never ratified it. Does this mean that it does not apply to our situation? The US has acknowledged that it treats UNCLOS as customary international law,[20] meaning that the US has agreed that it is the applicable law and they will respect it. In international law, this is a significant status. Ronald Regan, through executive decree, proclaimed an Exclusive Economic Zone around the US, matching what the UNCLOS stipulates.

What are Exclusive Economic Zones?

Exclusive Economic Zones (EEZ) is measured as 200 nautical miles from a shoreline, quite a distance. Because of size limitations, I cannot reproduce a detailed map of the world in this book, but you can search the Internet for world maps of Exclusive Economic Zones. [21]

Below is a diagram showing how Exclusive Economic Zones are between territorial waters and the high seas (international waters).

---

[20] Part V of UNCLOS was not included in the recognition as customary international law.

[21] (See sites.google.com/site/benarcjr/maps/exclusive-economic-zones for an excellent map based on GIS data, which allows you to zoom into areas of interest.)

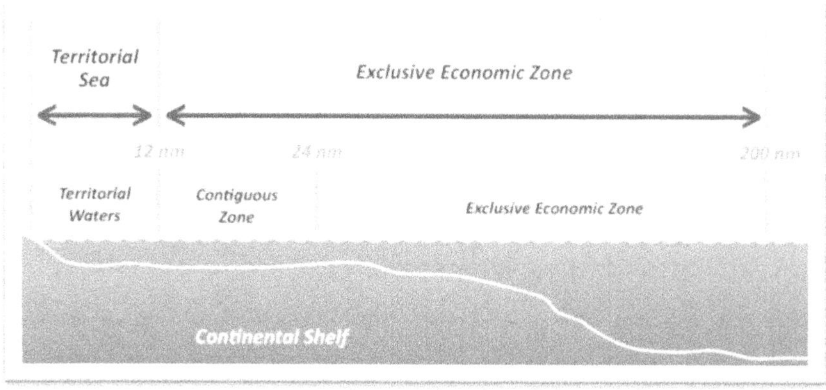

There are a couple of interesting things that happen on an EEZ map:

- The areas NOT in an EEZ are defined as international areas/waters/airspace.
- Little islands in the oceans suddenly look enormous.
- Most seas effectively disappear. The size of international waters is much smaller. Consider the disappearance of the Mediterranean Sea, Baltic Sea, North Sea, the Caribbean Sea, and most of South East Asian waters.

Consider the map below of Europe and North Africa. The map is unique. The Mediterranean, Baltic, North, and Adriatic Seas have all disappeared. It is as though it were a solid land mass. There is no international space shown except for the Atlantic Ocean. The format of this book doesn't permit showing giant world maps. Hopefully, this small picture gives you a taste for how UNCLOS redefines the world map as we used to think of it.

When we are counting full days in a foreign country or countries, there is less likelihood that you'd think that you were in international waters when traveling between countries.

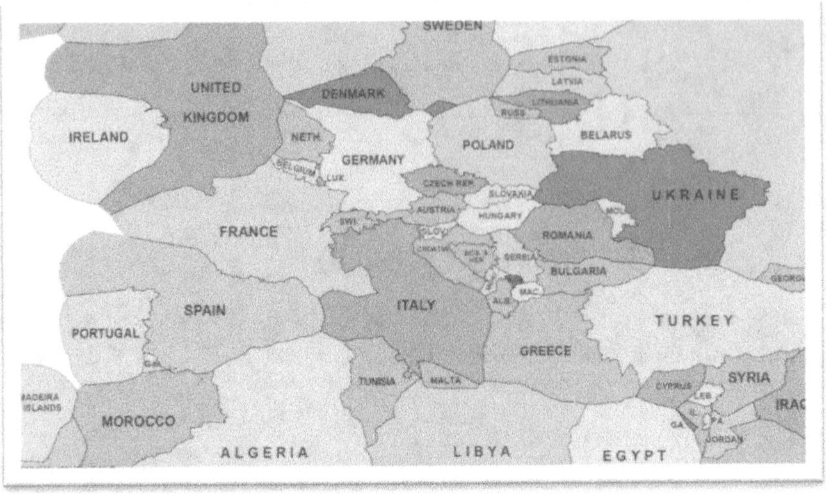

EEZs mean that more airline flight routes of airlines are over connected/adjacent foreign countries than a strictly political map would indicate. Even long distance air flights are more likely to be technically over foreign countries.

Note that Antarctica is not considered a foreign country. Antarctica has no native population or government. Dozens of US Tax Court cases on this issue have cemented this position.[22]

Further, special rules apply to US territories such as American Samoa, Guam, Commonwealth of Northern Mariana Islands, Puerto Rico and the US Virgin Islands. Do not assume these are treated as foreign countries.

What is a "full day?"

A "full day" is defined as 24 hours beginning at midnight and ending at the following midnight. However, this definition has issues because of changing time zones when travelling. I have not seen any rulings on this, but I would focus on a day starting at midnight in the time zone you were in when it was midnight, and a full day would continue for 24 hours. I would discount the phrase "following midnight" because the following midnight may come sooner or later than 24 hours. Further,

[22] D. Arnett, 2007-1 USTC 50,162, 473 F3d 790.

traveling over the International Date Line raises questions over what constitutes the "following midnight".

The key point is that a day starts at midnight. If time zone changes are significant, then you are living too close to the edge of the 330-day limit. If this is an issue, we can apply for a ruling or waiver from the IRS in advance.

What is a full day in a foreign country?

This question is related to movement between countries.

- Being in one country for a full day is clearly counted as a full day in a foreign country.
- Traveling between adjacent countries in a single day is counted as a full day in a foreign country.
- Traveling between two foreign countries where the flight path goes through international space and the duration of the trip is less than 24 hours is counted as a full day in a foreign country. The time in international space is considered time "not in a foreign country."

Examples:

- You fly from Barbados to England. Because the trip is less than 24 hours in duration though passing through international space, this would be counted as a full day in a foreign country.

- You take a ship from Barbados to England nonstop. The trip takes 5 days. Because you are in international waters for greater than 24 hours, none of the five days in international waters is considered a full day. The departure and arrival dates are only partial days in a foreign country. None of the days are considered foreign country time.

Travel between two foreign countries where the air flight is over the US is considered a full day(s) in the foreign country because time in US air space is considered time "not in a foreign country," but since it is less than 24 hours of travel, it qualifies as a full day in a foreign country.

Examples:

- You fly from Toronto, Canada to Mexico City, Mexico nonstop through US airspace. This would be treated as a full day in a foreign country.

- You fly from Toronto to Mexico City nonstop, but the plane lands in Mexico City after midnight the next day. The trip was less than 24 hours. You spent the departure day solely in Canada and you spent the arrival day solely in Mexico. Both days would be full days in a foreign country.

Travel between two foreign countries with brief layovers in the US does not count against full days if the travel is less than 24 hours.

- Example: You travel from Toronto to Mexico City on American Airlines with a four-hour layover in Houston. You spent the departure day solely in Canada and you spent the arrival day solely in Mexico. Since the entire travel duration is less than 24 hours, the entire time is considered full day(s) in a foreign country.

What is the 330 days test?

To qualify for the physical presence test, you must have:

- 330 full days in a foreign country or countries for twelve consecutive months.
- The days do not have to be consecutive.
- The days can be business or personal days.

This is not the same as "no more than 35 days in the US during a twelve-month period" because a day can fail to be a full day in a foreign country and still not be a day in the US. This is a common mistake because people would rather count days in the US than days in a foreign country.

What is the twelve months test?

The 330 days must be during a twelve-consecutive month period—basically a year. It includes leap day if applicable. The key requirement is that either the first day of the period or the final day of the period must be in the tax year. So, if your twelve-month period starts on July 4th, the period ends on July 3rd the following year.

Here are three strategies for picking when your twelve-month period starts and ends:

1. Understand that you want to maximize the number of days in the period during the tax year because the total amount for the exclusion limit is prorated or reduced by the fraction of days of the period during the tax year.

   Example: You are living in Japan from June 1, 2015 until November 30, 2016. For the tax year 2016, here are the options:

   a. The worst option is making your twelve-month period be light on the number of days in 2016. This would be choosing May 1, 2015 to April 30, 2016, resulting in 92 days of the period in 2016. The exclusion maximum of $101,300 is reduced to 92/366, resulting in $25,463 maximum foreign earned income exclusion for the year.

   b. The best option would be to choose January 1, 2016 to December 31, 2016. This results in 366 days of the period being in 2016. Then the exclusion maximum of $101,300 is reduced to 366/366 resulting in the full $101,300 maximum foreign earned income exclusion for the year.

2. The end date of the period can be in the year following the tax year. The complexity here is that you cannot put future dates in as the period because you cannot prove you were in the foreign country in the future. In this case, file an

extension until the twelve-month window completes. I had a client who moved to a foreign country June 10 during the tax year. In April of the following year, we filed an extension in order to file a return after June 10. You can use form 2350 to obtain approval for extending your return filing date. Remember, even though you get approved for an extension, the extension only applies to the filing date. Your taxes are still due on April 15. This client qualified for the physical presence test from June 10 of the tax year until June 9 of the following year.

3. Overlapping twelve month periods with other tax years are allowed.

Waiver of time requirements

If you are forced to flee a country because of war, civil unrest or other adverse conditions, you can seek relief for the time requirements of either the bona fide residence or physical presence tests. Annually, the IRS publishes a list of countries for which waivers are available. You must show that you would have otherwise qualified for one of the two tests had you not been forced to leave.

CHAPTER 7

Form Part IV – Foreign Earned Income

What is earned income?

Up until now, we have taken for granted the meaning of foreign earned income. Let's look more closely at what types of income are considered "earned." Foreign earned income generally is income you receive for services you perform.

- Earned income is salaries, wages, commissions, bonuses and professional fees.
- Unearned income consists of dividends, interest, capital gains, stock options, gambling winnings, alimony, social security benefits, pensions, and annuities.
- Variable types of income include business profits, royalties, rents, scholarships and fellowships.

Foreign earned income does *not* include:

- The value of meals and lodging furnished for the convenience of your employer. This is different than regular meals and lodging when traveling. "The convenience of employer" means the employer provided the meals and lodging to get more work out of the employees. Consider the example of a remote mining camp. The employer provides a camp with basic sleeping quarters and a cafeteria because the nearest alternatives are more than an hour's drive away. Providing food and lodging serves the employer's interest, so the value of the lodging and food is not treated as income.

- Pay you receive as an employee of the US government.
- Amounts you receive from employer's contribution to a nonexempt employee trust or to a nonqualified annuity contract.

Foreign earned income includes certain non-cash income, allowances, and reimbursements, such as:

- The fair market value of property or facilities provided to you by your employer in the form of lodging, meals, or use of a car
- Cost of living allowances
- Overseas differentials
- Family allowances
- Reimbursement for education or education allowances
- Home leave allowance
- Quarters allowance
- Reimbursement for moving (or moving allowance)

Foreign earned income includes some types of income not easily identified as "earned" or "unearned" income. This type of income is referred to as "variable income." Most of these situations occur because some degree of capital investment is required to make the income happen. Capital investment generates passive, unearned income, elaborated below:

Income from a sole proprietorship or partnership. If capital investment is an important part of producing income, no more than 30% of your share of the net profits of the business is earned income.

Rental Income. Generally, rental income is *unearned* income, but if you perform personal services connected with the production of rent, up to 30% of your net rental income can be considered earned income. Note that "personal services" do not include making minor repairs or collecting rents.

Income as an artist. Income from the sale of works of art is considered earned income.

Scholarships and fellowships. Any portion of a scholarship or fellowship grant that is paid to you for research, teaching, or other services is considered earned income and must be included in gross income.

Royalties. Royalties from the leasing of oil and mineral lands and patents generally are a form of rent or dividends and are *unearned* income; however, royalties received by a writer or artist are considered earned income.

Part IV All Taxpayers

Note: Enter on lines 19 through 23 all income, including noncash income, you earned and actually or constructively received during your 2016 tax year for services you performed in a foreign country. If any of the foreign earned income received this tax year was earned in a prior tax year, or will be earned in a later tax year (such as a bonus), see the instructions. **Don't** include income from line 14, column **(d)**, or line 18, column **(f)**. Report amounts in U.S. dollars, using the exchange rates in effect when you actually or constructively received the income.

If you are a cash basis taxpayer, report on Form 1040 all income you received in 2016, no matter when you performed the service.

	2016 Foreign Earned Income			Amount (in U.S. dollars)
19	Total wages, salaries, bonuses, commissions, etc.		19	
20	Allowable share of income for personal services performed (see instructions):			
a	In a business (including farming) or profession		20a	
b	In a partnership. List partnership's name and address and type of income ▶		20b	
21	Noncash income (market value of property or facilities furnished by employer – attach statement showing how it was determined):			
a	Home (lodging)		21a	
b	Meals		21b	
c	Car		21c	
d	Other property or facilities. List type and amount ▶		21d	
22	Allowances, reimbursements, or expenses paid on your behalf for services you performed:			
a	Cost of living and overseas differential	22a		
b	Family	22b		
c	Education	22c		
d	Home leave	22d		
e	Quarters	22e		
f	For any other purpose. List type and amount ▶	22f		
g	Add lines 22a through 22f		22g	
23	Other foreign earned income. List type and amount ▶		23	
24	Add lines 19 through 21d, line 22g, and line 23		24	
25	Total amount of meals and lodging included on line 24 that is excludable (see instructions)		25	
26	Subtract line 25 from line 24. Enter the result here and on line 27 on page 3. This is your **2016 foreign earned income** ▶		26	

Form **2555** (2016)

Which exchange rate to use?

All amounts on the form must be expressed in US Dollars. I recommend using the IRS published "Yearly Average Exchange Rates."

These are published on the IRS government website, which lists an average rate for the year for most countries. Alternately, you can use a daily bank exchange rate, but be prepared to defend the rate used. People living in countries with runaway inflation and without a reliable exchange rate must seek an alternate method outside the scope of this work.

If your income cannot be readily converted or is prevented from being converted to US dollars, then the income can be classified as "blocked." Blocked income can be deferred until it can be converted in the future. This must be clearly documented on separate paper for the IRS. How much was your income?

You must list all your wages, tips, commissions, bonuses and direct payments from foreign income. Do not include any amounts that you previously declared were earned while in the US. Your personal services income related to a foreign business or partnership should be entered. This does not include earnings paid as dividends or distributions from a foreign business or partnership, because these would be considered passive income, not earned income.

How much was your non-cash income?

The major non-cash wages in foreign employment are employer furnished living quarters, meals, and cars. When the employer furnishes these, the value must be reported here. If instead the employer reimbursed you or paid you an allowance towards quarters, meals, and car, list them in the allowance section. This non-cash income must be directly connected to the services you provided.

On the other hand, in certain circumstances, some meals and lodging costs, if these were provided by the employer for the employer's convenience, are *not* considered income. For example, if an employer provides lodging at a remote campsite where oil wells are being drilled, they provide the lodging and food because it benefits the employer to have the employee staying close to the work site.

How much were your allowances?

Foreign employers will often provide employees with a reimbursement or allowance on certain living expenses to be identified here. For example, an employer may reimburse you for the cost of education of children in private schools or give you a sum of money for the purpose of a home leave or trip to the US every year. Since these amounts were all earned because of foreign work, these allowances are included in foreign earned income.

Calculating foreign earned income

The final amount of this calculation is the total foreign earned income. This income should be included on form 1040 line 7 as wages. The next step is to first determine if a housing exclusion or deduction applies, then how much income can be excluded.

CHAPTER 8

Form Part V and VI: Housing Exclusion or Deduction

Before the FEIE can be calculated, the housing exclusion must be calculated. The housing exclusion is expressed as an addition to the maximum foreign earned income allowed. If you work for an employer, you are allowed exclusion. If you are self-employed, the calculated amount must be taken as a deduction on form 1040 and not as exclusion.

Form 2555 (2016) Page 3

Part V **All Taxpayers**

27	Enter the amount from line 26	27	
	Are you claiming the housing exclusion or housing deduction? ☐ **Yes.** Complete Part VI. ☐ **No.** Go to Part VII.		

Part VI **Taxpayers Claiming the Housing Exclusion and/or Deduction**

28	Qualified housing expenses for the tax year (see instructions)	28	
29a	Enter location where housing expenses incurred (see instructions) ▶		
b	Enter limit on housing expenses (see instructions)	29b	
30	Enter the **smaller** of line 28 or line 29b	30	
31	Number of days in your qualifying period that fall within your 2016 tax year (see instructions) — 31 ___ days		
32	Multiply $44.28 by the number of days on line 31. If 366 is entered on line 31, enter $16,208 here	32	
33	Subtract line 32 from line 30. If the result is zero or less, don't complete the rest of this part or any of Part IX	33	
34	Enter employer-provided amounts (see instructions) — 34		
35	Divide line 34 by line 27. Enter the result as a decimal (rounded to at least three places), but don't enter more than "1.000"	35	× .
36	**Housing exclusion.** Multiply line 33 by line 35. Enter the result but don't enter more than the amount on line 34. Also, complete Part VIII ▶	36	
	Note: The housing deduction is figured in Part IX. If you choose to claim the foreign earned income exclusion, complete Parts VII and VIII before Part IX.		

Which expenses can be excluded?

Your housing expenses are the reasonable expenses incurred during the tax year for housing costs. These reasonable expenses include rent (or deductible mortgage interest, taxes, and depreciation), utilities, property insurance, household repairs, and residential parking. Not included are unreasonable expenses, the cost of buying property and mortgage payments, domestic labor, the cost of capital improvements or furniture and accessories.

How much can be excluded?

The purpose of the housing exclusion is to not penalize workers from the US for higher costs of living in foreign countries. The amount of housing cost that can be excluded is related to the maximum amount of foreign earned income that can be excluded. The IRS has determined that a base amount of housing costs is the employee's burden. This base amount is 16% of the eligible foreign earned income exclusion limit. The IRS has also determined a level of reasonable housing expense. This amount of reasonable housing expense is either:

- 30% of the eligible foreign earned income exclusion limit, or

- a higher amount for specific high cost cities, expressed as a daily amount times the number of days worked in a foreign country

The base amount is then subtracted from the reasonable housing expense. This difference is the amount of housing exclusion. This exclusion is later added to the eligible foreign earned income exclusion to come up with the total exclusion.

If you worked partly for an employer and were partly self-employed, then you must prorate the amount excluded or deducted.

CHAPTER 9

Form Part VII – Foreign Earned Income Exclusion

The maximum foreign earned income exclusion is prorated by the number of days in the qualifying period. If the physical presence test was used, the number of days is the number of days in the tax year that are in the twelve-month test period. If the bona fide residence test was used, the number of days is the days in the year (365 or 366 days) reduced by the number of days spent in the US.

It is important to note that every day spent in the US or in international space reduces your excludable amount.

Part VII Taxpayers Claiming the Foreign Earned Income Exclusion

Line	Description		Line	Amount
37	Maximum foreign earned income exclusion		37	$101,300 .00
38	• If you completed Part VI, enter the number from line 31. • All others, enter the number of days in your qualifying period that fall within your 2016 tax year (see the instructions for line 31)	38 days		
39	• If line 38 and the number of days in your 2016 tax year (usually 366) are the same, enter "1.000." • Otherwise, divide line 38 by the number of days in your 2016 tax year and enter the result as a decimal (rounded to at least three places).		39	× .
40	Multiply line 37 by line 39		40	
41	Subtract line 36 from line 27		41	
42	**Foreign earned income exclusion.** Enter the **smaller** of line 40 or line 41. Also, complete Part VIII ▶		42	

CHAPTER 10

How Tax is Calculated under FEIE

Part VIII **Taxpayers Claiming the Housing Exclusion, Foreign Earned Income Exclusion, or Both**

43	Add lines 36 and 42	**43**	
44	Deductions allowed in figuring your adjusted gross income (Form 1040, line 37) that are allocable to the excluded income. See instructions and attach computation	**44**	
45	Subtract line 44 from line 43. Enter the result here and in parentheses on **Form 1040, line 21.** Next to the amount enter "Form 2555." On Form 1040, subtract this amount from your income to arrive at total income on Form 1040, line 22	**45**	

Part IX **Taxpayers Claiming the Housing Deduction**—Complete this part only if **(a)** line 33 is more than line 36 and **(b)** line 27 is more than line 43.

46	Subtract line 36 from line 33	**46**	
47	Subtract line 43 from line 27	**47**	
48	Enter the **smaller** of line 46 or line 47	**48**	
	Note: If line 47 is **more than** line 48 and you couldn't deduct all of your 2015 housing deduction because of the 2015 limit, use the housing deduction carryover worksheet in the instructions to figure the amount to enter on line 49. Otherwise, go to line 50.		
49	Housing deduction carryover from 2015 (from the housing deduction carryover worksheet in the instructions)	**49**	
50	**Housing deduction.** Add lines 48 and 49. Enter the total here and on Form 1040 to the left of line 36. Next to the amount on Form 1040, enter "Form 2555." Add it to the total adjustments reported on that line ▶	**50**	

Form **2555** (2016)

Reporting income

Your total foreign earnings should be included in the total on form 1040 line 7 as wages. On line 21, other income, put in an annotation "Form 2555" and subtract out the excluded income as a negative number.

Careful about itemizing deductions

Itemized deductions are deductions for unique personal expenses like home mortgage, medical costs, charitable gifts, etc. These are deductions from your income. If the income has already been excluded, it would be double dipping to also get a benefit related to how you spent the excluded income. You can still use the standard deductions unless you are self-employed and using the foreign housing deduction. Otherwise, you must prorate your itemized deductions by the percentage of excluded income divided by the adjusted gross income without the excluded income. Using the exclusion while also itemizing deductions is an easy IRS audit point.

What is stacking?

If you do not understand how your tax software is coming up with the amount of taxes you owe, it may be because of the practice of "stacking" introduced in 2006. This explanation only applies if you make more income than the limit. Since the amount excluded is subtracted out to give a lower adjusted gross income, what is your marginal tax rate? A marginal tax rate is the tax rate at which you would be taxed if you earned $1 more. When using the exclusion, the marginal tax rate is the highest tax bracket you would qualify for if none of your income were excluded.

Consider this example of a single person. You earned $120,000 working offshore all year. After you subtract out the exclusion of $101,300, the standard deduction of $6300, and personal exemption of $4050, then your taxable income is only $8350. But your tax is not calculated using the tax tables alone. There is a Foreign Earned Income Tax Worksheet that is used to determine taxes owed. So, in our example, instead of owing 10% or $830 in taxes, our single person owes 28% or $2340 in taxes.

There is a Foreign Earned Income Tax Worksheet, which is used to calculate the taxes due under the stacking principle.

Foreign Earned Income Tax Worksheet—Line 44 *Keep for Your Records*

CAUTION: If Form 1040, line 43, is zero, do not complete this worksheet

1.	Enter the amount from Form 1040, line 43	**1.**
2a.	Enter the amount from your (and your spouse's, if filing jointly) Form 2555, lines 45 and 50, or Form 2555-EZ, line 18	**2a.**
b.	Enter the total amount of any itemized deductions or exclusions you couldn't claim because they are related to excluded income	**b.**
c.	Subtract line 2b from line 2a. If zero or less, enter -0-	**c.**
3.	Add lines 1 and 2c	**3.**
4.	**Figure the tax on the amount on line 3.** Use the Tax Table, Tax Computation Worksheet, Qualified Dividends and Capital Gain Tax Worksheet*, Schedule D Tax Worksheet*, or Form 8615, whichever applies. See the instructions for line 44 to see which tax computation method applies. (Do not use a second Foreign Earned Income Tax Worksheet to figure the tax on this line.)	**4.**
5.	**Figure the tax on the amount on line 2c.** If the amount on line 2c is less than $100,000, use the Tax Table to figure this tax. If the amount on line 2c is $100,000 or more, use the Tax Computation Worksheet	**5.**
6.	Subtract line 5 from line 4. Enter the result. If zero or less, enter -0-. Also include this amount on Form 1040, line 44	**6.**

**Enter the amount from line 3 above on line 1 of the Qualified Dividends and Capital Gain Tax Worksheet or Schedule D Tax Worksheet if you use either of those worksheets to figure the tax on line 4 above. Complete the rest of that worksheet through line 6 (line 10 if you use the Schedule D Tax Worksheet). Next, you must determine if you have a capital gain excess. To find out if you have a capital gain excess, subtract Form 1040, line 43, from line 6 of your Qualified Dividends and Capital Gain Tax Worksheet (line 10 of your Schedule D Tax Worksheet). If the result is more than zero, that amount is your capital gain excess.*

If you do not have a capital gain excess, complete the rest of either of those worksheets according to the worksheet's instructions. Then complete lines 5 and 6 above.

If you have a capital gain excess, complete a second Qualified Dividends and Capital Gain Tax Worksheet or Schedule D Tax Worksheet (whichever applies) as instructed above but in its entirety and with the following additional modifications. Then complete lines 5 and 6 above. These modifications are to be made only for purposes of filling out the Foreign Earned Income Tax Worksheet above.

1. Reduce (but not below zero) the amount you would otherwise enter on line 3 of your Qualified Dividends and Capital Gain Tax Worksheet or line 9 of your Schedule D Tax Worksheet by your capital gain excess.

2. Reduce (but not below zero) the amount you would otherwise enter on line 2 of your Qualified Dividends and Capital Gain Tax Worksheet or line 6 of your Schedule D Tax Worksheet by any of your capital gain excess not used in (1) above.

3. Reduce (but not below zero) the amount on your Schedule D (Form 1040), line 18, by your capital gain excess.

4. Include your capital gain excess as a loss on line 16 of your Unrecaptured Section 1250 Gain Worksheet in the Instructions for Schedule D (Form 1040).

CHAPTER 11

Other Topics

Can spouse also exclude foreign income

If both you and your spouse have foreign earned income, you each claim the exclusion for your share of the income. Each spouse reports his or her foreign earnings on separate 2555 forms, whether filing jointly or separately, but each spouse would have to qualify.

Government personnel

The exclusion is not available to anyone who is paid by the US government or a governmental agency. There are several court cases on this point.

Keeping Records

You must keep accurate, permanent records and books to be able to show the different types of income, gains, losses, and expenses. These records need to be kept if they are relevant to any IRS investigation. There are statutes of limitation on how much time the IRS has to assess fines on any filed returns, usually either three or six years from when the return is filed depending on the type of form.

For foreign filers, the forms and limitations are intertwined. For instance, form 1040 is three years and form 8938 is six years. Because form 8938 is filed with form 1040, do not throw out those records until after six years or more has passed, if not longer. If you did not file, there is no statute of limitations clock, so records should be held indefinitely. Holding records *longer* than six years is prudent, preferably in electronic form to avoid the perils of paper and fading ink.

CHAPTER 12

Alternatives to FEIE

The FEIE has some significant limitations such as no exclusion for passive income and restrictions on your travel, several subjective aspects that are vulnerable during audits, and income in excess of the exclusion limit is fully taxed in the US.

However, one of the real strengths of the exclusion is that it can be used when living in any country in the world, whether or not the foreign country is also taxing your income.

A couple alternatives to the FEIE are the foreign tax credit (form 1116) and double taxation treaties (form 8833).

Remember, if you choose not to file form 2555 after having used it the year before, this possibly constitutes a revoking of your exclusion. You are then prohibited from re-electing the exclusion for five years.

Foreign tax credit

The foreign tax credit (FTC) is essentially a one-for-one credit against your US taxes for every income tax dollar paid to a foreign country. If the foreign country has higher taxes than the US, you would likely pay no US taxes. If the taxes were lower, you would have to pay the difference to the US.

One benefit of the FTC is there is no limit, so taxpayers of all income levels can use it.

The FTC can be used in conjunction with the exclusion in two ways. First, you can use it for foreign passive income in conjunction with excluding foreign earned income. Secondly, you can use it to offset US taxes on income in excess of the exclusion maximum income limit. Highly compensated foreign workers would either use the exclusion and the credit or just the credit.

The FTC also allows you to get a credit against passive income earned in a foreign country. In fact, you must file a separate form 1116 Foreign Tax Credit for your earned income (called "general income" on the form) and another form for the passive income.

Another benefit of the FTC is that unused credit can be carried forward for ten years and used later.

One drawback of FTC, though, is that completing the form is complex. It could take many hours just to understand the interactions of the data entered on this form. The form is long, counter-intuitive, poorly designed and confusing. In short, this form can give an aspirin a headache. Furthermore, if you use retail tax software to complete this form, your chances of making an error are very high because there is less error checking.

A second drawback of the FTC is that an alternative minimum tax (AMT) version of the form must be used in the AMT calculations. Depending on the support you have from your tax software, doing this yourself doubles the aggravation.

Treaty-based positions

With certain countries, the US has entered into double taxation treaties which, among other things, establishes rules over which county can tax a person's income when they operate between the two countries. For example, a person from the US working in England doing services would only be taxed on wages earned in England by the UK per the treaty between the US and the UK. The US agrees that the income is not taxable in the US.

Treaties are unique legal documents and overrule the Internal Revenue Code. They take priority. Treaties are interpreted only by their own accompanying technical explanation and the Vienna Convention on the Law of Treaties (VCLT).

One benefit of double taxation treaties is that if your income is taxed in a foreign country, it does not get treated as income on your US return, so there is no need to file for exclusion or the FTC.

Claiming a treaty benefit is done on form 8833. On the form, you must cite the articles and paragraphs of the treaty to substantiate your claim to a benefit. Your explanation should be detailed and logical. A word to the wise: treaties are written using complex legal language. Do not assume any noun, verb or phrase means what you would ordinarily think. In addition, the US often issues a technical explanation document of great length breaking down how both sides understand the treaty and its application. These are very nuanced and sophisticated legal documents and you must be very careful in citing them. Your explanations should reflect the same sophistication as the treaty documents.

Another benefit of a treaty-based claim is that, when done well, it is a stronger defense against an audit than the exclusion, which has several subjective elements. Recall that IRS auditors are hired because of their accounting knowledge. For an auditor to attack a treaty claim, he or she must get involved in reading treaties and following your written explanation. Legal analysis is not often an auditor's strength, and he or she does not have time for it. An error must be quite blatant before an auditor will challenge the claim.

A final benefit of a treaty-based claim is that it does not require the Bona Fide Resident Test or Physical Presence Tests. Usually, you only need to be in the foreign country an excess of 183 days in a year, but be aware that each treaty is different.

Countries with double taxation treaties with the US

- Australia
- Austria
- Bangladesh
- Barbados
- Belgium
- Bulgaria
- Canada
- China – does not include Hong Kong, Macau, or Taiwan
- Commonwealth of Independent States which includes
    - Armenia
    - Azerbaijan
    - Belarus
    - Georgia
    - Kyrgyzstan
    - Moldova
    - Tajikistan
    - Turkmenistan
    - Uzbekistan
- Cyprus
- Czech Republic
- Denmark
- Egypt
- Estonia
- Finland
- France
- Germany
- Greece
- Hungary
- Iceland
- India
- Indonesia
- Ireland

- Israel
- Italy
- Jamaica
- Japan
- Kazakhstan
- Korea, Republic of
- Latvia
- Lithuania
- Luxembourg
- Malta
- Mexico
- Morocco
- Netherlands
- New Zealand
- Norway
- Pakistan
- Philippines
- Poland
- Portugal
- Romania
- Russia
- Slovak Republic
- Slovenia
- South Africa
- Spain
- Sri Lanka
- Sweden
- Switzerland
- Thailand
- Trinidad and Tobago
- Tunisia
- Turkey
- Ukraine
- United Kingdom
- Venezuela

CHAPTER 13

Do You Owe Employment Tax?

If you live in the US and work for a US company, employment taxes (social security (FICA) and Medicare) are automatically withheld. If you are self-employed working in the US, you must pay the equivalent self-employment tax.

This chapter is about who pays the employment tax, when you work outside of the US. First, we'll look at the situation of working abroad for a foreign company; then, we'll consider the situation of a self-employed person, and lastly, we'll discuss how a self-employed person can eliminate paying self-employment tax.

Working for a foreign employer

To answer this question, we must dive into the complexities of the employment tax law. Social Security/Medicare are employment taxes. They are different than income taxes. While foreign earned income can be excluded from income taxes, it is still subject to employment taxes. But typically, no employment taxes are owed. Here's how:

For employment taxes, the term "wages" has a specific meaning under the law:

> *For purposes of this chapter, the term "wages" means all remuneration for employment, including the cash value of all remuneration (including benefits) paid in any medium other than cash23*

So, what is "employment" per employment tax law?

> *For purposes of this chapter, the term "employment" means any service, of whatever nature, performed ... outside the United States by a citizen or resident of the United States as an employee for an American employer[.]*[24]

What is a US employer according the to the employment tax law?

> *For purposes of this chapter, the term "American employer" means an employer which is—*
> *(1) the United States or any instrumentality thereof,*
> *(2) an individual who is a resident of the United States,*
> *(3) a partnership, if two-thirds or more of the partners are residents of the United States,*
> *(4) a trust, if all of the trustees are residents of the United States, or*
> *(5) a corporation organized under the laws of the United States or of any State.*[25]

The broadest definition is the fifth option, a corporation organized in the US or any state of the US.

So, if you are an employee for a US employer, the remuneration you receive are wages and subject to employment tax. If you are providing services for a non-US employer, then those services are not "employment". The remuneration for those services are not "wages" because they are not from "employment". Therefore, there are no employment taxes owed by you.

The employment tax is a tax on employee wages:

> *In addition to other taxes, there is hereby imposed on the income of every individual a tax equal to 6.2 percent of the wages (as defined in*

---

[23] 26 US Code 3121(a).

[24] 26 US Code 3121(b).

[25] 26 US Code 3121(h).

> *section 3121(a)) received by the individual with respect to employment (as defined in section 3121(b))*[26]

When working for a foreign employer, the money you receive is not wages from employment per the employment tax law. The tax is a percentage of wages. Wages would be zero; therefore, your taxes would be zero too.

Employers also pay employment tax.

> *In addition to other taxes, there is hereby imposed on every employer an excise tax, with respect to having individuals in his employ, equal to 6.2 percent of the wages (as defined in section 3121(a)) paid by the employer with respect to employment (as defined in section 3121(b)).*[27]

Again, for foreign employers, what is paid to their workers is not considered wages of employment under the employment tax law because the foreign employer doesn't have to pay the tax.

Welcome to reading the law. Words take on different meanings. Working for a foreign employer eliminates employment taxes.

Self-employed abroad

There is a special tax called self-employment tax that is imposed on self-employment income. The tax is 15.3% of your net earnings from self-employment.[28] Self-employment income, whether earned in the US or abroad, is reported on Schedule C of form 1040 and is subject to employment tax whether or not excluded from income tax. Here is what the law says:

---

[26] 26 US Code 3101(a).

[27] 26 US Code 3111(a).

[28] The combined rate of tax is 15.3%, which is comprised of 12.4% for social security and 2.9% for Medicare per IRC section 1401. The amount of income subject to social security tax is limited to ($118,500 for 2016; $127,200 for 2017). There is no cap on income subject to the Medicare tax. An additional 0.9% Medicare tax for income in excess of $200,000 for a single filer ($250,000 for married filing jointly; $125,000 for married filing separately).

> *In addition to other taxes, there shall be imposed for each taxable year, on the self-employment income of every individual, a tax equal to 12.4 percent of the amount of the self-employment income for such taxable year.*[29]

> *In addition to the tax imposed by the preceding subsection, there shall be imposed for each taxable year, on the self-employment income of every individual, a tax equal to 2.9 percent of the amount of the self-employment income for such taxable year.*[30]

> *In addition to the tax imposed by paragraph (1) and the preceding subsection, there is hereby imposed on every taxpayer (other than a corporation, estate, or trust) for each taxable year beginning after December 31, 2012, a tax equal to 0.9 percent of the self-employment income for such taxable year which is in excess of—*
> *(i) in the case of a joint return, $250,000,*
> *(ii) in the case of a married taxpayer (as defined in section 7703) filing a separate return, ½ of the dollar amount determined under clause (i), and*
> *(iii) in any other case, $200,000.*[31]

What is "self-employment income" per the law?

> *The term "self-employment income" means the net earnings from self-employment derived by an individual (other than a nonresident alien individual, except as provided by an agreement under section 233 of the Social Security Act) during any taxable year*[32]

Following the logic, what is "net earnings from self-employment"?

The term "net earnings from self-employment" means the gross income derived by an individual from any trade or business carried on by such individual, less the deductions allowed by this subtitle which are attributable to such trade or business.[33]

Only a person directly engaged in trade or business him or herself (or as a partner in a partnership) is subject to self-employment tax. If

---

[29] 26 US Code 1401(a).
[30] 26 US Code 1401(b)(1).
[31] 26 US Code 1401(b)(2).
[32] 26 US Code 1402(b).
[33] 26 US Code 1402(a).

you don't have net earnings from self-employment, then there is no self-employment tax.

How to eliminate self-employment tax

From the preceding discussion, we see that when working abroad, if your work is self-employment, there is an employment tax, but if you work for a foreign company, then there is no tax. So instead of being self-employed, create a foreign company and work for the foreign company. This eliminates your self-employment tax liability.

There are numerous considerations in putting such a strategy in place.

This strategy only works if the company is a foreign company and not a US company. You can be the sole shareholder and officer of the company. Be careful to create a foreign company that would be classified by the IRS as a corporation and not a partnership.

You should write a basic employment contract between you and your company. Any contracts with clients should be written in the name of the company. Your foreign company may need to provide a W-8BEN-E withholding statement to US employers.

Also, your foreign company should open a bank account to which you receive business income and pays your wages. These days, with the restrictions on bank accounts, opening a foreign bank account in the name of a foreign corporation isn't always simple. This foreign bank account should be reported on your tax return on form 8938 and FinCen-114(FBAR).

A foreign company costs money to create. There are usually annual corporation renewal taxes to be paid. A foreign company can be subject to foreign taxes on income. You may need to pay a foreign tax preparer to do your foreign taxes. These costs and liabilities offset the savings of self-employment tax. Pick carefully which country you choose to open a company and bank account in.

Also, the IRS requires ownership of foreign companies to be reported each year on your individual tax return form 1040. Failure to report the company is subject to a $10,000 fine plus 50% of the value of the company. That's an enormous penalty, so always report your foreign company on your tax return.

A foreign company which is wholly owned by you can be reported on form 8621 for Passive Foreign Investment Corporation (PFIC), as a foreign disregarded entity (form 8858), or on form 5471 for Controlled Foreign Corporation (CFC).

You don't want your corporation to be a PFIC because there is a punishing and complex tax, which is about 39% or more of profits.

Nor do you want to elect to treat your foreign company as a disregarded entity, because then the IRS will not treat the company as a foreign company which was the goal in the first place.

With CFCs, to avoid a complexity and tax for "subpart F"[34] income, take all the profits of the company each year as wages.

Another consideration is that by eliminating your self-employment tax, you are not paying into the Social Security Trust Fund. This can reduce the amount of social security income you could receive when you are older and want to collect payments (assuming social security is still around then).

All these extra complexities and costs may make paying self-employment tax the easiest and possibly cheaper solution. The more you earn, the less attractive paying self-employment tax will be.

Each person's situation is different. You should review your plans with an experience tax professional to make sure you have all the bases covered before acting on any of the thoughts provided in this chapter.

IRS per se foreign corporations

The following is a list of foreign corporation types which the IRS has determine are always treated as foreign corporations as opposed to a partnership, trust etc.

American Samoa, Corporation

[34] Subpart F of form 5471 creates a tax on retained earnings. This means you have to pay tax on income you haven't received yet.

Argentina, Sociedad Anonima

Australia, Public Limited Company

Austria, Aktiengesellschaft

Barbados, Limited Company

Belgium, Societe Anonyme

Belize, Public Limited Company

Bolivia, Sociedad Anonima

Brazil, Sociedade Anonima

Bulgaria, Aktsionerno Druzhestvo.

Canada, Corporation and Company

Chile, Sociedad Anonima

People's Republic of China, Gufen Youxian Gongsi

Republic of China (Taiwan), Ku-fen Yu-hsien Kung-szu

Colombia, Sociedad Anonima

Costa Rica, Sociedad Anonima

Cyprus, Public Limited Company

Czech Republic, Akciova Spolecnost

Denmark, Aktieselskab

Ecuador, Sociedad Anonima or Compania Anonima

Egypt, Sharikat Al-Mossahamah

El Salvador, Sociedad Anonima

Estonia, Aktsiaselts

European Economic Area/European Union, Societas Europaea

Finland, Julkinen Osakeyhtio/Publikt Aktiebolag

France, Societe Anonyme

Germany, Aktiengesellschaft

Greece, Anonymos Etairia

Guam, Corporation

Guatemala, Sociedad Anonima

Guyana, Public Limited Company

Honduras, Sociedad Anonima

Hong Kong, Public Limited Company
Hungary, Reszvenytarsasag
Iceland, Hlutafelag
India, Public Limited Company
Indonesia, Perseroan Terbuka
Ireland, Public Limited Company
Israel, Public Limited Company
Italy, Societa per Azioni
Jamaica, Public Limited Company
Japan, Kabushiki Kaisha
Kazakstan, Ashyk Aktsionerlik Kogham
Republic of Korea, Chusik Hoesa
Latvia, Akciju Sabiedriba
Liberia, Corporation
Liechtenstein, Aktiengesellschaft
Lithuania, Akcine Bendroves
Luxembourg, Societe Anonyme
Malaysia, Berhad
Malta, Public Limited Company
Mexico, Sociedad Anonima
Morocco, Societe Anonyme
Netherlands, Naamloze Vennootschap
New Zealand, Limited Company
Nicaragua, Compania Anonima
Nigeria, Public Limited Company
Northern Mariana Islands, Corporation
Norway, Allment Aksjeselskap
Pakistan, Public Limited Company
Panama, Sociedad Anonima
Paraguay, Sociedad Anonima
Peru, Sociedad Anonima

Philippines, Stock Corporation

Poland, Spolka Akcyjna

Portugal, Sociedade Anonima

Puerto Rico, Corporation

Romania, Societate pe Actiuni

Russia, Otkrytoye Aktsionernoy Obshchestvo

Saudi Arabia, Sharikat Al-Mossahamah

Singapore, Public Limited Company

Slovak Republic, Akciova Spolocnost

Slovenia, Delniska Druzba

South Africa, Public Limited Company

Spain, Sociedad Anonima

Surinam, Naamloze Vennootschap

Sweden, Publika Aktiebolag

Switzerland, Aktiengesellschaft

Thailand, Borisat Chamkad (Mahachon)

Trinidad and Tobago, Limited Company

Tunisia, Societe Anonyme

Turkey, Anonim Sirket

Ukraine, Aktsionerne Tovaristvo Vidkritogo Tipu

United Kingdom, Public Limited Company

United States Virgin Islands, Corporation

Uruguay, Sociedad Anonima

Venezuela, Sociedad Anonima or Compania Anonima[35]

---

[35] 26 CFR 301.7701-2(b)(8)(i).

CHAPTER 14

Convention on Mutual Administrative Assistance in Tax Matters

The following jurisdictions participate in the Convention on Mutual Assistance in Tax Matters:[36]

Albania, Andorra, Argentina, Anguilla, Aruba, Australia, Austria, Azerbaijan, Barbados, Belgium, Belize, Bermuda, Brazil, British Virgin Islands, Bulgaria, Burkina Faso, Cameroon, Canada, Cayman Islands, Chile, China, Colombia, Cook Islands, Costa Rica, Croatia, Curacao, Cyprus, Czech Republic, Denmark, Dominican Republic, El Salvador, Estonia, Finland, Faroe Islands, France, Gabon, Georgia, Germany, Ghana, Gibraltar, Greece, Greenland, Guatemala, Guernsey, Hungary, Iceland, India, Indonesia, Ireland, Israel, Isle of Man, Italy, Jamaica, Japan, Jersey, Kazakhstan, Kenya, Korea, Latvia, Liechtenstein, Lithuania, Luxembourg, Malaysia, Malta, Marshall Islands, Mauritius, Mexico, Moldova, Monaco, Montserrat, Morocco, Nauru, Netherlands, New Zealand, Nigeria, Niue, Norway, Pakistan, Panama, Philippines, Poland, Portugal, Romania, Russia, Saint Kitts and Nevis, Saint Lucia, Saint Vincent and the Grenadines, Samoa, San Marino, Saudi Arabia, Senegal, Seychelles, Singapore, Saint Maarten, Slovakia, Slovenia, South Africa, Spain, Sweden, Switzerland, Tunisia, Turkey, Turks and Caicos Islands, Uganda, Ukraine, United Kingdom, United States, Uruguay.

[36] For the current list of participating jurisdictions, go to http://www.oecd.org/tax/exchange-of-tax-information/convention-on-mutual-administrative-assistance-in-tax-matters.htm

CHAPTER 15

Cases and Rulings

Here are brief summaries of real tax court cases or applications of IRS rulings. Each case has unique characteristics that led to a challenge of the IRS in tax court. These are real stories of real people, Sometimes they win; sometimes they lose. If a case seems even remotely similar to your situation, read the full court case where the judge summarizes the facts of the case, the applicable law, and why they made their decision.

To see the full court case, which goes into detail of the facts and decision, search on the Internet for the court case. For example, for the first case below, search on "51-1 USTC 9114."

Some of the older decisions may contain law references that were later changed. Some of these that occur in the cases are:

- Old references to section 116 are now section 119
- The United Nations Relief and Rehabilitation Administration (UNRRA) is an agency was broken up in 1947 into the World Health Organization, International Refugee Organization and other UN agencies.
- The Physical Presence Test was once 510 full days over 18 months. This was later relaxed to the current 330 full days in 12 months.
- Also, in reading the cases, the term petitioner is usually the taxpayer and the term respondent is usually the IRS.

Abandonment of foreign residence

1. Temporary absence in the United States on a "business trip" or "vacation" does not necessarily result in the loss of an established foreign residence for purposes of the exemption under Code Sec. 116(a)(2). However, it is held that the exemption is lost in the case of a taxpayer who is absent on business in this country, even at the direction of his company and in connection with its foreign business, when the taxpayer subsequently engages in unrelated work. Under such circumstances, it cannot be said that taxpayer is still on a "business trip" after assignment to other work in the US.

   Seely, CA-2, 51-1 USTC 9114, 186 F2d 541. Rehearing denied, 51-1 USTC 9152, 186 F2d 541.

2. A US citizen residing in foreign countries for several years as an employee of UNRRA had her foreign assignment terminated in December 1947 and obtained an assignment to the US to which she desired to return for necessary medical treatment. She returned, had the treatment, and her employment by UNRRA was permanently terminated on January 31, 1948. Later in that year, after a period of convalescence, she applied for a position with a new employer, obtained such employment and left the US for a new foreign post on October 15, 1948. She was not "a bona fide resident of a foreign country or countries during the entire taxable year" and her income from sources outside the US was not excluded from tax under section 116(a)(1).

   Laughlin, 27 TC 23, Dec. 21, 970.

3. Although it was conceded that the taxpayer established bona fide residence in Beirut from October 31, 1957 to December 16, 1958, upon his departure on that date, with no intention of

returning, he severed all his ties there and abandoned his foreign residence.

A.E. Adams, 22 TCM 1215, Dec. 26, 295(M), TC Memo. 1963-241.

4. The taxpayer did not meet his burden of proof relating to whether he was a bona fide resident of a foreign country, thereby entitling his income earned there to be exempt from taxation. His employment abroad was terminated before the end of the taxable year, and even though he remained there beyond the end of the year, his status after termination was that of a mere transient.

F.J. Sherman, 24 TCM 650, Dec. 27,379(M), TC Memo. 1965-126.

5. Held: a bona fide resident of Switzerland since 1968, petitioner abandoned his Swiss residence on May 12, 1974 when he and his family severed all community ties, took all their possessions, and left for the US with the definite intention of not returning. Therefore, under sec. 911, I.R.C. 1954, as amended, the individual was entitled to exclude, as earned income from sources outside the US, $8,973 from the gross income for 1974.

R.A. Craig, 73 TC 1034, Dec. 36, 811 (Acq.).

6. Petitioner, a US citizen, went to Canada in 1973 to teach at a university. He intended to remain in Canada indefinitely but returned to the US within two years of his entrance into Canada because his teaching contract was terminated and he was unable to find other employment. Upon leaving Canada, petitioner applied for exemption from Canadian income taxes as a visiting teacher under Article VIIIA of the US-Canada Income Tax Convention and obtained refunds of Canadian income taxes for

the years 1973 and 1974. In claiming exemption from Canadian income tax under Article VIIIA of the US-Canada Income Tax Convention, petitioner did not make a statement to Canadian authorities, either explicitly or implicitly, that he was not a resident of Canada during 1973 and 1974 and is, therefore, not precluded by sec. 911(c)(6), I.R.C. 1954, from claiming the benefits of sec. 911(a)(1) as a bona fide resident of Canada during those years.

P.V. Riley, Jr., 74 TC 414, Dec. 36, 975.

Administrative assistance

7. A district court lacked jurisdiction over a Danish citizen's action to stop the US from collecting his Danish taxes because the US had not waived its sovereign immunity. Article 27 of the treaty explicitly requires that the Danish revenue claim be treated like US federal income taxes, but it does not provide the Danish citizen with the same rights to challenge the taxes that a US citizen might have. The treaty required the US to accept that taxes are due by certification by Denmark. The US accepted Denmark's revenue claim, and, therefore, the claim was treated like a US tax assessment and was subject to the Anti-Injunction Act (AIA) and the Declaratory Judgement Act (DJA).

   T. Dileng, D.C.-Ga., 2016-1 USTC 50, 150.

Airline employee

8. A commercial airline pilot did not qualify for the foreign earned income exclusion or the excess foreign living expense deduction because his identifiable principal place of business was a domestic airport. However, he was entitled to an interest expense deduction for loan losses that his S corporations

incurred because he established that the loan was bona fide. The S corporations were formed as aircraft leasing businesses. The taxpayer never realized a profit from the leasing operations, but he was entitled to deduct business expenses related to them because he organized and operated his businesses with the objective of making a profit. Although the fraud penalty was not imposed, additions to tax were assessed for failure to pay estimated tax and for a substantial understatement of income.

I.M. Sislik, 58 TCM 115, Dec. 46, 015(M), TC Memo. 1989-495.

9. An airline pilot was a bona fide resident of Japan and, therefore, entitled to the foreign earned income exclusion and to certain deductions for expenses incurred while living abroad. The pilot worked for a Japanese airline and left that country only when business required or when taking a vacation. Although the taxpayer maintained a home in Anchorage, Alaska, where his wife lived and worked, he visited only on vacations or during layovers. Additionally, the taxpayer had Japanese taxes withheld from his paychecks and filed Japanese income tax returns. These factors proved that the taxpayer intended to establish and maintain residence in Japan despite the fact that he lived in a Tokyo hotel, maintained no Japanese bank accounts, and was not assimilated into the culture. Furthermore, based on his ties to Japan, the taxpayer's abode and tax home were found to be in Japan, thereby enabling him to qualify for the tax benefits available to bona fide residents.

G.H. Jones, CA-5, 91-1 USTC 50,174, 927 F2d 849.

10. A pilot for a business that furnished flight crew personnel to aircraft operators was a bona fide resident of Japan because of a permanent duty assignment in that country. The pilot's tax home was located at his base airport in Japan, which was his principal place of business, rather than in California where his

family resided. Thus, the individual qualified for the foreign earned income exclusion.

J.S. Cobb, 62 TCM 408, Dec. 47,535(M), TC Memo. 1991-376.

11. A pilot was not entitled to a foreign earned income exclusion because his tax home was the vicinity of his principal place of employment which was in the US. The taxpayer's legal residence for appeal was the Eleventh Circuit Court of Appeals because his presence in North Carolina at the time the petition was filed was only temporary and he stipulated that the case was not appealable to the D.C. Circuit. The taxpayer did not qualify for the foreign earned income exclusion for income received in the Bahamas because his principal place of employment was New York City. Although a deduction for a paging device was permitted, the taxpayer's hotel room fees, inter-airport bus fares in New York and parking expenses in Florida were nondeductible commuting expenses.

    B.L. Swicegood, 57 TCM 1456, Dec. 45, 984(M), TC Memo. 1989-467.

12. The tax home of a flight engineer for an international air cargo service, who resided in the Bahamas and worked various US flight assignments, was in the vicinity of New York City, which was the base for his assignments. Thus, the individual did not have a foreign residency for tax purposes and his income did not qualify for the foreign earned income exclusion.

    M.H. Wojciechowski, 61 TCM 2758, Dec. 47, 373(M), TC Memo. 1991-239.

13. An airline pilot was not a "qualified individual" for purposes of claiming a foreign earned income exclusion because his tax home was not located outside of the US. He was based by his

employer in the US even though he flew all his flights between European cities. He had no headquarters or base station in Europe.

E.T. Dougherty, 62 TCM 680, Dec. 47, 605(M), TC Memo. 1991-442.

14. In allocating income for purposes of the foreign earned income exclusion, a flight attendant could not treat income earned in international airspace as income earned in a foreign country because such airspace is not under the sovereignty of a government other than the US. Furthermore, the flight attendant had to allocate unpaid pre-flight and post-flight service time when calculating foreign earned income, and allocate income from sick and vacation leave between foreign earned income and income subject to federal income tax.

    W.D. Rogers, 97 TCM 1573, Dec. 57, 827(M), TC Memo. 2009-111.

15. A flight attendant stationed in Hong Kong, whose duties were performed in and out of the US, could not exclude all of her income using the foreign earned income exclusion. Only that portion of her wages attributable to services performed in a foreign country was excludible. Income earned over international waters is not income earned in a foreign country. The flight-time percentages stipulated by the parties applied to all of her compensation, including compensation for her preflight and post-flight duties, as well as for non-flight time such as vacation and sick time.

    W.D. Rogers, CA-D.C., 2015-1 USTC 50,273.

Alien resident of United States

16. Under nondiscrimination clauses in various tax treaties with foreign countries, citizens of such countries who are resident aliens of the US may qualify for the Code Sec. 911 exclusions and deduction under the bona fide resident test. These countries include:
    - Australia
    - Austria
    - Barbados
    - Belgium
    - Canada
    - Cyprus
    - Denmark
    - Egypt
    - Finland
    - France
    - The Federal Republic of Germany
    - Greece
    - Hungary
    - Iceland
    - India
    - Indonesia
    - Ireland
    - Italy
    - Jamaica
    - Japan
    - Korea
    - Luxembourg
    - Malta
    - Morocco
    - The Netherlands
    - New Zealand
    - Norway

- Pakistan
- People's Republic of China
- The Philippines
- Poland
- Romania
- Spain
- Sweden
- Switzerland
- Trinidad and Tobago
- Tunisia
- Union of Soviet Socialist Republics
- United Kingdom

Rev. Rul. 91-58, 1991-2 CB 340.

Allocation of compensation

17. Petitioner, a US citizen residing in France, was employed by J-M Europe Corp., a Delaware corporation subsidiary of Johns-Manville Corp., as an executive overseeing the operations of various subsidiaries of Johns-Manville Corp. doing business in Europe. Petitioner worked part of the time within the US and part of the time outside of the US. Petitioner received from his employer as compensation for his services a basic salary and bonuses based on the earnings of the foreign subsidiaries of Johns-Manville Corp. and on the export earnings of Johns-Manville Corp. The bonuses received by petitioner do not qualify as compensation for services performed wholly outside of the US and thus are not wholly exempt from tax under sec. 911, I.R.C. 1954. Respondent's allocation on a time basis approved.

    A.L. Cini, 67 TC 857, Dec. 34,272.

18. The salary paid to a professional hockey player, who was a Canadian citizen and resident, by his employer, a US professional hockey club, is allocable between sources within the US and outside the US. Rev. Rul. 76-66 revoked.
    Rev. Rul. 87-38, 1987-1 CB 176.

19. Compensation based on actual flight time paid to an airline pilot who is a US citizen and bona fide resident of a foreign country must be allocated between US and foreign sources by comparing the hours of both flight and required preflight services performed in the US to the total hours of such services. Rev. Rul. 76-66 distinguished.

    Rev. Rul. 77-167, 1977-1 CB 239.

20. A US citizen, a bona fide foreign resident, working partly within the US and partly abroad, must allocate his annual living allowance and regular salary for purposes of section 911 of the Code if his employment contract does not so provide.

    Rev. Rul. 69-238, 1969-1 CB 195.

    W.D. Rogers, 97 TCM 1573, Dec. 57,827(M), TC Memo. 2009-111.

    W.D. Rogers, CA-D.C., 2015-1 USTC 50,273..

Allocation of deductions

21. Examples are given to show the computation of US citizens' earned foreign income excludable from gross income under section 911(a) of the Code, and deductions allocable to the excluded income, in situations involving sole proprietors and

partners who receive fees from services in excess of the maximum exclusion, income from services and capital in excess of the maximum exclusion, and expenses in excess of income.

Rev. Rul. 75-86, 1975-1 CB 242.

American Institute of Taiwan

22. Thus, all laws, including the Internal Revenue Code, treaties, international agreements, and conventions between the US and Taiwan that were in force on December 31, 1978, are continued in force unless and until terminated by law.

Rev. Rul. 80-208, 1980-2 CB 212.

Amounts paid by United States

23. An architect who was employed by the US Department of State, Office of Foreign Buildings Operations (FBO) as director of a construction project in Colombia was not entitled to the foreign earned income exclusion because he was an employee of a US agency and not an independent contractor. The FBO retained the right to control his work and restrict his authority, required him to provide regular progress reports and contracted with and paid the workers he hired. The FBO also controlled his work hours and leave time and provided him with some employee benefits. Further, the taxpayer's position was permanent rather than transitory; he worked exclusively for the FBO for several years and the FBO intended to create an employer-employee relationship with him. In addition, he had no investment in the work facilities and no opportunity for profit or loss, either party could terminate his employment contract, and the project was within the scope of the FBO's regular business.

E. Eren, CA-4, 99-1 USTC 50,599, 180 F3d 594.

24. A world-renowned specialist in malariology working in Pakistan with its Ministry of Health was entitled to a tax refund pursuant to the foreign earned income exclusion because he was an independent contractor rather than an employee of a US agency. Despite having a personal service contract with the agency, which provided for tax withholding, report schedules and leave accrual, the agency did not supervise or have actual control over the doctor's work for the Pakistani government. Furthermore, the evidence indicated that the agency improperly used the personal service contract for hiring the doctor and that it lacked the intent to retain control over his work.

W. Chin, CA-9, 95-1 USTC 50,302, 57 F3d 722.

25. The salary received by a US citizen while employed by the United States Bureau of Public Roads to work on a highway project of the Government of Iran, which had entered into a credit agreement with the Export-Import Bank in Washington under which the proceeds of a loan to Iran were to be used exclusively to finance the road project, was not exempt from federal income tax. The amounts received as salary were "amounts paid by the United States or an agency thereof," although the employee's basic salary was reimbursed by Iran. One dissent.

E.E. Wolfe, CA-D.C., 66-1 USTC 9375, 361 F2d 62. Cert. denied, 385 US 838, 87 SCt 86.

F. Morris, CtCls, Commissioner's Report, 677 CCH 8182.
J.C. Johnson, CA-5, 68-1 USTC 9106, 386 F2d 824.

26. Payments received by taxpayer for services performed as second officer on a government-owned vessel operated in

foreign waters by a shipping line which pays crew members from funds supplied specifically for that purpose by a US agency were wages "paid by the United States or an agency thereof." Such compensation was not excludable from gross income under Code Sec. 911(a)(2).

G.Y. Erlandson, CA-9, 60-1 USTC 9364, 277 F2d 70.

R.W. Teskey, 30 TC 456, Dec. 23, 006.

27. A citizen of the US, employed on a vessel owned—or owned for the time being—by an agency of the US and operated by the US is paid wages by a private shipping line as agent of the US from funds provided specifically for that purpose by the US. Such compensation constitutes an amount paid by the US or an agency thereof within the meaning of section 911(a) of the Internal Revenue Code of 1954 and is not excludable from gross income under section 911(a)(2) of the Code even though the employee may be physically present in a foreign country or countries for 510 full days or more of an 18 consecutive month period to which such wages are attributable. Section 1(a) of the Clarification Act of March 24, 1943, 57 Stat. 45, 50 U. S. C. 1291(a) affords no basis for holding that such compensation is entitled to exemption from taxation under section 911(a)(2) of the Code.

Rev. Rul. 58-4, 1958-1 CB 268.

28. Amounts earned by US citizens present in a foreign country for at least 510 full days during any period of 18 consecutive months, which are paid from sources outside this country are excludable from income unless actually paid by the US or an agency thereof. The Court of Appeals for the First Circuit, in affirming the Tax Court, stated that since the Air Force Child Guidance Center in Germany was, in actuality, a US agency,

wages paid by it to the taxpayer-employees could not be excluded from their taxable incomes. The Center was not a mere conduit for money paid to the taxpayers by private sources because it was both the obligor and payor of the taxpayers' salaries.

B.D. Kalinski, CA-1, 76-1 USTC 9177, 528 F2d 969.

29. Wages paid to a US citizen by the Panama Canal Commission (PCC) were not exempt from taxes because the PCC was an agency of the US. The PCC was controlled by the US government, operated to serve governmental purposes, did not benefit private interests, and was limited to government-connected persons. Accordingly, the PCC was an agency of the US, and the wages were not exempt from taxes. Summary judgment in favor of the IRS was affirmed.

A.J. Payne, CA-2, 92-2 USTC 50,609. Cert. denied, 6/21/93.

30. Individuals who resided in West Germany and who worked for and were paid by non-appropriated fund instrumentalities (NAFIs) concerning services provided to the US Army were employees of a US agency. Thus, amounts received by such individuals from such sources were not excludable as foreign earned income.

D.W. Matthews, CA-D.C., 90-2 USTC 50,363, 907 F2d 1173.

31. The Trust Territory Government of the Pacific Islands is an agency of the US.

K.R. Groves, CA-5, 76-2 USTC 9509, 533 F2d 1376. Cert. denied, 429 US 1000, 97 SCt 529.

32. A US customs inspector, who was paid overtime for off-hours services in the Bahamas to accommodate an airline, was paid by the US rather than by the airline, even though the airline was

obligated by statute to pay the government for the cost of these services. Thus, the compensation did not constitute foreign earned income. The court noted that: (1) the airline paid the government, not the inspector, for the services; (2) the government compensated the inspector; (3) the government, not the airline, could hire, fire and supervise the inspector, under a contract; (4) the inspector continued to perform the same duties during overtime as he did during regular hours; (5) the government bore the risk of nonpayment by the airline; and (6) the inspector's position that he was employed by the airline was inconsistent with the purpose of the tax on government payments.

J.T. Smith, CA-9, 83-1 USTC 9255, 701 F2d 807.

33. Compensation paid to an individual by the US Employees Association of Tehran, Iran, for services performed in Tehran was not excludable from his gross income because the association was held to be an agency of the US government within the meaning of Code Sec. 911(a)(2). The association was organized to provide recreational activities and commissary benefits to embassy employees and their dependents and was under the control of the Ambassador.
A.A. Morse, Sr., CtCls, 71-1 USTC 9482, 443 F2d 1185.

34. Amounts paid to the taxpayer as an employee by the US Officers' Open Mess, Taipei, Formosa, were excludible from her income. The above organization, before January 9, 1961, was not an instrumentality of the US since it was not a military non-appropriated fund activity.

L.D.Brummitt, CtCls, 64-1 USTC 9310, 329 F2d 966.

35. Taxpayer was not taxable on that part of his 1951 income, which was earned in Ethiopia, even though it was paid to him by the

US Bureau of Public Roads, Department of Commerce out of funds transferred to it by a board of directors set up by the Ethiopian Government. Income tax was withheld by the US Bureau of Public Roads Department of Commerce. The taxpayer received the benefits of the Social Security laws as an employee of the US and was paid compensation benefits for an injury sustained while in Ethiopia under the federal employees' compensation act. (The compensation benefits were charged back to the Ethiopian Government.) Here, the US was not the debtor but simply paid the amount which was in fact a debt of another debtor. It is immaterial that taxpayer did not pay any income taxes to Ethiopia. He is entitled to recover the amounts withheld from the part of his 1951 salary that was earned in Ethiopia since he satisfied the 510 full days[37] requirement in 1939 Code Sec. 116(a)(2).

Krichbaum, DC Tenn., 56-1 USTC 9362, 138 FSupp 515.

36. Amounts received by a US citizen while employed by the US Army Corps of Engineers to work on the construction of various facilities in Saudi Arabia under a construction contract between that country and the US were not excludable from his gross income. Although the construction projects were covered by an irrevocable letter of credit deposited by Saudi Arabia with a New York bank in an amount sufficient to fund the projects (including compensation for employees such as the taxpayer), the amounts received by the taxpayer were "amounts paid by the United States or an agency thereof."

    A.T. Wagner, DC Colo., 86-1 USTC 9186, 628 FSupp 1184.

37. An employee of the United States Army Corps of Engineers who worked in Saudi Arabia pursuant to an engineering assistance agreement between the Army Corps and the government of

---

[37] The 510 days was later changed to 330 full days.

Saudi Arabia was not entitled to the foreign earned income exclusion for the amount of his wages. Where the United States has the primary obligation to pay the taxpayer's salary, as was the case here, the foreign earned income exclusion does not apply, even if the taxpayer's salary will ultimately be reimbursed by a foreign government.

H.B. Davidson, DC Ga., 87-2 USTC 9473, 670 FSupp 998.

38. Petitioner, an individual citizen of the US, was a bona fide nonresident of the US for more than six months during the taxable year 1942. As a member of an engineering partnership, he received in 1942 the amount of $36,279.30 as his distributive share of the net amount derived from four contracts which the partnership entered into with the US and which were performed by the partnership and another party under a joint venture agreement. He was also paid in 1942 the amount of $5,000 by the joint venture as additional compensation because of the nature of the work done by him in the performance of the above contracts. Both these amounts were received from sources outside of the US and would have constituted earned income as defined in section 25(a), Internal Revenue Code (as in effect for the year 1942) had they been received from sources within the US. (1) The amount of $36,279.30 was not excludable from petitioner's gross income in 1942 under section 116(a), Internal Revenue Code, since it was an "amount paid by the United States" within the meaning and intent of the parenthetical exception to the exemption provided by that section. (2) The amount of $5,000 was excludable from petitioner's gross income in 1942 under section 116(a), Internal Revenue Code.
Sverdrup, 14 TC 859, Dec. 17,644 (Acq.).

39. A US citizen employed in Spain as a civilian by the US Air Force, and a resident of Spain was married to a Spanish citizen who has no US residence. The marriage ceremony took place outside

Spain. The Civil Code of Spain contains comprehensive community property provisions governing the rights and interests of one spouse in the other's earnings. Explicit provisions of article 1325 of the Spanish Civil Code render the community property laws therein inapplicable to couples like this, and thus no portion of husband-petitioner's earnings belonged to the wife under Spanish law. Husband petitioner, who filed US income tax returns without his wife, was therefore required to report his full earnings on such returns.

R.R. Santiago, 61 TC 53, Dec. 32,177. Aff'd, *per curiam*, CA-D.C., 75-1 USTC 9273.

40. During 1963, petitioner was employed by the US Embassy Cooperative Commissary in Pakistan. The Commissary was organized and operated under Government regulations; policy and management direction of the Commissary was vested in the State Department; and the Commissary was engaged in governmental functions and had no commercial objectives. The Commissary was an agency of the US for the purpose of sec. 911(a), I. R. C. 1954, and, consequently, petitioner is not entitled to exclude from his gross income the compensation he received therefrom.

    C.A. Donaldson, 51 TC 830, Dec. 29,467.

    Rev. Rul. 64-255, 1964-2 CB 189.

41. An Air Force officer assigned to NATO did not receive tax-free foreign-earned income because, while he was working overseas, he was subject to the supervision of and had pay checks issued by the US Air Force. He was not, however, liable for penalties for failure to file a return because his failure was due to his reliance on the advice of an overseas IRS agent and an Air Force attorney. The deduction of undocumented interest payments on

a family residence, a second home, and a car were denied with the exception of a conservative estimate of the interest paid on the family residence. The taxpayer's claimed deduction for the destruction of his automobile was denied because he received insurance compensation for the loss and he failed to establish the fair market value of the vehicle prior to the accident.

W.A. Gillis, 52 TCM 1128, Dec. 43,532(M), TC Memo. 1986-576.

42. A defense contractor who was deployed to a North Atlantic Treaty Organization (NATO) mission in Afghanistan was not allowed to characterize the compensation he received during his deployment as foreign earned income because he was an employee of the US Government. Although the taxpayer worked under the supervision of NATO officers, the US Army hired him, paid his salary, assigned him to the NATO post, had exclusive authority to discharge him from military service, and subjected him to the same periodic Defense Civilian Intelligence Personnel System performance evaluations to which all Department of Defense intelligence personnel were subject. Therefore, the US Army had the right to control the taxpayer's work. The taxpayer failed to carry his burden of proving that he was an employee of NATO rather than the US Army during the period of his deployment. Therefore, as an employee of the US during those years, the taxpayer was subject to the exception under Code Sec. 911(b)(1)(B)(ii) and was not entitled to a foreign earned income exclusion.

S. Striker, 110 TCM 623, Dec. 60,479(M), TC Memo. 2015-248.

43. Pursuant to the US Code, US employees may be either detailed or transferred to international organizations for foreign service. Petitioner was transferred from the US Army to NATO. After 1981, sec. 911 IRC was amended to exclude from the definition

of foreign earned income amounts "paid by the United States or an agency thereof to an employee of the United States or an agency thereof." Petitioner was an employee of NATO and not an employee of the US.

W.H. Adair, 70 TCM 998, Dec. 50,946(M), TC Memo. 1995-493 (Acq.).

44. A citizen of the US employed as an offset press operator by the Army and Air Force Exchange Service (AAFES) in Munich, Federal Republic of Germany, was not entitled to exclude the wages from such employment from his gross income for the tax years in question. Since the printer was paid by AAFES, an instrumentality of the US, the wages constituted amounts paid by the US and not foreign earned income. Although the press operator argued that a US treaty obligation deemed his AAFES wages as paid from a source other than the US or an agency or instrumentality thereof, the exception to the foreign earned income definition was unaffected by such treaty.

    H.J. Shelonzek, Jr., 55 TCM 515, Dec. 44,673(M), TC Memo. 1988-137.

45. An economic advisor performing personal services in Haiti was employed by the US Agency for International Development (USAID) and therefore was not entitled to exclude from income compensation received from this federal agency. USAID exercised considerable control over the advisor's work and, thus, the advisor's claim that she was an independent contractor receiving foreign earned income was unsubstantiated. The applicable statute specifically provides that the proffered exclusion from income does not apply to amounts paid by a US agency to an employee. Additions to tax for negligence were also properly imposed.

L.M. Matt, 59 TCM 472, Dec. 46, 547(M) TC Memo. 1990-209.

46. Although Code Sec. 911(b)(1)(B)(ii) does not define the term "employee," an individual engaged by the US Agency for International Development in Haiti was considered an employee of such agency under the common law meaning of the term "employee." Thus, amounts received by the individual from such agency did not qualify for the foreign earned income exclusion.

    C.L. Juliard, 61 TCM 2683, Dec. 47,363(M), TC Memo. 1991-230.

47. A demographer working in Peru under a written contract with the US Agency for International Development was an employee of an agency of the US and was not eligible for the foreign earned income exclusion. He was not, however, liable for additions to tax due to negligence. Under the circumstances, he could have reasonably believed that he was an independent contractor of an agency of the US, which would have made him eligible for the exclusion.

    A.M. Marckwardt, 62 TCM 262, Dec. 47,497(M), TC Memo. 1991-347.

48. A US citizen was not an employee of the US or a US government agency but an independent contractor and, therefore, was entitled to the foreign earned income exclusion. The US government agency (USAID) that administered the emergency disaster relief project in Ecuador that the taxpayer, a civil engineer, was hired to oversee did not have the right or ability to control the taxpayer's activities. Further, the work and leave schedule and termination provisions in the contract at issue were common in the industry; USAID did not withhold income or social security taxes; the taxpayer's liability for Ecuadorean

taxes and any double benefit from his failure to pay them was beyond the scope of the inquiry; and the contract was, on its face, a personal service contract.

J.R. deTorres, 65 TCM 2381, Dec. 48,983(M), TC Memo. 1993-161.

C.F. Hawkins, 66 TCM 332, Dec. 49,202(M), TC Memo. 1993-350.

49. A US taxpayer employed by the US Agency for International Development in Turkey was not entitled to exclude amounts received as compensation for services rendered because the amounts were paid in Turkish Lira, which were subject to certain currency restrictions. The expenditure of the Turkish Lira conferred an economic benefit upon the taxpayer, and it is this benefit that was taxable.

V.G. Marty, Jr., 31 TCM 26, Dec. 31,212(M), TC Memo. 1972-11.

50. Payments received by an employee of the US Employees' Association of Tehran, Iran, were not excludable since that organization was an agency of the US.

D.R. Dykes, 30 TCM 1141, Dec. 31,036(M), TC Memo. 1971-266.

51. Per diem payments received by an employee who provided field team services for the maintenance and modification of weapons systems and support equipment in the US were includible in his gross income.

D.R. Wyrick, 35 TCM 1176, Dec. 33,991(M), TC Memo. 1976-268.

52. A nonresident alien individual married to and filing a joint return with a US citizen was not entitled to exclude from income wages she received as an employee of the US army in Germany. The individual (a German citizen) was a receptionist at the Friedberg, Germany, US Army Dental Clinic and entered into a termination agreement with the US Army during the tax year at issue. The US Army provided the funds that the Pay Office Foreign Forces (POFF) disbursed to the taxpayer. However, the POFF did not employ the taxpayer; the individual was a US Army employee, subject to hiring, firing, and supervision by that US government agency. Although POFF was the immediate source of the funds paid to the taxpayer, as an employee of the US, she was paid by a US "an agency" and, therefore, was not entitled to the foreign earned income exclusion. Moreover, collateral estoppel did not apply because the exclusion issue was not litigated and decided in a prior proceeding.

    H. Dinger, 110 TCM 130, Dec. 60,367(M), TC Memo. 2015-145.

53. A US citizen employed by an agency of the US performed services in a foreign country under the terms of an agreement between the governments of that country and of the US whereby the US agency agreed to furnish certain technical training to nationals of such foreign country. The foreign government agreed to reimburse the agency for the cost of salaries paid its employees assigned to give such technical assistance. The compensation of such employees constitutes amounts paid by the US or an agency thereof within the meaning of section 911(a)(2) of the Internal Revenue Code of 1954. Therefore, such compensation is not excludable from the gross income of the taxpayer even though he was physically present in the foreign country for 510 full days or more of the 18 consecutive-month period to which such compensation is attributable.

Rev. Rul. 58-485, 1958-2 CB 388.

54. Compensation received by a US citizen for services performed in a foreign country under a contract with the foreign government which required him to render advisory services for a period of two years is not an amount paid by the US or any agency thereof within the meaning of section 911(a)(2) of the Internal Revenue Code of 1954, even though the project on which he worked was financed in part by an agency of the US. Therefore, such compensation is excludable from the gross income of the taxpayer to the extent provided by section 911(c)(1) of the Code if he otherwise meets the requirements for exemption under section 911(a)(2) of the Code.
Rev. Rul. 67-87, 1967-1 CB 186.

Rev. Rul. 68-81, 1968-1 CB 40.

55. The above ruling is modified to make it applicable only to tax years beginning on and after February 19, 1968.

Rev. Rul. 69-213, 1969-1 CB 34.

56. Amounts paid by the US Government to an individual US citizen under a contract performed in a foreign country are not exempt from taxation. US citizens employed and paid by the contractor, however, may receive the exemption if they satisfy the other requirements of Sec. 911.

Rev. Rul. 54-483, 1954-2 CB 168.

57. US Armed Forces exchanges, commissioned and noncommissioned officers' messes, Armed Forces motion picture services, and other organizations similarly organized and operated under US Army, Navy, or Air Force regulations are

integral parts of the Armed Forces, agencies, or instrumentalities of the US. Compensation received from such organizations by a US citizen for personal services performed abroad, whether paid from appropriated or non-appropriated funds, constitutes "amounts paid by the United States or any agency thereof" within the meaning of section 116(a)(1) of the Internal Revenue Code of 1939. The term "agency" as used in that section includes an instrumentality of the United States. See section 39.116-1 of Regulations 118. Also, such amounts are deemed to be "derived from sources within the United States" within the meaning of section 251(j) of the Code. Accordingly, such amounts must be included in gross income, for Federal income tax purposes.

Rev. Rul. 54-612, 1954-2 CB 169.

58. Amounts received by a U.S. citizen and an employee of the U.S. Corps of Engineers for services performed in a foreign country are not foreign earned income within the meaning of section 911 of the Code since the individual is an employee of, and paid by, the Corps even though the ultimate "source" of such amounts is foreign. Rev. Rul. 80-78 clarified.

Rev. Rul. 85-29, 1985-1 CB 223; clarifying Rev. Rul. 80-78, 1980-1 CB 171.

Antarctic region

59. An individual could not exclude income earned for services rendered in Antarctica from his gross income because Antarctica is not a "foreign country" as that term is employed in Reg. §1.911-2(h). The definition of foreign country in the regulation is reasonable and consistent with the congressional purpose underlying the exclusion. An essential component of

the definition of a foreign country is the requirement that the territory be under the sovereignty of a government that is not the US government. The regulation should not be read to include the limitless class of sovereign-less territory, such as Antarctica, in the definition of "foreign country."

D. Arnett, CA-7, 2007-1 USTC 50,162, 473 F3d 790, aff'g, 126 TC 89, Dec. 56,415.

Rev. Rul. 67-52, 1967-1 CB 186.

Armed forces service

60. A US citizen who is a bona fide resident of a foreign country does not lose that status by reason of absence from the foreign country while serving in the US Armed Forces. I.T. 3797 superseded.

Rev. Rul. 70-374, 1970-2 CB 154.

Army civilian club

61. The Union Club of Tokyo was a non-appropriated fund activity established and operated under Army regulations and as such was an agency of the US during the year 1953, and the salary paid to petitioner as civilian manager thereof was not excludable from his gross income under section 116(a), I. R. C. 1939.

F.E. Raffensperger, 33 TC 1097, Dec. 24,114.

Artist's sale of paintings

62. The amounts received from the sale of a petitioner's paintings constituted "earned income" as defined in section 911(b), I. R.

C. 1954.

M. Tobey, 60 TC 227, Dec. 31,971 (Acq.).

R.H. Cook, CtCls, 79-1 USTC 9335, 599 F2d 400.

63. Rev. Ruls. 71-182 and 71-183 held that income from the sale of musical or artistic property created by certain taxpayers is not earned income within the meaning of section 911(b) of the Code and is revoked.

Rev. Rul. 79-85, 1979-1 CB 246.

Author's compensation

64. Royalties paid to a writer by a publisher for the transfer of property rights of the writer in the writer's products are earned income under section 911(b) of the Code.

Rev. Rul. 80-254, 1980-2 CB 222, modifying Rev. Rul. 71-315, 1971-2 CB 271.

Applicable test of bona fide residence

65. Taxpayer worked for a China Trade Act corporation in China from 1929 to November 1941. He was a bona fide resident of China during that period. However, when war broke out between the US and Japan in 1941, taxpayer returned to the US. He returned to China in February, 1946, and remained there until November, 1947, when he returned to the US after selling out his interest in the China Trade Act corporation. Under these circumstances, the Tax Court properly held that the taxpayer had not returned to the US in 1941 for a temporary period with the intention of returning to his domicile when the purpose for

which he had returned had been consummated. Accordingly, taxpayer was not a bona fide resident of China, nor was he present in a foreign country for at least two years before he left China in November, 1947. Consequently, the income earned in 1946 and 1947 in China was not exempt.

R.A. Henningsen, CA-4, 57-1 USTC 9637, 243 F2d 954.

66. Amounts received by a married couple from a corporation for which they held majority interest were constructive dividends, not loans. There was no collateral, no fixed repayment schedule, no limits were set on the amounts to be borrowed, and the proceeds were used for personal purposes. Since the corporation, a possessions corporation with its plant located in Puerto Rico, accumulated huge earnings but never paid dividends, the couple, which intended to move to Puerto Rico, was effectively given permanent tax-free control over the funds. The Tax Court did not make a mistake of law construing Code Sec. 933 because Congressional policy permitted the company to accumulate earnings in Puerto Rico free of tax but did not authorize tax-free dividends to residents of a state (Illinois).

E.O. Bergersen, CA-1, 97-1 USTC 50,295, 109 F3d 56.

67. A petroleum engineer, who was employed by foreign petroleum companies in foreign countries over the course of several years, did not qualify for the foreign earned income exclusion because he maintained his tax home in the US and was not a bona fide resident of a foreign country for an entire tax year. The taxpayer retained strong economic, familial, and personal ties to his US home and maintained only transitory ties to the foreign countries during the years at issue. Further, he had no actual intent to remain in the foreign countries, his employment was for a limited duration, his status was that of a transient at foreign worksites, he did not assume the obligations of a foreign home,

and he was not assimilated into the foreign communities.

D.P. Lansdown, 68 TCM 680, Dec. 50, 114(M), TC Memo. 1994-452.

68. Income received in 1946 by a US citizen from a US company for services performed by him in Germany was exempt from income tax. The taxpayer maintained his own apartment in Frankfort and later married a German girl, and his overseas employment was intended to be of unlimited duration. The Court ruled that taxpayer's bona fide residence in Germany was established in spite of the Government's contentions that he did not pay a German income tax, that he was reimbursed by his employer for expenses incurred for living quarters and food, that he maintained his bank account in the US, and that he never applied for German citizenship.

W.B. Meals, DC Calif., 53-1 USTC 9225, 110 FSupp 658.

69. Taxpayer was a bona fide resident of a foreign country during all of 1948 and is entitled to refund of federal income taxes paid on his salary earned in Okinawa for that year. He had gone to Okinawa in April of 1947 to work for a construction company under a one-year contract, subject to indefinite renewal on an informal basis. He constructed a three-bedroom home in November, 1947, and lived in it thereafter. He was married in 1948 to a native of Okinawa and was still living on the island at the time of this action.

Seki, DC Hawaii, 54-2 USTC 9563.

70. Taxpayer, an US citizen, worked in Saudi Arabia as a carpenter for a private concern during the entire taxable year 1949, gave notice of the termination of his contract in April, 1950, and returned to the US in May, 1950. Taxpayer did not speak Arabic,

did not enter into the social life of the community, nor become assimilated into the foreign environment. He did not pay any Saudi Arabian income taxes, nor apply for Saudi Arabian citizenship. The Court held that the fact that taxpayer contracted to work in Saudi Arabia for a period extending beyond the end of the tax year in question took him out of the class of a transient and sojourner, and that he was entitled to the exemption claimed under 1939 Code Sec. 116(a) as a bona fide resident of a foreign country.

Ditman, DC Md., 56-1 USTC 9186, 136 FSupp 542.

71. In 1947, taxpayer went to Saudi Arabia to work for an oil company. His employment contract terminated in the fall of 1948 and he returned to the US, where he remained until after December 31, 1948. He seeks to recover income taxes paid for the year 1948 on the ground that he was a bona fide resident of Saudi Arabia and had returned to the US only on a vacation. The jury returned a verdict in favor of the taxpayer on his suit for refund.

J.D. Carter, DC Tex., 58-2 USTC 9570.

72. The taxpayer, a US citizen working as a tugboat captain in the North Sea during 1967 and 1968, was denied exclusion of income earned abroad. While the taxpayer was in the North Sea or in countries contiguous to it for at least 510 days of a consecutive 18-month period, he failed to prove that the North Sea was under the sovereignty of the United Kingdom or of any other foreign government. Parliamentary acts passed that purportedly extended British sovereignty over all of the continental shelf underlying the North Sea, as applied, only regulated natural resource development in the area. Furthermore, during 1967 and 1968, the US did not recognize national sovereignty extending beyond three miles from shore.

L.A. Plaisance, DC La., 77-2 USTC 9485, 433 FSupp 936.

73. In determining whether US citizens are bona fide residents of a foreign country or countries, the tests generally applicable will be those used in ascertaining whether an alien is a resident of the US. Mere physical presence in a foreign country for the entire tax year is not of itself sufficient to establish a US citizen as a bona fide resident of such country.
Mim. 5632, February 9, 1944, 443 CCH 6154.

74. During 1949, petitioner earned and was paid $7,350 from sources outside of the US as an accountant employed by Lockheed Aircraft Overseas Corporation at the Keflavik Airport, an International Airport in Keflavik, Iceland. None of the amounts received by petitioner were paid by the US or any agency or instrumentality thereof. The petitioner was held a bona fide resident of Iceland throughout the taxable year 1949 and the $7,350 is exempt from tax under section 116(a)(1), IRC.

F.H. Pierce, 22 TC 493, Dec. 20,373 (Acq.).

75. When a taxpayer left Saudi Arabia in November 1949, it was understood that he would return, and indeed he left most of his belongings there with that expectation. Such temporary absence from the foreign country does not interrupt his period of foreign residence.

L. Larsen, 23 TC 599, Dec. 20,801.

76. A farm management specialist and his wife moved from Iowa to China for employment first with UNRRA and later with the Food and Agricultural Organization of the United Nations. They were found to have been bona fide residents of China during 1948, where they established their home in that country, joined

local organizations and participated in local social life.

B.B. Hamer, 22 TC 343, Dec. 20,341 (Acq.).

77. University professors on leave working for the Food and Agriculture Organization were bona fide residents of Argentina while they were present there in the performance of their duties. The fact that neither taxpayer intended to remain in Argentina after completion of their assignments, which were for a definite period, but planned to return to their teaching jobs in the US, and the fact that each enjoyed privileges and immunities as officials of the US, including freedom from the Argentina income tax, did not prevent them from establishing bona fide residence in Argentina, where they integrated into the community life. Also, the tax exempt status conferred by the treaty was not equivalent to a "statement" made by the taxpayer that he was a nonresident for tax purposes, which would prevent recovery.

Scott, Jr., CtCls, 70-2 USTC 9652, 432 F2d 1388.

78. The petitioner was not a bona fide resident of a foreign country or countries for a period of at least two years prior to the date in 1946 on which he changed his residence to the US, under section 116(a)(2), I. R. C., where he abandoned his foreign residence before the end of the two-year period, even though he may have acquired no other residence until after that period.

L. White, 22 TC 585, Dec. 20,398.

H. Lindsay, 13 TCM 168, Dec. 20,168(M).

79. A proceeding involving a deficiency in income tax for the year 1947 in the amount of $483 raises two questions: Whether a deficiency may be claimed for a year for which the respondent

has previously refunded taxes paid principally by withholding; and whether the petitioner was a bona fide resident of a foreign country in 1947 and thus exempt from income taxes under section 116(a) of the Internal Revenue Code of 1939.

L.K. Stierhout, 24 TC 483, Dec. 21,080 (Acq.).

80. During 1946, petitioner earned and was paid from sources outside of the US while working in Europe, principally France. None of this income was paid by the US or any agency thereof. Petitioner was held a bona fide resident of France during 1946 and the income is exempt from tax under section 116(a)(1), Internal Revenue Code of 1939.

E.D. Sass, 13 TCM 1091, Dec. 20,692(M), TC Memo. 1954-212.

81. Essentially, although petitioner kept certain ties to California and to Ohio, his intentions to return to California seem to be floating intentions. Compared to the roots petitioner maintained in Japan, these factors are less significant. Therefore, we find that, for 1972 through 1975, petitioner was domiciled in Japan.

T.F. Pope, 40 TCM 1045, Dec. 37,176(M), TC Memo. 1980-332.

82. From October 4, 1973 until late 1976, petitioner was assigned to an offshore drilling rig anchored outside the territorial waters of Singapore. Petitioner worked two out of every three weeks during this period. He spent his free time in Singapore, where he leased an apartment. In December 1976, petitioner was transferred to Malta, where he again took up lodgings. Petitioner remained in Malta until the early part of 1979. During 1975 and 1976, petitioner returned to the US three times. Petitioner was held to have established "strong proof" that he was a bona fide resident of a foreign country for the 1975 and 1976 taxable years.

K. Van Yost, 44 TCM 1071, Dec. 39, 328(M), TC Memo. 1982-516.

83. A mechanic on an offshore oilrig located near Brazil and later relocated to the Gulf of Mexico was not a qualified person eligible to exclude foreign earned income. During the years he was employed abroad, he owned a home in Louisiana, where his wife and children resided, had a Louisiana driver's license and a car that was registered in that state, and also maintained bank accounts there. When working, the taxpayer lived on the rig and ate his meals there; when off-duty, he would leave his clothing and other personal belongings on the rig and leave only to visit friends living in the country. He did not seek or obtain any employment as a mechanic with the countries where the rig was docked when he was not employed on the rig. He retained his US citizenship and was permitted to work in the countries under a visa, but did not pay taxes to either country. Because he did not establish a tax home abroad, the Court ruled that he was not a qualified individual for the purposes of the bona fide resident test or the physical presence test.

J.M. Steel, 55 TCM 1721, Dec. 45,012(M), TC Memo. 1988-399.

84. An engineer who worked on oil rigs outside the US for 28-day rotation periods was not a qualified individual for purposes of the foreign earned income exclusion.

J.R. Richard, 55 TCM 864, Dec. 44,785(M), TC Memo. 1988-217.

85. A US citizen who worked on an off-shore oil rig was not a "qualified individual" who could deduct foreign earned income from his US taxes. Although he worked on the rig for 28-day periods with 28-day periods off, he maintained only the smallest relationship with the country in whose territorial waters the rig

was located (Chile), staying in the country only for one-day periods while on his way to or from the oil rig. He at all times maintained his residence in the US, where his family lived, where he maintained his bank accounts, and where he spent virtually all his time away from work. Thus, he was not a bona fide resident of Chile. Further, because his abode was in the US, his tax home could not be elsewhere.
L.L. Harper, 58 TCM 1509, Dec. 46,404(M), TC Memo. 1990-94.

86. An individual employed by a US corporation in Saudi Arabia who worked a rotational schedule comprised of 42 work days and 21 off-days did not establish a bona fide residency abroad where he was required to leave Saudi Arabia during his off-duty shifts. Such individual was considered a global commuter regularly traveling between his home in the US and work in Saudi Arabia. Thus, he was not entitled to claim a foreign earned income exclusion.

    H.A. Woodward, 58 TCM 1133, Dec. 46,308(M), TC Memo. 1990-7.

87. An airline pilot was employed by a US corporation, but lived in the United Kingdom for the years in issue. He elected to exclude a portion of his income pursuant to sec. 911 IRC but was held not qualified to elect under sec. 911 IRC because he did not have a tax home in a foreign country for the years at issue.

    T.M. Stright, 66 TCM 1490, Dec. 49,451(M), TC Memo. 1993-576.

88. An individual who serviced and installed printing press equipment in the US, Australia and Canada was not a qualified person eligible to exclude foreign earned income because he was not present in a foreign country for the requisite 330 days during any of the relevant tax years and because his tax home

and principal abode remained in the United States. The taxpayer was not entitled to a reduced, pro-rata credit for income earned during the days he spent abroad because failure to meet the 330-day requirement precluded him from reaching the status of a qualified individual for purposes of the credit. Further, the US could constitutionally tax the individual's worldwide income because the power to tax derives from a person's status as a US citizen rather than the situs of property taxed or the domicile of the citizen.

J.B. Coker, 67 TCM 2515, Dec. 49,747(M), TC Memo. 1994-129.

89. In 1942, petitioner, a married man whose wife was deceased, went to Edmonton, Canada, as an employee of a contractor who was engaged in construction work on the Canol oil project. For years, petitioner had suffered from a chronic sinus trouble. Owing to the dry climate in Edmonton, petitioner's health immediately improved, and the relief was so great that sometime during the year 1942, he definitely determined to make his permanent residence in Edmonton. Petitioner has made proof of acts and statements which establish his definite intention prior to 1943 to acquire a residence in Canada and has shown that his stay in Canada has been of such an extended nature as to constitute Canadian residency. During the entire year of 1943, it was held that the petitioner was a bona fide resident of Canada and the compensation which he earned from his work on the Canol oil project in Canada should be excluded from his gross income under section 116(a)(1) IRC

Bouldin, 8 TC 959, Dec. 15,765 (Acq.).

90. On or about August 23, 1942, petitioner, a US citizen, left the US for Canada in pursuance of his employment concerning a war contract. About 10 days after his arrival in Canada, petitioner moved out of his hotel room and arranged for the arrival of his

family. Petitioner's family, his wife and two children, went to Canada in September 1942 with all of petitioner's possessions, including furniture and automobile, with intent to reside there for an indefinite period. Petitioner and his family lived in an apartment in Edmonton, Canada, until October 1, 1944, at which time petitioner and his family departed for the US. For at least two years prior to October 1, 1944, petitioner and his family had no home other than their apartment in Edmonton, and during this period, they took part in various community activities. Petitioner did not pay any Canadian income tax. Petitioner was held to be a bona fide resident of Canada for at least two years prior to October 1, 1944, and the compensation received from his work in Canada during 1943 and 1944 to be excluded from his gross income under section 116(a)(1) and (2). Further, the income received from his work in Canada in 1942 is not excludible from gross income within the meaning of section 116(a)(2).
Baehre, 15 TC 236, Dec. 17,841 (Acq.).

91. A ferry pilot in Canada with temporary visits and investments in the US, having established an intent to make aviation a career but unsuccessful in obtaining employment in the US, had gone to Canada in an attempt to enter the aviation field there, so was not taxable on earned income received as a Canadian aircraft ferry pilot, even though he (1) resided at a hotel while in Canada, (2) made a number of visits to the US while on leave, and (3) had a part interest in one US business and bought and sold another small business during the taxable period involved.

P. Yaross, DC Conn., 49-1 USTC 9207, 83 FSupp 411.

92. Taxpayer was employed on a construction project in the Bahamas during 1943. He moved his family to Nassau with the idea and intention of establishing a permanent residence there. Although he made several short visits to the US, he was a bona

fide resident of a foreign country in 1943 within the meaning of Code Sec. 116(a)(1). Income from his services in the Bahamas was excluded from US tax.

Myers, CA-4, 50-1 USTC 9253, 180 F2d 969.

93. Petitioner, a supervising brick mason, who lived in Iran for some 22 months in barracks provided by his employer, whose wife and children remained behind in the US and whose right to remain in Iran was limited first by a visa and then by a "residence permit", was not a bona fide resident of Iran within the meaning of Section 116(a), IRC 1939.
J.A. McCurnin, 30 TC 143, Dec. 22,953.

94. Petitioner, a citizen of the US, worked in China for UNRRA from March 1946 to September 1947. He had worked in Honduras from 1942 to September 1945 for The Institute of Inter-American Affairs and received terminal pay from that organization until March 1946, but his work in Honduras had ceased in September 1945 and he had returned to the US with his family, found employment with UNRRA and was on its payroll from November 1945. He was not a held a resident of Honduras in 1946 and therefore was not a resident of a foreign country or countries during the entire year of 1946 under section 116(a) of the Internal Revenue Code.

Lovald, 16 TC 909, Dec. 18,249.

95. Petitioner was offered and accepted employment in Ethiopia on a project expected to last approximately 15 or 20 years. He left the US on November 21, 1951, and arrived seven days later in Paris, France, to take care of certain matters preliminary to proceeding to Ethiopia. Unexpected difficulties arose, keeping petitioner from proceeding to Ethiopia until March 2, 1952. Thereafter, unforeseen problems made it impossible to continue

with the project, and petitioner returned to the US on March 13, 1953. Petitioner is a calendar year taxpayer. On the facts, petitioner was not a bona fide resident of a foreign country or countries for a period including an entire taxable year within the meaning of section 116(a)(1) of the Internal Revenue Code of 1939 as amended by the Revenue Act of 1942.

D.H. Nelson, 30 TC 1151, Dec. 23,145.

96. Taxpayer performed services in Greenland under an off-continent employment contract that also contemplated duties in the US. His domicile was in Massachusetts, where his wife and family lived. During two of the three years, taxpayer spent over half of his time in the US. In the other year, he spent 48 percent of his time in the US. Taxpayer was not a resident of Greenland within the meaning of section 911(a)(1) IRC of 1954 during any of the three years.

J.J. Scheuren, Jr., 20 TCM 289, Dec. 24,684(M), TC Memo. 1961-52.

97. The taxpayer, a US citizen, failed to prove that he ever became a bona fide resident of a foreign country during his employment from 1961 to 1964 in places outside the US by his US-based company. There was no evidence that he became a part of the society in those countries to which he was assigned. Taxpayer's income received during this period was, therefore, not exempt from taxation.

E.K. Nold, 26 TCM 802, Dec. 28,582(M), TC Memo. 1967-171.

98. On the facts, the taxpayer-pilot was not a bona fide resident of the Bahamas during 1962. No legitimate business purpose compelled or motivated his leasing an apartment in Nassau. During 1962, the taxpayer also rented an apartment in Miami,

his home base with Pan American Airways. The taxpayer's extensive use of the Miami apartment, the scope of financial and business transactions carried on by him in Miami, and the lack of similar activities by him in Nassau discredited his claim of being a bona fide resident of the Bahamas.

G.L. Fly, DC Fla., 67-2 USTC 9601.

99. Petitioner traveled to India to work on a television production show and became a bona fide resident of that country in late 1966 or early 1967. His wife. Joined him in India in July 1967. They took enough clothing and personal effects for an indefinite period, retaining a condominium and car in California. On a business trip, they returned to the US in September 1967. While in the US, the television show was cancelled and petitioner lost his job. He remained in the US until July 1968, when he went to Japan to work. He was not a bona fide resident of a foreign country or countries for an uninterrupted period of a year for purposes of applying the exclusion of foreign source income under section 911(a) IRC 1954. They were domiciled in the State of California during the entire taxable year 1967.

D.L. Young, 33 TCM 488, Dec. 32,553(M), TC Memo. 1974-99.

100. Taxpayer-husband was held not to be a bona fide resident of Thailand during an entire taxable year for purposes of the exclusion provided by Code Sec. 911(a)(1).
M. Fugit, 34 TCM 646, Dec. 33,195(M), TC Memo. 1975-140.

101. Per diem payments received by an employee who provided filed team services for the maintenance and modification of weapons systems and support equipment were includible in his gross income.
D.R. Galistel, 35 TCM 1107, Dec. 33,974(M), TC Memo. 1976-

253.

102. Held: amount of deductions allowable under section 162 determined. Held further: amount of exclusion from income tax under section 911 determined: petitioner did not prove that he was a bona fide resident of a foreign country or that capital was not a material income-producing factor; further, amount of deductions excluded from section 162 under section 911(a) is determined from gross income, not net income, Brewster v. Commissioner [Dec. 34,125], 67 T. C. 352 (1976), followed. Held further, negligence penalty is not warranted for 1968 but warranted for 1969.

103. Petitioner did not prove that he was a bona fide resident of a foreign country or that capital was not a material income-producing factor; further, amount of deductions excluded from section 162 under section 911(a) is determined from gross income, not net income, Brewster v. Commissioner [Dec. 34,125], 67 T. C. 352 (1976), followed. Held, further, negligence penalty is not warranted for 1968 but warranted for 1969.

W.D. Alexander, 37 TCM 1849-75, Dec. 35,571(M), TC Memo. 1978-487.

104. A New York-based airline pilot who flew international flights between New York and Paris was not a bona fide resident of France and was not entitled to the earned income exclusion. Although the taxpayer leased a Paris apartment and lived there except as required by his employment, he had not made any efforts to become assimilated into the French environment, had not applied for a French visa and had not paid any French income taxes. The taxpayer maintained extensive ties with the US, where his employment was based in New York, his children continued to reside in the US, he maintained US bank accounts, he owned real estate in the US and possessed a valid New Jersey

driver's license. Additionally, the court was unconvinced that tax avoidance considerations had not influenced the taxpayer's decision to live in Paris and commute to New York to report for his assigned international flights.

S.B. Croyle, 41 TCM 339, Dec. 37,388(M). TC Memo. 1980-501.

105. Held: 1. Wages received by William and Erna Howell in 1976 and by Erna Howell in 1977, and military retirement pay received by William Howell in 1976 and 1977 are includable in petitioners' taxable income and subject to Federal income tax. 2. The Form 1040s filed by petitioners for both 1976 and 1977 on which they checked the box for "married filing joint return" but entered no amounts for income or deductions in reliance on various constitutional grounds did not constitute income tax returns within the meaning of secs. 1(a), 6012 and 6013, I. R. C. 1954; hence petitioners are not entitled to have their tax liability computed under the rates applicable to married individuals filing joint returns. 3. Petitioners are liable for additions to tax under sec. 6651(a)(1) for failure to file timely returns. 4. Petitioners are liable for additions to tax under sec. 6653(a) for negligent or intentional disregard of rules and regulations.
W. Howell, 42 TCM 1564, Dec. 38,387(M), TC Memo. 1981-631.

106. A mechanical technician who worked in Angola did not qualify for the foreign earned income exclusion because his home was in the US during the years at issue, not in Angola. His contacts in Angola were minimal; he never left the company compound for recreational purposes and he remained there except for short periods of time when performing maintenance or repair work. The taxpayer returned to the US during each off-duty period, maintained a bank account in Florida, and was registered to vote there.

C.O. James, 55 TCM 1112, Dec. 44,845(M), TC Memo. 1988-266.

107. A taxpayer whose abode remained in the US while he worked on an overseas oil rig did not satisfy the "bona fide resident" test of Code Sec. 911. Thus, he did not qualify for the foreign earned income exclusion.

H.E. Howe, 55 TCM 1153, Dec. 44,860(M), TC Memo. 1988-277.

108. Held: Petitioner is not entitled to exclude from Federal income tax under section 911 compensation earned in Angola because his abode remained in the US. Held further, a refund of state income tax and a trust fund distribution are taxable income.

F.D. Brobst, 56 TCM 282, Dec. 45,082(M), TC Memo. 1988-456.

109. Petitioner was employed as a tool pusher on a mobile rig off the coast of England in the North Sea during 1982, 1983, and 1984. Petitioner's work schedule consisted of a 28-day work period followed by a 28-day rest period. The entire work period was spent on the rig, and the rest period was spent either at his residence in Milton, Florida, or in transit to or from the rig. Petitioner was required by his employer to maintain a residence in the US, wherein petitioner's wife and their children resided during the years in issue. Held: Petitioner is not a qualified individual eligible to exclude foreign-earned income from his gross income under section 911(a), IRS of 1954.

J.H. Cameron, 56 TCM 496, Dec. 45,129(M), TC Memo. 1988-496.

110. Petitioner is not entitled to exclude compensation earned in Saudi Arabia from Federal income tax under section

911 because his abode remained in the US.

L.D. Welsh, 56 TCM 560, Dec. 45,149(M), TC Memo. 1988-512.

111. A taxpayer who worked on a schedule of 42 days in Angola and 28 days off outside of Angola was not eligible for the foreign earned income exclusion because his abode was in Florida, the locus of his non-employment life, financial affairs and civic duties. The taxpayer was liable for a penalty for negligence in preparing his income tax return, but the 50 percent penalty could only be applied to his deficiency relating to filing as a single taxpayer rather than as married filing separately; the case law on the issue of foreign income exclusion was too indefinite to apply the 50percent penalty to that part of his deficiency.

J.R. Hummer, 56 TCM 657, Dec. 45,168(M), TC Memo. 1988-528.

112. An individual who was employed as a senior electrician on an offshore oilrig located in the territorial waters of the Netherlands did not have a tax home in the Netherlands and was not entitled to a claimed foreign earned income exclusion. The electrician was a resident of Arkansas and had strong economic, familial, and personal ties to his family residence there. He worked alternating 14-day periods on the oilrig and returned to his residence in Arkansas for 14-day rest periods. Thus, he spent approximately one-half of his time in Arkansas with his family. Since the taxpayer's abode was in the US during the three years in issue, he was ineligible for the foreign earned income exclusion. Although the Court declined to award damages to the government under Code Sec. 6673 in this case, it advised similarly situated taxpayers that further litigation of this issue might result in an award of damages to the US.

J.L. Lovelady, 56 TCM 689, Dec. 45,173(M), TC Memo. 1988-533.

113. A crane operator who alternated between 28-day work periods on an offshore drilling rig in foreign territorial waters and 28-day rest periods in the US did not qualify for the foreign earned income exclusion. The IRS conceded that the crane operator's 1982 and 1983 tax home, for purposes of determining deductible traveling expenses, was in Indonesia, Thailand or Cameroon. However, the worker was not a bona fide resident of the foreign countries because he had significant ties to the US and his abode remained there during the years in issue. The crane operator's family lived in Alabama during his work periods, his home and bank accounts were in Alabama, he had an Alabama driver's license, and was registered to vote in Alabama. Further, his only contact with the mainland of the foreign countries was for layovers en route to and from Alabama.

W.H. Bosarge, 56 TCM 1043, Dec. 45,418(M), TC Memo. 1989-15.

114. An individual who worked as a driller and a tool pusher on offshore oil drilling rigs located in the territorial waters of Brazil and India was not entitled to a foreign earned income exclusion. The taxpayer's work schedule consisted of alternate 28-day work and rest periods. During the years in issue the taxpayer maintained significant ties to the United States. At the beginning of each rest period, he immediately returned to Mississippi, where his family resided in a home they purchased well before the years in question. Thus, during the years in issue, the taxpayer spent about half of his time with his family in Mississippi. The taxpayer also maintained bank accounts in Mississippi, held a Mississippi driver's license, and was registered to vote there. Since the taxpayer had only minimal

contact with India or Brazil (work periods were spent on the offshore rig and his mainland contact was only during layovers of a few hours en route to or from Mississippi on each of his rest periods), it was determined that his abode remained in the US during the years in issue. Since it was stipulated that the taxpayer did not meet the "physical presence test" of Code Sec. 911(d)(1)(B), and since he did not meet the bona fide residence test of Code Sec. 911(d)(1)(A), he was not a qualified individual for purposes of the foreign earned income exclusion.

W.M. Adams, Jr., 56 TCM 1394, Dec. 45,518(M), TC Memo. 1989-91.

115. An assistant construction engineer who was transferred to Saudi Arabia by his oil company in connection with a pipeline construction project merely worked within Saudi Arabia and his "abode" was in the US during the tax year. Therefore, during the tax year, his tax home was not in a foreign country for purposes of the foreign earned income exclusion, he was not a "qualified individual," and he was not entitled to exclude any portion of his wages from gross income as foreign earned income. In addition, because at the trial and on brief the only issue addressed by the engineer was the availability of the foreign earned income exclusion, he was deemed to have conceded the adjustments relating to additional interest income, was disallowed the foreign tax credit, and was penalized in taxes for negligence.

D.A. Benham, 57 TCM 323, Dec. 45,670(M), TC Memo. 1989-215.

116. Since an oilrig worker's tax home was not in Nigeria during the years at issue, he could not exclude any portion of the wages he earned while working there. Although the worker had a checking account with a Nigerian bank and held a Nigerian driver's license, his ties to that country were merely transitory.

The worker not only maintained a dwelling in the US during the years in question, he retained strong economic, familial, and personal ties with the US.

J.R. Moudy, 57 TCM 327, Dec. 45,671(M), TC Memo. 1989-216.

117. A driller who was stationed in the United Arab Emirates in 1982 on indefinite assignment and who possessed a valid resident visa issued by that country failed to carry his burden of showing by strong proof that, for purposes of the foreign earned income exclusion, he was a bona fide resident of the United Arab Emirates during the year in issue. A citizen of the US, the driller maintained a bank account in Nebraska throughout the period of his employment in the United Arab Emirates and returned to the US shortly after terminating his employment in September 1982. The driller made no effort to participate in social or cultural activities in the United Arab Emirates, learn the language of the region, or become assimilated into its environment. He paid no foreign income taxes on his 1982 income, and was neither registered to vote nor licensed to drive in the United Arab Emirates. The driller was physically present in the United Arab Emirates for less than four months in 1982 but maintained a checking account and leased an apartment in Spain for much of that year. These factors militated against his being a bona fide resident of the United Arab Emirates in 1982.

D.L. Hoppes, 57 TCM 366, Dec. 45,691(M), TC Memo. 1989-228.

118. A nonresident US citizen was not a bona fide resident of Nigeria. The taxpayer worked on an offshore oilrig within the territorial waters of Nigeria and had a Nigerian work permit as was required. Further, the taxpayer's employer paid Nigerian income taxes on his behalf, and this amount was included by the taxpayer on his returns as part of his income. He had alternate

work and rest periods of 28 days each. However, work periods were spent entirely on the rig and rest periods were spent either at one of his two residences in the US or in transit between Nigeria and the US. No time other than transit time was spent in Nigeria. The taxpayer's family remained in the US during the entire period at issue. No household was ever established in Nigeria. Thus, considering all the facts and circumstances, the taxpayer's abode remained in the US during the tax years at issue.

J. Eubanks, 57 TCM 391, Dec. 45,696(M), TC Memo. 1989-233.

119. Individual taxpayers were not entitled to the foreign earned income exclusion because their bona fide residences were in the US. The fact that they worked on a rotating schedule on oilrigs that were on- and offshore of the United Arab Emirates did not shift their tax homes away from Louisiana. Each taxpayer maintained a home in Louisiana and returned there to his family during rest periods. Each had a US driver's license, had US bank accounts, and was registered to vote in Louisiana. Furthermore, no evidence was offered to show that the taxpayers remained overseas during their entire rest periods or that they had or actively sought housing in the United Arab Emirates. The IRS was not stopped from asserting its position by purportedly contrary guidance provided in one of its publications.

W.D. Mount, 57 TCM 1188, Dec. 45,915(M), TC Memo. 1989-405.

120. A divorced taxpayer was entitled to deduct, as alimony payments, deposits that he made to a joint checking account used by his former spouse except to the extent that the payments exceeded the amount specified in the divorce decree. Evidence and testimony produced by the taxpayer were

sufficient to demonstrate that the taxpayer deposited his required alimony payments to a joint checking account from which he made no withdrawals. The taxpayer's deduction for one alimony payment was limited because his payment was in excess of the amount specified.

C.R. Ritchie, 57 TCM 1282, Dec. 45,939(M), TC Memo. 1989-426.

121. A carpenter who worked for an oil company at a drilling site in Angola was not entitled to the foreign earned income exclusion because his abode remained in the US. The carpenter maintained strong economic, familial, and personal ties to Florida, but his contacts with Angola were minimal. The carpenter's only connection with Angola was his job. The Angolan government required him to leave the country during off-duty periods. While working there, he lived in a compound provided by his employer, and he did not maintain a bank account or receive wages in Angola.

J.S. Doyle, 57 TCM 1436, Dec. 45,980(M), TC Memo. 1989-463.

122. A pilot was not entitled to a foreign earned income exclusion because his tax home was the vicinity of his principal place of employment, which was in the US. The taxpayer's legal residence for appeal was the Eleventh Circuit Court of Appeals because his presence in North Carolina at the time the petition was filed was only temporary and he stipulated that the case was not appealable to the D.C. Circuit. The taxpayer did not qualify for the foreign earned income exclusion for income received in the Bahamas because his principal place of employment was New York City. Although a deduction for a paging device was permitted, the taxpayer's hotel room fees and inter-airport bus fares in New York and parking expenses in Florida were nondeductible commuting expenses.

B.L. Swicegood, 57 TCM 1456, Dec. 45,984(M), TC Memo. 1989-467.

123. A US citizen who worked as a consultant for an oil company failed to establish a tax home in Brunei and was ineligible for the foreign-earned income exclusion. Based on the consultant's economic, familial, and personal ties to Texas and his lack of such ties to Brunei, the court concluded that his abode remained in the US.

J.R. Dye, 60 TCM 446, Dec. 46,787(M), TC Memo. 1990-420.

124. An individual employed as a cementer on an offshore oilrig located in territorial waters failed to establish a tax home in India or Angola because his abode remained in the US. Accordingly, he was not entitled to the foreign earned income exclusion. The individual did not make an effort to acquire a home or maintain an apartment in either India or Angola and he maintained significant ties with the US.

P.J. Abrams, 60 TCM 915, Dec. 46,901(M), TC Memo. 1990-517.

125. An individual who worked as an oil driller on offshore drilling rigs did not establish that he was a bona fide resident of Brazil for purposes of the foreign earned income exclusion.

IRS Letter Ruling 8526002, Feb. 25, 1985.

126. A US citizen who worked on an offshore oil rig located off the coast of a foreign country was not entitled to exclude foreign earned income from his gross income because his tax home was in the US. For purposes of the foreign earned income exclusion, a taxpayer's tax home is his abode. Half his days were spent working and living on the oilrig and the other half were

spent with his wife in the US. The nexus of his economic, familial, and personal ties were to the US community where he maintained a residence with his wife and not the foreign country that was host to the offshore oilrig. The IRS was not stopped from determining by a deficiency based on a return on which the IRS had earlier mailed a refund to the taxpayer.

W.R. Wilson, 62 TCM 900, Dec. 47,662(M), TC Memo. 1991-491.

127. The petitioner, a member of a partnership, was the managing partner of the firm's Paris office for a period of time and received payments from the partnership attributable to such period. Held: Some of the payments were guaranteed payments within the meaning of sec. 707(c) IRC 1954 and are fully excludable from gross income under sec. 911 IRC 1954 as income from sources outside the US.

A.O. Miller, Jr., 52 TC 752, Dec. 29,690.

128. The petitioner, who was employed during the taxable years on a guided missile range in the Bahamas, was not a bona fide resident of a foreign country during this time. He was not, therefore, entitled to exclude amounts received during this period from his gross income.

J.D. Allen, 27 TCM 1082, Dec. 29,157(M), TC Memo. 1968-218.

129. Jose V. Ferrer, a movie actor and US citizen who was present in certain foreign countries for limited periods in connection with work on various films was a transient and not a bona fide resident of the foreign countries involved. Tax Court affirmed.

J.V.Ferrer, 50 TC 177, Dec. 28,937.Aff'd, *per curiam,* CA-2, 69-1 USTC 9425.

130. Under employment contracts, the petitioner lived and worked in Viet Nam for a year's duration on two discrete occasions. He definitely intended not to stay more than temporarily, he lived as a transient, and he did not participate in community activities. Moreover, his income was not subject to Vietnamese income taxation. The court held that he was not a bona fide resident of Viet Nam. His earnings there were taxable income.

D.Y. Coyle, 28 TCM 299, Dec. 29,497(M), TC Memo. 1969-53.

131. In reversing the decision of the Tax Court, the Court of Appeals held that the taxpayer foreign correspondent, as a matter of law, was a bona fide resident of Singapore during all of 1954 within the meaning of Code Sec. 911(a)(1) and was not a transient or sojourner. His 1954 wages received from his U. S. employer were therefore exempt from taxation.

H.J. Sochurek, CA-7, 62-1 USTC 9293, 300 F2d 34.

132. The court held that an employee of a missile tracking station, as a matter of law, was a bona fide resident of Grand Turk Island and was entitled to a refund of the income taxes withheld from his wages for the taxable years 1958 and 1959. The factors considered by the court in reaching its decision were the following: the taxpayer was unmarried with no dependents, his intention, apparently, was to remain on the island indefinitely when he went to work there, he participated in the social life of the island, his physical presence there was consistent with his employment, his temporary absences were for vacations, his work was of indefinite duration, and there was no showing of a tax evasion purpose in making the trip abroad.

E.M. Brueck, DC, 63-2 USTC 9786, 228 FSupp 112.

133. During the taxable year 1958, petitioners were employed by Pan American World Airways, Inc., Guided Missiles Range Division, in connection with the performance of its contract with the US Air Force for the maintenance and operation of a down range missile-tracking station located on the island of Trinidad, where petitioners were stationed. The missile base was established by the Air Force pursuant to treaties executed by the US and Great Britain, which provided certain extraterritorial rights for military and civilian personnel involved in the missile program. While stationed down range petitioners lived off the base in facilities furnished by themselves. During the taxable year involved, petitioners were not bona fide residents of a foreign country or countries within the meaning of section 911(a)(1) IRC 1954 and are not entitled to exclude from gross income amounts received in those years for services performed at the down range missile site.

Nahacky, 26 TCM 572, Dec. 28,492(M), TC Memo. 1967-128.

134. During 1963 and the major portion of 1964, petitioners traveled throughout Europe selling the products of a US corporation. In October of 1964, they returned to Europe, settling in France, to assist their customers in merchandising the products sold in the earlier years, to create and test new marketing and advertising ideas for the US corporation and to form a European sales office which would take over the selling activities of the US corporation. Petitioners returned to the US in June of 1966. Petitioners were bona fide residents of a foreign country for one entire taxable year and the income received while residents of France was attributable to services performed in a foreign country and therefore such income is excludable under sec. 911.

C.P. Hagerty, 32 TCM 788, Dec. 32,060(M), TC Memo. 1973-162.

135. Petitioner, a TWA pilot based in New York and flying primarily international flights, began in April 1974 to spend all his time, insofar as the demands of his employment allowed, in France. A taxpayer must offer "strong proof" of bona fide residency in a foreign country to qualify for an exclusion from gross income under section 911(a)(1), which provides that such bona fide residency must be established "to the satisfaction of the Secretary or his delegate." Applying this standard of proof to the circumstances revealed in the record herein, petitioner was a bona fide resident of France for an uninterrupted period beginning April 15, 1975, and continuing throughout the year 1976, but was not a bona fide resident of France prior to April 15, 1975.

B.J. Schoneberger, 74 TC 1016, Dec. 37,138.

136. A taxpayer who met the applicable criteria to be a bona fide resident of a foreign country from January 1, 1973, through November 1, 1974, was entitled to exclude from income his earnings for the period from January 1, 1974, through October 31, 1974.

R.E. Heinzelman, 41 TCM 1423, Dec. 37,877(M), TC Memo. 1981-218.

Belgian nonresident returns

137. U.S. citizen temporarily working and residing in Belgium who would be classified as a resident of Belgium under the principles of section 1.871-2(b) of the regulations, has not,

by filing a Belgian "nonresident" income tax return, made a statement that would disqualify such individual under section 911(c)(6) of the Code from being considered a bona fide resident of Belgium for purposes of section 911(a)(1). The return, made a statement that would disqualify such individual under section 911(c)(6) of the Code from being considered a bona fide resident of Belgium for purposes of section 911(a)(1).

Rev. Rul. 78-254, 1978-1 CB 243.

Bonus

138. Petitioner received, in the taxable year and as an employee of a corporation, installments of stock bonuses declared in previous years. He was a nonresident citizen of the US for a portion of the taxable year and a portion of the years during which the bonuses were set up. The plan provided, inter alia, that the bonus was payable over a period of four years, one-fourth down, three-fourths credited monthly, but to be delivered at the end of the four years, or upon death and (within the discretion of the corporation), upon discharge without fault and with good record. Voluntary leaving the service or dismissal for cause would deprive the employee of the credited stock except up to the date of leaving the service. The bonus was earned by services over the period of service rendered up to four years, and not merely in the year of declaration of bonus; therefore, petitioner earned one-fourth of each year's bonus in 1939, the taxable year, so is entitled to exemption of 198/365ths because of non-residence for 198 days during the taxable year.

Mooney, 9 TC 713, Dec. 16,080 (Acq.).

Business profits as earned income

139. Examples are given to show the computation of US citizens' earned foreign income excludable from gross income under section 911(a) of the Code and deductions allocable to the excluded income in situations involving sole proprietors and partners who receive fees from services in excess of the maximum exclusion, income from services and capital in excess of the maximum exclusion, and expenses in excess of income.

Rev. Rul. 75-86, 1975-1 CB 242.

140. The taxpayer, a US citizen and a partner in a Danish accounting firm, was entitled to apply the foreign earned income exclusion against his share of the partnership net income for 1969 and 1970 rather than, as contended by the government, against his share of partnership gross income. In view of the government's prior long-standing interpretation, as shown in its publications and actions, of following the "net income" position in this matter, the court refused to give any effect to an IRS Revenue Ruling issued in 1975, which for the first time clearly indicated that the government follows the "gross income" position.

Vogt, CtCls, 76-2 USTC 9482, 537 F2d 405.

141. Petitioner, a US citizen, was a bona fide nonresident of the US for more than six months of each of the taxable years. During the taxable years, he was a general partner and manager of the London office of a domestic brokerage firm, in which capital was a material income-producing factor. Petitioner at no time contributed capital to the firm but received a percentage of its profits plus a sum designated "salary." Held: the petitioner's earned income from sources outside the US, excludable from

gross income under section 116(a) of the Revenue Acts of 1936 and 1938, is limited to 20 percent of his share of the partnership's net profits, which included the amounts designated "salary."

Tweedy, 47 BTA 341, Dec. 12,588.

142. The monthly drawing account received by a taxpayer-partner while employed abroad by the partnership, a partnership distribution, was not completely excludable from his gross income as earned income from sources outside the US. The “entity” approach was not applicable to the drawing account and, under the “conduit” approach, the taxpayer’s exclusion for income earned from sources outside the US was limited to the proportion of the partnership’s income which was earned income from sources outside the US.

T.B. Foster, CA-2, 64-1 USTC 9362, 329 F2d 717.

143. Guaranteed payments received by a partner in charge of the US partnership's Tokyo office were treated as compensation for personal services performed outside the US.

E.L. Carey, CtCls, 70-1 USTC 9455, 427 F2d 763.

144. Interest income is derived from the investment of capital and is not "earned income" for the purpose of computing allowable contributions and deductions under a self-employed retirement plan qualified under section 401 of the Internal Revenue Code of 1954. However, if interest income is derived from financing activities which are an integral part of a taxpayer's business in which he also renders personal services, such interest income would enter into the computation of the amount which may be considered "earned income" where both personal services and capital are material income-producing

factors.

Rev. Rul. 66-56, 1966-1 CB 87.

145. The Tax Court found that the taxpayer, a US citizen and resident of Cuba, owned and operated mining and sugar cane corporations located in Cuba, and that all profits realized from the mining and sugar cane operations were taxpayer's earnings and not the corporation's.

M.R. Leeder, 19 TCM 352, Dec. 24,125(M), TC Memo. 1960-69.

Community property

146. The division of income on the community property basis does not alter the exempt character of income entitled to exemption under section 911(a) of the Internal Revenue Code of 1954.

Rev. Rul. 55-246, 1955-1 CB 92.

147. The tax exemption for income earned outside of the US was not available to the wife of a member of the Navy for her one-half community property share of salary paid to her husband while he served in Japan. The wife's half of her husband's salary was ruled to be not tax-exempt because it was earned income paid by the US. The court agreed with Rev. Rul. 55-246, 1955-1 CB 129, which states that community property laws cannot alter the exempt or non-exempt character of income. Furthermore, the court found that, under the community property laws of the state where the couple resided (Washington), both spouses are deemed to have provided services in earning income for services rendered.

E.R. Fink, CtCls, 72-1 USTC 9254, 454 F2d 1387. Cert. denied, 409 US 844, 93 SCt 46.

148. Petitioner a US citizen, and her husband, who was a nonresident alien, resided in Spain, a community property jurisdiction. Husband received compensation for services performed in Spain. Held: Sec. 911 IRC 1954 is not applicable to the income earned by husband and attributed to petitioner under the community property law; further, sec. 872 IRC 1954 is not applicable to petitioner to allow her to exclude the portion of husband's income attributed to her by reason of the community property law.
H.R. Solano, 62 TC 562, Dec. 32,705.

149. As used in Code Sec. 911(a)(2), the words "taxable year" mean the year in which income attributable to foreign service was received rather than the year in which services were performed. Domicile in a community property state does not entitle a married couple to a double foreign income exclusion.

J. Renoir, CA-9, 63-2 USTC 9665, 321 F2d 605.

Compensation received abroad from private non-federal funds

150. Compensation received by a US citizen from private (non-Federal) funds for employment during an 18 consecutive month period in a foreign country as an employee of the Smithsonian Institution qualifies as income from sources outside the US.

Rev. Rul. 71-199, 1971-1 CB 216.

Election

151. An engineer employed abroad and was a bona fide foreign resident for the years at issue could not claim the foreign earned income exclusion because he did not make a timely election pursuant to the requirements set forth in Reg. §1.911-7(a). Further, the IRS did not abuse its discretion in refusing to grant an extension of the election period because the taxpayer did not request an extension until long after the election period had expired.

W.J. Faltesek, 92 TC 1204, Dec. 45,743.

152. Petitioner was not entitled to exclude her foreign earned income for the tax year at issue because she failed to make a timely election under Reg §1.911-7(a)(2). The taxpayer's argument that Reg §1.911-7(a)(2) was invalid because the additional timing requirement rule imposed is absent from the statute, was rejected. The statute authorizes the IRS to impose a deadline for filing the election. These deadlines are not unreasonable or arbitrary and are within the specific authority granted to the IRS by Congress to prescribe regulations necessary and appropriate to carry out the purposes of the statute.

110 TCM 239, Dec. 60,391(M), TC Memo. 2015-169.

153. If a qualified individual's claiming of a foreign tax credit with respect to foreign earned income eligible for exclusion under Code Sec. 911 and which the taxpayer has elected to exclude is inconsistent with the previously made election or elections, it will generally result in the revocation of one or both elections.

Rev. Rul. 90-77, 1990-2 CB 183.

Election of exclusion

154. A taxpayer who revoked his foreign income exclusion when he moved to England was given consent to reelect the exclusion when he moved to Hong Kong to work for a new employer. Since England and Hong Kong have differing tax rates and the taxpayer changed employers, the IRS determined that the facts and circumstances paralleled those described in Reg. §1.911-7(b)(2).

IRS Letter Ruling 9625060, March 28, 1996.

Employment of capital

155. Petitioner, as sole proprietor, operated an automobile body repair business during 1967, when he was a bona fide resident of Canada. For use in his business, he rented and later purchased garage space, owned necessary machinery, including air compressors, welding equipment, grinders, sanders, and paint spraying equipment, and carried an inventory of fenders, bumpers, and other parts. Held: petitioner was engaged in a business in which capital was a material income-producing factor and is subject to the 30 percent limitation on the exclusion from gross income prescribed by sec. 911(b) IRC 1954.

G. Rousku, 56 TC 548, Dec. 30,839.

156. Held: amount of deductions allowable under section 162 determined. Held, further: amount of exclusion from income tax under section 911 determined: petitioner did not prove that he

was a bona fide resident of a foreign country or that capital was not a material income-producing factor; further, amount of deductions excluded from section 162 under section 911(a) is determined from gross income, not net income, Brewster v. Commissioner [Dec. 34,125], 67 T. C. 352 (1976), followed. Held further; negligence penalty is not warranted for 1968 but warranted for 1969.

W.D. Alexander, 37 TCM 1849-75, Dec. 35,571(M), TC Memo. 1978-487.

Evidence

157. A taxpayer engaged in setting up manufacturing branches for his employer in foreign countries was a bona fide resident of the foreign countries during 1947-1949. It was found that he was in the countries for a purpose requiring indefinite extended foreign residence.

G. Weible, CA-9, 57-1 USTC 9589, 244 F2d 158.

158. The decision of the District Court was reversed and the case remanded on the ground that taxpayer was clearly a bona fide resident of Soviet Russia during the taxable year 1944. The Sixth Circuit stated that "in determining the issue, it is necessary to consider the circumstances surrounding taxpayer's journey to Russia, the services he performed there and the nature of his stay in that country, as evidence of his intentions as to residence in Russia."

N.C. Fuller, CA-6, 53-1 USTC 9405, 204 F2d 592.

159. A taxpayer who worked under contract for a US firm in Afghanistan during 1947 and 1948 contended that income

earned in such years was excludible from gross income since he was, at such time, a resident of Afghanistan. It was brought out that taxpayer would willingly accept work in almost any foreign country. Held: residence in Afghanistan, or any other foreign country, during 1947 and 1948 was not sufficiently established, and therefore his income for such years was includible in gross income.

S. Meso, DC Ida., 52-1 USTC 9159, 102 FSupp 173.

160. Married taxpayers who lived and worked on a yacht that primarily operated in international waters qualified for the foreign earned income exclusion. The taxpayers satisfied the foreign tax home requirement during the days they were physically present in foreign countries. They had neither a regular or principal place of business, nor any abode in a real and substantial sense and thus were itinerants whose tax home was located wherever they were physically located from day to day. Although the taxpayers owned a townhouse in the US, they did not have a US abode because the property was owned and leased to others and was not available for their use, and they had limited additional ties to the US. The taxpayers also satisfied the alternate physical presence test because they spent more than 330 days in foreign countries during the applicable periods. The 330 days did not include days spent in international waters, but it did include partial days spent in international waters while traveling between foreign locations. The IRS failed to meet its burden of proof that the taxpayers spent one entire month in the US during one of the tax years at issue. Further, a slight adjustment that the court made to the applicable period the taxpayers originally reported did not amount to the introduction of a new issue.

M.R. Struck, 93 TCM 928, Dec. 56,845(M), TC Memo. 2007-42.

161. A worker who failed to file federal income tax returns or report income for two tax years was required to pay taxes and penalties relating to wages, interest and pension monies that he received. He had no foreign-earned income and was not a qualified individual for purposes of the foreign-earned income exclusion. The interest he received from the federal government and his compensation for labor or personal services performed in the US were items of gross income that were treated as income from US sources. During the years at issue, he resided in one state and therefore was a resident of the US for tax purposes. His argument that the state was not part of the US and that therefore he was not subject to the jurisdiction of the Tax Court was a stale tax protestor contention. Accordingly, he was penalized for instituting a proceeding in the Tax Court primarily for delay.

L.G. Solomon, 66 TCM 1201, Dec. 49,376(M), TC Memo. 1993-509.

162. A controlled corporation was entitled to claim a net operating loss based upon a deductible business bad debt, as computed from the evidence and an application of the Cohan rule. A portion of its unrepaid advances to a corporation under common control and a portion of payments to that corporation's creditors were shown, from a history of repayments, to have been bona fide loans. The computation of the net operating loss, however, properly excluded payments that were made when the second corporation's impending failure and/or actual termination was manifest. At that time, the first corporation did not have a reasonable expectation of repayment. In addition, it failed to show that it was contractually liable to pay the creditors in question or that its business reputation would suffer from nonpayment of them.

H. Kalicak Construction Co., 48 TCM 1403, Dec. 41,558(M), TC

Memo. 1984-552.

163. A US citizen who was employed as an overseas bank inspector did not qualify as a bona fide foreign resident. In 1957 he was merely a traveler while working overseas. In 1958 he abandoned his foreign residence before he could qualify as a foreign resident for one year.

A.E. Adams, 22 TCM 1215, Dec. 26,295(M), TC Memo. 1963-241.

164. On the facts, the taxpayer, who was employed by a civilian company engaged in construction work on Okinawa Island, was not a bona fide resident of the island and, consequently, the Commissioner's determination of deficiencies for the taxable years was correct.
L.S. Crane, 11 TCM 516, Dec. 19,992(M).

165. Amounts transferred to an individual by his employer were not bona fide loans and should, therefore, have been reported as income. No promissory notes or other instruments were executed with respect to two series of amounts, and neither party intended to comply with the terms of a loan agreement or promissory note with respect to another such series. Furthermore, no collateral was pledged to secure repayment, there was no fixed schedule for repayment, it was not reasonable to expect at the time the funds were advanced that the taxpayer could repay them, no interest was charged or paid, and the taxpayer did not intend at the time the funds were advanced to actually make any payments. Moreover, the evidence showed that the individual also received, but did not report, income from the sale of several properties. The fact that the individual did not report income earned or claim losses incurred from leasing one of the properties did not prove lack of ownership.

R.B. Talmage, CA-9, 2010-2 USTC 50,550.

Expenses

166. Taxpayer, an opera and concert singer of international fame, claimed deductions for advertising, entertainment of concert managers, traveling expenses to place of concert, salaries and fees of pianist, accompanist, flutist, maid and secretary, an office, special music, professional coaches, special theatrical costumes and make-up. It was held that taxpayer was engaged in a business and that her expenses were proper business expenses. However, the Court held that since the proof of the expenses was inadequate, it estimated that taxpayer's expenses for 1937 were $4,100 and $5,530 for 1938. Expenses incurred while taxpayer toured Europe were not estimated.

Hempel, 6 TCM 743, Dec. 15,888(M).

167. The Commissioner properly determined that petitioner, who had earned income from sources outside the US, could not claim a deduction from gross income of a portion of her expenses, since a portion of such expenses was properly allocable to or chargeable against amounts excluded from gross income. Secs. 911(a) and (b) IRC 1954.

A.M.B. Brewster, 55 TC 251, Dec. 30,402.

168. The taxpayer, a US citizen and a partner in a Danish accounting firm, was entitled to apply the foreign earned income exclusion against his share of the partnership net income for 1969 and 1970 rather than, as contended by the government, against his share of partnership gross income. In view of the government's prior long-standing interpretation, as

shown in its publications and actions, that it had previously followed the "net income" position in this matter, the court refused to give any effect to an IRS Revenue Ruling issued in 1975, which for the first time clearly indicated that the government follows the "gross income" position.

F.H. Vogt, CtCls, 76-2 USTC 9482, 537 F2d 405.

169. An actor was not entitled to deduct certain travel expenses (including meals and lodging) incurred in connection with preliminary research for making a motion picture beyond the amount allowed by the Commissioner where he was unable to substantiate those expenses by adequate records or other sufficient evidence.

Quinn, 33 TCM 310, Dec. 32,501(M), TC Memo. 1976-64.

170. A US citizen who operated a farm in Mexico could not deduct the portion of his farming expenses that was properly chargeable against amounts excluded from his gross income as foreign source earned income. The earned income exclusion was an exclusion of an amount taken from gross income rather than net income after deducting all expenses for earned income from sources other than partnerships. Since the excluded income was therefore a part of gross income, a proportionate part of total expenses had to be allocated to the exclusion.

L.F. Jones, 38 TCM 1064, Dec. 36,183(M), TC Memo. 1979-271.

171. A technical consultant for a Saudi Arabian airport project was not entitled to deduct per diem payments as reimbursements for expenses because his employment in Saudi Arabia was of indefinite rather than temporary duration. The taxpayer remained in Saudi Arabia for 37 months, and his wife spent approximately 23 of those months with him and the

remainder with their children, who were attending college in the US. Although a letter agreement indicated that the job was to last no more than 6 months, the taxpayer did not adequately explain how the job was extended or the mechanism by which he was retained beyond his original agreement. Furthermore, a Code Sec. 911 exclusion claimed on the taxpayer's Form 2555 based on his bona fide residence in Saudi Arabia conflicted with his simultaneous claim for travel expenses "while away from home" under Code Sec. 162(a).

C.K. Brooke, 54 TCM 132, Dec. 44,114(M), TC Memo. 1987-400.

172. Petitioner, a US taxpayer residing in a foreign country, earned no income from biological research activities in 1970. He did, however, deduct expenses related to these activities on his joint Federal income tax return for 1970. Respondent disallowed such expenses on the ground that they were allocable to income, which would be exempt from taxation under sec. 911(a), I.R.C. 1954 if earned. Held: petitioner is entitled to deduct the biological research expenses under sec. 162(a), where he received no “earned income” within the intended scope of sec. 911(a) to which his expenses would be properly allocable or against which they would be chargeable.

Cornman, 63 TC 653, Dec. 33,085 (Acq.).

173. The method is provided to compute the amount of partnership loss deductible and earned foreign income excludable from gross income under section 911 of the Code by a US citizen receiving a salary as an employee of a foreign corporation and owning a 50 percent interest in a foreign partnership in which personal services and capital are material income producing factors.

Rev. Rul. 76-163, 1976-1 CB 199.

Farm income

174. Up to 30 percent of the net profit derived by a US citizen, a bona fide resident of Mexico, who rents and operates a truck farm in that country with the use of farm equipment of comparatively little value, represents earned income for the purpose of the exclusion provided by section 911(a) of the Internal Revenue Code of 1954.

Rev. Rul. 66-326, 1966-2 CB 281.

Federal credit union

175. Amounts paid to a US citizen as compensation for services by a Federal credit union in a foreign country may be excludable from gross income under section 911 of the Code. Rev. Rul. 69-448, 1969-2 CB 154.

Fisherman's income

176. Petitioner was employed as a crew member of a US ship registered in San Diego, California. During the taxable year, all fishing was done outside the territorial waters of the US, but at all times the ship sailed from and returned to San Diego, and all fish were sold there. His earnings were a part of the net proceeds of sales in San Diego of all fish caught. None of petitioner's earnings were from business conducted in a foreign country. Petitioner did not reside in any foreign country. His residence was in San Diego, from which he was absent, temporarily, when he went on fishing trips. Held: petitioner's earned income was not exempt from income tax under section 116(a) of the Revenue Act of 1936.

Balestreri, 47 BTA 241, Dec. 12,572.

177. Petitioner, captain of a fishing vessel, took his vessel to Peru and fished in the waters within 200 miles of the Peruvian coastline. Peru claimed sovereignty and jurisdiction over the waters adjoining its coast to a distance of 200 miles and confiscated vessels fishing therein without a Peruvian permit. Petitioner's operations were subjected to extensive regulation by the Peruvian Government. The Executive Branch of the US Government does not recognize the Peruvian claims to sovereignty and jurisdiction beyond three miles from the Peruvian coast.[38] Petitoner arrived in Peru June 7, 1953, and during 1953 and 1954 he spent some of his time ashore in Paita, Peru, part of his time fishing within three miles of Peru, and part of his time fishing beyond three miles off the coast of Peru, but within 200 miles of the coast. There is no proof that he spent 510 days ashore in Peru and fishing within three miles from Peru during 1953 and 1954. Held: petitioner was not present in a foreign country 510 days during the period in question within the provisions of section 911(a)(2) IRC 1954, and therefore his earnings in 1953 and 1954 are not excludable from gross income under the provisions of such section.

F. Souza, 33 TC 817, Dec. 24,036.

178. Held: petitioner Raymond C. Lewis was a bona fide resident of Peru for the entire year 1954 and his earnings as engineer of the fishing boat Sun Splendor in that year were excludable from his gross income under the provisions of section 911(a)(1) IRC 1954. The Sun Splendor did all of its fishing during 1954 either within 3 miles of the coast of Peru or within 200 miles of the coast of Peru. None of its fishing was

[38] This court case is from 1933 and predates the UNCLOS treaty, which supports the 200 mile zone.

done within waters under the jurisdiction of the US.

R.C. Lewis, 18 TCM 1059, Dec. 23,856(M), TC Memo. 1959-219.

179. A US citizen employed on a fishing vessel operating over the continental shelf area adjacent to a foreign country's territorial waters over which that country exercises taxing authority does not meet the presence requirement of section 911(a)(2) of the Code.
Rev. Rul. 73-181, 1973-1 CB 347.

Foreign tax credit

180. A US citizen who worked as a North Atlantic Treaty Organization (NATO) contractor in Germany was not entitled to a foreign tax credit because he had already excluded his wages from income using the foreign earned income and housing cost exclusions. Thus, allowing a foreign tax credit would violate the double benefit rule of Code Sec. 911(d)(6), even if he had paid or accrued foreign tax on these wages, which he did not. Further, the taxpayer was not entitled to a foreign tax credit relating to his non-NATO income because he did not pay any foreign tax for the tax years at issue. In addition, the taxpayer would not receive the benefit of accrued foreign taxes because he did not pay any taxes within two years after the close of the tax years at issue. Moreover, the taxpayer's argument that because he was a resident of Germany, his income was exempt from US tax under the treaty was dismissed, as the taxpayer did not pay any income taxes to Germany. Further, the taxpayer's conflict arguments failed because the saving clause of the treaty barred him from obtaining relief and there was no conflict between the code and the treaty.

E.S. Gerencser, 112 TCM 218, Dec. 60,671(M), TC Memo. 2016-

151.

181. An individual entitled to a foreign tax credit under a US income tax treaty may not claim the credit if it is allocable to income the individual chooses to exclude from gross income under section 911 of the Code.

Rev. Rul. 79-199, 1979-1 CB 246.

Fulbright lecturer

182. Petitioner was in Japan from October of 1955 until July of 1957 as a Fulbright lecturer at Kobe University and paid in inconvertible Japanese currency by the US Educational Commission in Japan. Held: 1. Amounts paid to petitioner in 1956 and 1957 as a Fulbright lecturer were "paid by the United States or an agency thereof" within the meaning of Section 911(a)(2) of the 1954 Code and thus were not excludible from gross income. 2. Petitioner's tax residence remained in the US during 1956 and 1957. As a Fulbright lecturer in Japan, petitioner was temporarily "away from home" in the pursuit of his trade or profession of teaching and was entitled to deduct his traveling expenses under Section 162(a)(2) of the 1954 Code. Amount of such expenses in 1956 and 1957 determined.

L.P. Dowd, 37 TC 399, Dec. 25,158.

Husband and wife

183. Husband and wife were employed abroad under a joint employment contract, which provided a stock option for petitioner-husband alone. Held: petitioners were free to structure the provisions of their joint employment contract as they wished, and abided by the contract as they made it, so

must accept the tax consequences of their structural choice. Commissioner v. National Alfalfa Dehydrating & Milling Co. [74 1 ustc 9456], 417 U.S. 134, 149 (1974). Therefore, petitioners may not allocate any of the gain from petitioner-husband's 1978 disposition of the stock to petitioner-wife for the purpose of computing her foreign earned income exclusion under section 911, I.R.C. 1954. Held further: petitioners may attribute petitioner-husband's stock upon proceeds to their 1977 gross income under the attribution rule of section 911(c)(2) for the limited purpose of computing the foreign earned income exclusion for 1977 under section 911(a)(1) and (c)(1)(B).

R.S. Groetzinger, 87 TC 533, Dec. 43,307.

Identification card

184. A taxpayer who lived and worked in the Panama Canal Zone was unable to exclude any of his earned income since his residence was not within a foreign country.

W.T. Coffey, 31 TCM 344, Dec. 31,339(M), TC Memo. 1972-87.

Indefinite appointment

185. Taxpayer was entitled to exclude from income amounts paid him as a foreign service representative of a US company for the taxable years 1943-1946 even though he paid no income taxes to the countries wherein he served, stated that he intended to return to the US within six months when registering at the consulate, and made extensive visits to the US when recalled for consultation, his return to the foreign country being delayed to some extent by wartime travel restrictions. His appointment was for an indefinite period, and he included in his taxable income compensation covering periods when he was in

the US for consultative purposes.

White, DC Md., 50-1 USTC 9197, 88 FSupp 457.

186. Petitioner left the US in 1938 in order to take a position as the managing director of all subsidiaries of Paramount Pictures Inc. in the United Kingdom. This was a permanent and continuing position, and one of the conditions of petitioner's employment was that he move to and reside in England. This he did, taking his family, personal effects, and furniture with him, and renting an apartment in London under a five-year lease. During the years 1943, 1944, 1945, and 1946, petitioner made a number of trips to the US in order to visit his family who had returned to the US upon the fall of the Low Countries in 1940. Upon the end of the war in Europe, petitioner's family returned to England. Held: Petitioner was a bona fide resident of Great Britain during the entire taxable year in 1943, 1944, and 1945, and during 1946 until September 30 of that year.

D.E. Rose, 16 TC 232, Dec. 18,072 (Acq.).

187. Taxpayer, a US citizen, was away from the US during 1950, leaving December 28, 1949. He was under contract with a US airline company to represent it in Saudi Arabia and other foreign countries. Upon completion of his work on December 28, 1950, taxpayer returned to the US, arriving in New York on January 1, 1951. During the period he was overseas, he was not restricted by his employer as to housing accommodations, nor did his employer provide his meals or lodging. Taxpayer paid income taxes to the government of Iraq. It was determined that he was a bona fide resident of a foreign country or countries during the entire taxable year 1950 within the meaning of Sec. 116(a)(1) and that the wages paid to him were received from sources outside the US. Accordingly, such wages were exempt. Refund allowed.

G.A. Glackin, DC Ill., 53-1 USTC 9103, 110 F2d 372.

188. The taxpayer, a construction engineer, entered into a two-year employment contract in 1946 under which he worked in Afghanistan. The employer furnished board and lodging and agreed to pay any income taxes, which might be levied against the taxpayer by foreign countries. The taxpayer returned to the US on abandonment of the project in 1949. Although he had intended to remain somewhere abroad for from ten to twenty years, he was unable to find another job abroad. The taxpayer was not a bona fide resident of Afghanistan during 1947-1948.

E.R. Hertig, 19 TC 109, Dec. 19,272.

189. Taxpayer left the US in May 1947 to work on a construction project in the Philippines and returned to the US in May 1949 on completion of the project. From July to August 1949, he worked for another firm in Okinawa and then returned to the US to engage in consulting engineering work. In December, he departed for the Marshall Islands. The Tax Court had held that during 1948-1949, the taxpayer was not a bona fide resident of the Philippines. The Tax Court was affirmed on the ground that its finding was supported by substantial evidence and was not clearly erroneous.
E.M. Dunn, CA-9, 55-1 USTC 9297, 220 F2d 323.

190. As taxpayer was not a bona fide resident of Saudi Arabia in 1948. Held: his wages, earned under a temporary employment contract, were not excludible from gross income.

E. Benbow, 12 TCM 380, Dec. 19,570(M).

191. Taxpayer, a millwright, was employed in Saudi Arabia from December, 1947 to September, 1949, at which time he

returned to the US because of his wife's serious illness. Upon the facts, held: taxpayer was not a bona fide resident of Kuwait, Saudi Arabia, during 1948 and 1949 within the meaning of Sec. 116(a) as amended by the Revenue Acts of 1942 and 1943.

J.R. Vance, 12 TCM 966, Dec. 19,861(M).

192. From September 1943 to September 1952, petitioner's only employment was outside of the US. He returned approximately at two-year intervals only for vacations. From August 1947 to March 1949, he was employed in Saudi Arabia. Held: petitioner was a bona fide resident of Saudi Arabia during the year 1948 within the meaning of section 116(a) IRS 193.

H.W. Dickinson, 14 TCM 82, Dec. 20,851(M), TC Memo. 1955-24.

193. The taxpayer's husband accepted work in Vietnam for an indefinite period but for a minimum of 18 months. During his stay, his wife filed a joint return, in which his income from this foreign project was excluded. After six months, the project was cancelled. The taxpayer and her husband filed separate amended returns. The husband included his salary earned in Vietnam, but deducted over $4,000 as away from home expenses. Since the taxpayer's husband did not meet the time requirement for excluding income earned outside the US, his salary was not excludable. Moreover, he was not entitled to any living expense deduction since his stay in Vietnam was for an indefinite period. The Court also found that separate returns may not be filed after a joint return has been filed once the time for filing returns has expired. The taxpayer was therefore jointly liable for the tax on her husband's income. The Court was wholly sympathetic to the taxpayer's plight and recognized the unfairness of determining a deficiency against her based solely upon income realized by her husband, who was living apart

from her; however, the Court saw no escape from this unfortunate result in view of the law as it is presently constituted.

A.E. Wilson, 29 TCM 481, Dec. 30,092(M), TC Memo. 1970-105.

194. Per diem payments received by an employee who provided filed team services for the maintenance and modification of weapons systems and support equipment were includible in his gross income.

D.R. Galistel, 35 TCM 1107, Dec. 33,974(M), TC Memo. 1976-253.

International Waters

195. Income that a US citizen residing in Scotland earned while traveling in international waters was not foreign earned income excludable from gross income. International waters are not under the sovereignty of any nation; thus, they are not a "foreign country" for purposes of Code Sec. 911.

E.D. Clark, Dec. 57,376(M), TC Memo. 2008-71.

196. A flight attendant for a major US airline who was a US citizen and had been living in France for several years was entitled to claim a foreign income exclusion. However, the exclusion only applied to a portion of the wages that she earned because the foreign income exclusion only applies to wages earned while in a foreign country. International airspace is not under the sovereignty of a foreign government and, therefore, is not a foreign county. Since the flights she worked on flew through international airspace and landed in the US, her foreign income exclusion was properly calculated using the airline's duty time apportionment tables.

C.J. LeTourneau, 103 TCM 1229, Dec. 58,951(M), TC Memo. 2012-45.

Island residence

197. Married individuals were not entitled to exclude from gross income money earned while working on Johnston Island, a possession of the US. Code Sec. 911 was inapplicable because the island did not qualify as a foreign country for the purposes of the statute and, therefore, income earned there was subject to tax.

P.E. Farrell, CA-9, 2003-1 USTC 50,149, 313 F3d 1214.

198. An individual who resided on Johnston Island could not exclude amounts earned there from gross income under Code Sec. 911 because Johnston Island is a US possession, not a foreign country. Thus, his income earned there was not foreign earned income.

S. Jones, 85 TCM 767, Dec. 55,016(M), TC Memo. 2003-14.

199. Canton Island, which is under a form of joint control of the Governments of the US and the United Kingdom until 1989, is not a possession of the US for the purposes of section 931 of the Internal Revenue Code of 1954, but is considered to be a foreign country for the purposes of section 911 of the Code.

Rev. Rul. 63-50, 1963-1 CB 129.

Kindergartens on US bases

200. A teacher was not entitled to exclude the salary received from her work at a US air base in the Philippines since

the school was a nonappropriated fund instrumentality of the US Government. The exclusion is allowable in the case of schools operated on a permissive basis rather than under official regulations.

C.D. Taylor, Jr., 30 TCM 233, Dec. 30,700(M), TC Memo. 1971-53.

201. Kindergarten and nursery schools organized and operated on US bases or installations located in foreign countries or possessions of the US when operated on a permissive basis rather than under official instructions or regulations and the support of which is furnished by the parents of the pupils are not agencies or instrumentalities of the US within the meaning of section 911(a) or 931(i) of the Internal Revenue Code of 1954 (sections 116(a) or 251(j) of the 1939 Code). Accordingly, US citizens who receive compensation from such organizations are entitled to the benefits accorded by section 911(a)(1) or section 911(a)(2) or section 931 of the Code with respect to such income, provided the provisions of the applicable section of the Code are otherwise met.

Rev. Rul. 55-384, 1955-1 CB 94.

Life insurance commissions

202. An US insurance agent who operated a business in Costa Rica could not deduct the portion of his subagent commission expenses, which was properly chargeable against amounts excluded from his gross income as foreign source earned income. The earned income exclusion was an exclusion of an amount taken from gross income, rather than net income after deducting all expenses, for earned income from non-partnership sources. Since the excluded income was therefore a part of gross

income, a proportionate part of total expenses had to be allocated to the exclusion.

H. Hernandez, 38 TCM 1068, Dec. 36,184(M), TC Memo. 1979-272.

203. "First year" and "renewal" commission income received by a citizen of the US for life insurance policies written during a period of bona fide foreign residence for an uninterrupted period which includes an entire taxable year may be excluded from gross income whenever and wherever received. All "earned income," including "first year" and "renewal" commission income, received by an individual citizen of the US which is attributable to a period of "physical presence" in a foreign country or countries for at least 510 full days during any period of 18 consecutive months may be excluded from gross income in the amount which bears the same ratio to $20,000 as the number of days in the part of the taxable year within the 18 month period bears to the total number of days in such year. Commission income, attributable to a period of "physical presence" in a foreign country received in a subsequent year, no part of which falls within the 18-month period, may not be excluded from gross income.

Rev. Rul. 55-497, 1955-2 CB 292.

Moving expenses

204. Petitioner moved from the US to Australia and in doing so incurred unreimbursed moving expenses. Respondent concedes that petitioner satisfied the requirements for a sec. 217, I. R. C. 1954, moving expense deduction but contends that the expenses are properly allocable to tax-exempt income earned subsequent to the move and as such are disallowed by

sec. 911(a), I. R. C. 1954. Held, petitioner is entitled to a deduction under sec. 217. Moving expenses are personal family expenses, and as such, are not disallowed by sec. 911(a).

J.F. Hartung, CA-9, 73-2 USTC 9616, 484 F2d 953.

205. Under authority of Hartung, 722 CCH 2052.011, a chemist was entitled to deduct unreimbursed expenses incurred in moving to Switzerland, even though the income he earned on his new job was exempt. However, he was not entitled to a business expense deduction due to lack of evidence.

R.L. Markus, 55 TC 1, Dec. 30,357.

206. Petitioner was transferred to Spain by his employer, which reimbursed him for expenses incurred in the move. Respondent concedes that petitioner satisfies all the requirements for a moving expense deduction under sec. 217, I.R.C. 1954, but contends that the portion of such expenses allocable to tax-exempt income earned subsequent to the move cannot be deducted. Held: Petitioner is not entitled to deduct fully his moving expenses incurred under sec. 217. Such expenses are partially allocable to or chargeable against exempt earned income and consequently partially disallowed by sec. 911(a).

W. Hughes, 65 TC 566, Dec. 33,547.

207. Moving expenses incurred by US citizens in a move from US to Israel were not deductible. Income earned by taxpayers while in Israel was exempt from US taxation.

M. Painter, 35 TCM 731, Dec. 33,842(M), TC Memo. 1976-164.

208. A retired accountant was not entitled to a refund of taxes paid incident to a reimbursement of moving expenses because the Code Sec. 911 foreign income exclusion that supported his claim was not in effect for the year in question. The Foreign Earned Income Act of 1978 (P.L. 95-615) repealed section 11(c) of the 1962 Act and converted what would have been exclusions for most US citizens working abroad into exclusions for some citizens working in hardship areas and deductions of certain foreign living costs for all other citizens. Even though the appellate court affirmed the lower court's dismissal of the accountant's claim on the ground that the statute was repealed, the lower court erred in finding that it lacked subject matter jurisdiction. The lower court had subject matter jurisdiction because the accountant's claim was founded upon Code Sec. 7422, which granted taxpayers the right to sue the US for the recovery of taxes alleged to have been erroneously or illegally assessed or collected.

R.J. Foreman, CA-FC, 95-2 USTC 50,386.

209. A deduction for moving expenses incurred by the taxpayers in moving from Bellevue, Washington to Divonne-les-Bains, France, in 1976 was disallowed to the extent that the expenses were allocable to foreign earned income under Code Sec. 911 and Reg. Sec. 1.911-2(d)(6) applicable to the 1976 taxable year. The moving expenses were properly allocable to or chargeable against the taxpayers' foreign earned income, were not inherently personal in nature, and the provisions of Code Sec. 911 excepting moving expenses from the allocation requirement effective for taxable years beginning after December 31, 1977 were not retroactive.

E.K. Morley, 44 TCM 1337, Dec. 39,408(M), TC Memo. 1982-586.

210. Examples discussing the treatment of reimbursed moving expenses of a US citizen who performs services abroad for his domestic employer, and whose foreign earnings qualify for exclusion from gross income under Code Sec. 911(a) are provided. The extent to which the moving expenses are deductible and the extent to which the reimbursement is includable in gross income and subject to withholding is explained. The examples cover moving to a foreign country and moving back to the US (1) to work for the same employer, (2) to work for a different employer, and (3) to retire. In general, the IRS ruled that (1) expenses incurred in moving to a foreign country are allocable to or chargeable against foreign earned income in the year of the move; (2) expenses incurred in moving from a foreign country to work in the US are allocable to US source income and not to foreign earned income; and (3) where the employee moves to the US and is no longer employed after the move, the moving expense reimbursement will be viewed as attributable to compensation for past services performed by the employee for the employer in the foreign country.

Rev. Rul. 75-84, 1975-1 CB 236, amplified by Rev. Rul. 76-162, 1976-1 CB 197.

211. The treatment is prescribed, under section 217 of the Code, for moving expenses incurred and paid in one year by a US citizen who moved to a foreign country to seek employment, became a bona fide resident there, and in the following year became entitled to the exclusion provisions of section 911.

Rev. Rul. 75-85, 1975-1 CB 239, amplified by Rev. Rul. 76-162, 1976-1 CB 197.

212. Petitioner was employed as an attorney in a law firm, and in 1971, the firm requested petitioner to transfer to its Paris office. As an inducement for petitioner to accept the transfer,

the firm agreed to pay for all expenses incurred in moving to Paris as well as for all moving expenses incurred in returning to this country. In 1973, the firm requested petitioner to transfer to its London office, and reiterated its promise to pay for petitioner's expenses in returning to this country. In 1975, after two years in the Paris office and two years in the London office, petitioner moved back to the US, and the firm paid for the return moving expenses. Held: for the purposes of the foreign tax credit, the reimbursement for petitioner's move back to the US is compensation for personal services performed without the US.

C. Dammers, 76 TC 835, Dec. 37,919.

213. Irrespective of whether the taxpayer continued to work for a domestic corporation, he properly treated reimbursed expenses for his move back to the US as foreign source income, thereby increasing the foreign tax credit available to him. The reimbursement was earned outside the US by means of a fulfillment of his employer's conditions before the move and the reimbursement was not contingent upon his performance of future services in the US. Rev. Rul. 75-84 did not control as to whether income was earned without the US.

D.R. Redding, 43 TCM 719, Dec. 38,837(M), TC Memo. 1982-111.

214. Petitioners excluded from income reimbursements they received for moving expenses incurred when they retired in 1973 from employment with Aramco in Saudi Arabia and returned to the US. Held: the reimbursements were properly excluded from income under sec. 911, I.R.C. 1954, pursuant to the "grandfather clause" thereto, sec. 1.911-1(c)(2), Income Tax Regs., because they were amounts to which petitioners had a "right" as of March 12, 1962, based on the Aramco employment

contract in force at that time, and they constitute "determinable" amounts, as required by sec. 911 and the implementing regulations.

L.F. Hills, 72 TC 958, Dec. 36,276.

215. Taxpayer was denied a moving expense deduction for reimbursed moving expenses that were treated as foreign earned income (thereby excluding such amounts from his gross income) because such deduction is disallowed by reason of Code Sec. 911(d)(6) as being properly allocable or chargeable against amounts excluded from gross income under Code Sec. 911(a). Further, Reg. §1.911-6(b)(1), which explicitly disallows the moving expense deduction in situations where otherwise deductible moving expenses are attributable to a move that will be allocable to foreign earned income, is valid.

D.J. Butka, 91 TC 110, Dec. 44,913.

Naturalized citizen

216. These factors were indicative of a (naturalized) taxpayer's bona fide residence in a foreign country, entitling him to exclude income earned during the period of foreign residence: (1) an understanding that the foreign employment would be permanent; (2) moving his family from the US to France; (3) purchasing a house abroad and expending money to renovate it; (4) obtaining a permanent resident card in France; and (5) maintaining his family abroad except for sending his children to school in US when English-speaking schools were not available in France. A portion of income, during the years in question, which arose from the settlement of litigation in the US was income earned in the US and was subject to tax.

R.J. Supino, DC N.J., 61-1 USTC 9375, 192 FSupp 389.

Okinawa

217. Okinawa is not a possession of the US but is a foreign country.

Rev. Rul. 55-6, 1955-1 CB 409.

Partnership Income

218. If a US citizen is a resident partner in charge of a foreign branch of a US partnership and the partnership agreement does not provide that he is to receive his share of partnership income from a specific source, only that portion of his distributive share of partnership income which the partnership's earned income from foreign sources bears to its total earned income is earned income "from sources without the United States" for purposes of the exemption for foreign earned income under Code Sec. 911(a).

A partnership is engaged, in the US and abroad, in a business in which both personal services and capital are material income-producing factors. The partnership agreement provides that a partner assigned to a foreign branch is to receive his entire distributive share of partnership income only from the profits of the foreign branch with which a partner is associated. The principal purpose of such provision is not the avoidance or evasion of any income tax. Held: the partner's entire distributive share of partnership income is considered income from sources outside the US and a reasonable allowance as compensation for personal services rendered by the partner, not in excess of 30% of the partner's distributive share of the net profits, is "earned income" from sources outside the US for purposes of Code Sec. 911(b).

Rev. Rul. 67-158, 1967-1 CB 188.

Rev. Proc. 80-16, 1980-1 CB 619.

Payment in year following services

219. Where a taxpayer meets the requirements of section 116(a)(2) of the IRS regarding presence in a foreign country or countries during at least 510 full days during any period of 18 consecutive months, but receives compensation attributable to such period in a taxable year ending subsequent to December 31, 1952, no portion of which falls within the 18 month period, no portion of such compensation received in such taxable year is excludable from his gross income.

Rev. Rul. 54-72, 1954-1 CB 117.

220. An individual who was employed by a construction conglomerate during the years 1968 and 1969 in Vietnam could not exclude as compensation income received for personal services performed abroad the $6,580 that she received in 1974 in settlement of a wage discrimination suit. Such compensation was received more than one year after the year in which the underlying services were performed.
H.T. Johnson, Jr., 36 TCM 1531, Dec. 34,720(M), TC Memo. 1977-377.

221. Married US taxpayers who lived and worked in a foreign country properly included foreign earned income in the denominator of their foreign tax credit disallowance fraction for the year that it was received, rather than the year that it was

earned. They were cash basis taxpayers and the income was attributable to personal services they performed in a foreign country while they were qualified individuals. Rules that related foreign earned income to the year in which it was earned applied only for purposes of determining limitations on the amount excludable from gross income. Since the disallowance fraction was used only to determine the amount of foreign tax attributable to the excluded income, it did not affect the timing of the foreign tax deduction or credit or the timing of the income exclusion.

IRS Letter Ruling 199918055, August 26, 1998.

Penalties

222. The Code Sec. 6654 penalty for calendar year 2006 for an underpayment of estimated tax will be waived for certain US citizens and residents living abroad, to the extent the underpayment is attributable to changes made by section 515 of the Tax Increase Prevention and Reconciliation Act of 2005 (P.L. 109-222). Section 515 made changes to the foreign earned income exclusion limitation and the foreign housing cost exclusion available under Code Sec. 911. These changes include the imposition of a "stacking" rule, under which excluded income is taken into consideration in determining the rate of tax on taxable income. Taxpayers relying on the law as it existed prior to the changes made by section 515 of (P.L. 109-222) may have underpaid their estimated tax liabilities for 2006. Accordingly, the IRS will waive the penalty to the extent the underpayment is attributable to those changes. The waiver is available only to qualified individuals who file a Form 2555, Foreign Earned Income, or Form 2555-EZ, with their timely filed Form 1040, US. Individual Income Tax Return or Form 1040X, Amended US Individual Income Tax Return.

Notice 2007-16, 2007-8 I.R.B. 536.

Red Cross workers

223. The American National Red Cross is not an agency of the US within the meaning of section 911(a)(2) IRC 1954. Rev. Rul. 60-36, 1960-1 CB 279.

Reimbursed expenses

224. An employee who has been reimbursed by his employer for expenses incurred on behalf of his employer should omit the reimbursement from earned income to the extent of expenses incurred. Where the expenses are equal to the reimbursements, no amount remains to be allocated to excluded earned income in determining non-deductible expenses under Code Sec. 911(a). If expenses exceed reimbursements, the excess is considered to have been incurred in producing earned income and this amount must be allocated. If reimbursements exceed expenditures, no expenses remain to be allocated. In this event, the excess reimbursements must be included in earned income.

Rev. Proc. 64-48, 1964-2 CB 993.

Permanence of work

225. A US citizen who had continuous residence in England since March 12, 1945, was a bona fide resident of a foreign country throughout the entire year 1946. Consequently, his income earned outside the US during 1946 is not subject to US income tax, but his 1945 income is fully taxable by the US.

Special Ruling, Feb. 25, 1947, 474 CCH 6136.

226. A US citizen who, while doing geophysical work in Colombia, lived there for four years and during the taxable years, and who paid taxes to that country for several years continuously, was a bona fide resident of Colombia, although he established no fixed home there, or even a settled place of abode (his work requiring him to be continuously on the move).

Swenson, CA-5, 47-2 USTC 9404, 164 F2d 783.

A.G. Harvey, 10 TC 183, Dec. 16,231 (Acq.).

227. Where taxpayer sought to take advantage of the exclusion granted by Code Sec. 116(a)(1) in the first year in which he was absent from the US, but did not establish that, during such year, he had a definite intention to remain in Saudi Arabia as a bona fide resident, income earned there was not exempt from tax.

Lockhart, 11 TCM 254, Dec. 18,860(M).

228. A script supervisor for a film company was a bona fide resident of Mexico during the entire taxable year and, consequently, was entitled to exclude her foreign earned income under Code Sec. 911(a)(1). Though she planned to return to the US eventually, she had not traveled to Mexico for a specific purpose that could be accomplished promptly.
D. Ross, 33 TCM 982, Dec. 32, 740(M), TC Memo. 1974-221.

229. Because the taxpayer was unable to prove that he was a bona fide resident of Nassau, he was not entitled to exclude the income he earned while employed in that country.

Barocas, 34 TCM 755, Dec. 33, 243(M), TC Memo. 1975-172.

230. Taxpayer was in charge of a road construction project in Costa Rica during the taxable years 1943 and 1944 and was required to remain in that country to perform his duties. While there, taxpayer and his wife actively participated in the social and economic life of their community. Upon their return to this country on business and on vacation, they reported that they were non-residents of the US. It was the intention of taxpayer to reside in Costa Rica with his wife until his work was finished. He actually did so, and the Commissioner erroneously required him to pay income taxes to the US on the basis of the inclusion of his Costa Rican income as taxable income.

C.H. Wood, DC Ky., 50-2 USTC 9351, 92 FSupp 1.

231. A professor who worked temporarily in Australia and New Zealand while on a sabbatical leave was not a "qualified person" within the meaning of Code Sec. 911. The taxpayer traveled to many foreign countries for a period of 345 days and therefore satisfied the physical presence test. However, due to the temporary nature of the foreign employment, the taxpayer failed to prove she had a "tax home" in Australia and New Zealand. Thus, the taxpayer was unable to exclude foreign earned income from gross income.

L.W. Gelhar, 63 TCM 2466, Dec. 48,086(M), TC Memo. 1992-162.

Return to United States

232. Taxpayer, a US citizen who registered his intention with the Canadian government to remain permanently in Canada, was a bona fide resident of Canada during the taxable year in

question, even though he subsequently returned to the US. Income earned in Canada during the taxable year was held exempt from tax.

H.E. Powell, 10 TCM 928, Dec. 18, 565(M).

233. Held: petitioner Gerald L. Walker was a bona fide resident of Japan for the entire year 1950, and the insurance commissions which he earned in 1950 under his contract for writing life insurance policies on the lives of American military personnel stationed in Japan, having been earned in Japan, were excludible from his gross income under the provisions of section 116(a)(1) IRC 1939.

G.L. Walker, 16 TCM 171, Dec. 22, 283(M), TC Memo. 1957-40.

234. A petroleum engineer who had established a bona fide residence in the Middle East lost it when he returned to the US for ten months in 1962 and 1963. Thus, he was not entitled to the foreign-earned income exclusion. Although prior to his departure he had agreed return to the Middle East to form a partnership following a minimum US stay of six months, the agreement was indefinite as to when the partnership would commence. Moreover, he failed to establish a physical residence at the location to which eventual departure was planned.

M.A. Carpenter, Jr., 74-1 USTC 9473, 495 F2d 175.

235. Taxpayer was not a bona fide resident of Newfoundland so as to qualify for exemption under Code Sec. 116. Moreover, he was not entitled to deduct the cost of meals and lodging while there for an indefinite or indeterminate period on the business of his employer.
Lambach, 11 TCM 330, Dec. 18, 888(M).

236. Taxpayer sought refund of his income taxes for 1945 on the ground that he had been a bona fide resident of foreign countries during the entire taxable year and all of his income was earned income from those countries. He had been employed in the Netherlands West Indies from June, 1944 to March, 1945, when he returned to the US. In May, 1945, he went to Saudi Arabia, where he worked for the rest of the year. Refund was denied because the taxpayer was not a bona fide resident of a foreign country for the entire taxable year. His West Indies residence ended when he returned to the US, or at least when he decided not to return there. His residence in Saudi Arabia could not begin until his arrival there.

R.C. DeFir, DC Calif., 57-1 USTC 9403.

237. Amounts paid by a taxpayer to his brother in connection with the proposed publication of a newspaper supplement were paid with the primary intention and good faith expectation of making a profit, so they were deductible as losses from an activity engaged in for profit. No partnership was found to exist between the brothers, so the taxpayer's loss deduction was not limited by an agreement concerning the venture. Amounts paid to help his brother and his family relocate in California were paid out of the desire to help in a time of need and were, therefore, nondeductible gifts. Amounts given to the brother in connection with a second venture were nondeductible personal expenditures because they were used in a general search for business, and not in the conduct of a profit-making activity.

C.D. Duley, 41 TCM 1521, Dec. 37, 915(M), TC Memo. 1981-246.

238. A sole proprietor engaged in the highway construction business in Venezuela incorporated his business of which he

became the president and dominant stockholder. During the years 1949-1956, the business prospered and the taxpayer made substantial withdrawals from the corporation's London and New York bank accounts for personal purposes. On the evidence, the Tax Court sustained the Commissioner's determination that the withdrawals for the taxpayer's personal benefit were includible in his income. The taxpayer was the true owner of the outstanding shares of the corporation at all times and treated the corporation as his own and used the accounts indiscriminately for the benefit of the corporation as well as for his own personal purposes. The Court, taking into consideration all of the evidence before it, including information as to whether or not a particular withdrawal was personal and giving appropriate affect to the fact that there may have been a redeposit in connection with certain withdrawals, determined that the amount of withdrawals which were includible in the petitioner's income.

G. Foster, 24 TCM 1268, Dec. 27,557(M), TC Memo. 1965-246. Aff'd and rev'd on other issues, CA-4, 68-1 USTC 9256, 391 F2d 727 .

239. In October 1947, when he was in Argentina on company business, the taxpayer was advised that he was to become a permanent employee of the company's subsidiary in that country and returned with his family to Argentina in February 1948. Since then they have been living in Argentina. The taxpayer was a bona fide resident of Argentina during the entire year of 1948 because of his physical presence in that country in October 1947, coupled with his intention to become a permanent employee there.

G.A. Page, 24 TC 52, Dec. 20, 968 (Acq.).

240. A US citizen employed by a domestic corporation was assigned to a foreign country where he established a bona fide residence. He returned to the US for an intended training period

of 7 months that actually extended over a 13-month period. Prior to his departure, he sold his residence in the foreign country and had no intention of returning to that country. After the training period, he was assigned to another foreign country where he established a permanent place of residence. Held: taxpayer did not maintain his status as a foreign resident for purposes of section 911(a)(1) of the Code during the period he was present in the US.

Rev. Rul. 73-492, 1973-2 CB 291.

241. The master of a cable ship operating in foreign waters lived in Peru with his family until 1946, when they moved to the US so that the children might secure a higher education. The taxpayer renewed his contract for service abroad. He and his wife intended that upon attainment of the education goals the family, or at least taxpayer's wife, would rejoin him at his principal base of operations abroad. After the taxpayer moved his family to the US in 1946, he secured a letter ruling as to his tax status. In this ruling, the IRS held that the taxpayer had been a bona fide resident of a foreign country for the preceding ten years and found that he intended to maintain that status for at least three more years (the period of the contract). He was regarded as coming under the exclusion. Subsequent to the tax years in issue (1947-1953), and unrelated to any conduct of taxpayer or course of events initiated by him, he was permanently transferred to the US. The court found that the taxpayer was a bona fide resident of a foreign country or countries.

F.F. Hack, 33 TC 1089, Dec. 24,112 (Acq.).

242. The District Court was affirmed per curiam in its finding that a seismograph operator, employed in Mexico, who returned to the US for four days rest in every fourteen-day period, was

not a bona fide resident of a foreign country. Income could not be excluded.

F.A. Moore, CA-5, 61-1 USTC 9441, 289 F2d 926.

Return trip on business

243. The taxpayer, manager of the Swedish branch of an American corporation since 1937, was called back to the US in February, 1941, because of the war. On June 20, 1942, he was sent to London, whence he returned to the US on June 15, 1944, and during this period he made three visits to the US of approximately two months each, the first two weeks of each being counted as a vacation. The taxpayer's wife did not accompany him to England, because of restrictions on travel, but had lived with him in Sweden both prior to the war and after he resumed his old duties there in August, 1945. Held: the taxpayer was entitled to exemption under Sec. 116(a) for 1943, but not for that part of his 1944 income paid for British activities, since he was five days short of the two years required by Sec. 116(a)(2). In so holding, the court refused to consider the vacation of three months, which he was given on his return from London as part of the period of foreign residence.

Seeley, CA-2, 51-1 USTC 9114, 186 F2d 541.

Royalties v. wages

244. An amount received by a nonresident citizen of the US from the *Reader's Digest* for foreign rights to an article written while the taxpayer was abroad, which rights were sold in this country after the article had been written, does not constitute

earned income within the meaning of section 116(a)(3) and is not exempt.

F.L. Kluckhohn, 18 TC 892, Dec. 19,158.

245. Rev. Ruls. 71-182 and 71-183, holding that income from the sale of musical or artistic property created by certain taxpayers is not earned income within the meaning of section 911(b) of the Code, are revoked.

Rev. Rul. 79-85, 1979-1 CB 246, revoking, Rev. Rul. 71-182, 1971-1 CB 214.

Self-employment income

246. The amounts allowed by the IRS as reasonable exempt earned income tax allowances and for self-employment tax were upheld where taxpayer failed to overcome the presumption of correctness as to the amounts.

F.B. Rexach, DC P.R., 71-1 USTC 9340, 341 FSupp 524.

Services rendered

247. So-called salary payments received by a nonresident citizen are not exempt earned income where evidence fails to show any services rendered, and the greater part of the payments were made by the corporations which were holding companies for petitioner's securities.

Beaumont, CA-D.C., 4 USTC 1320, 73 F2d 110.

248. Taxpayer in 1935 set up a trust with broad powers of management and control with himself as trustee. Such part of the income and principal as the trustee might in his discretion

deem necessary or proper for comfort, support or happiness was payable to grantor's wife, and after her death to their two children until they reached the age of 45 years. All income from 1935 to 1939, inclusive, less trust expenses, was accumulated and added to principal. Held: the trust income is includible in taxpayer's gross income for 1937, 1938, and 1939.

Jones, 6 TC 412, Dec. 15, 018.

249. A corporation was entitled to a business expense deduction for a portion of the amounts paid to its president as compensation. In order for such payments to be deductible, they must be paid purely as compensation for services rendered and be reasonable in amount. Even though the president was industrious and there was a special need for his services, the Court considered the following factors: corporate dividend payments on equity held by the president, the sole shareholder, were unreasonably low considering cash availability; the increase in sales was due to a boom in the industry and inflation; and there was a vast discrepancy between the president's salary and the salaries of the other employees. Accordingly, the Court held that only a portion of the payments was reasonable and deductible.

Ken Miller Supply, Inc., 37 TCM 974, Dec. 35,224(M), TC Memo. 1978-228.

250. Salary paid to an individual for management services performed for his employer by mail and telephone while on extended leave to conduct activities for his church in a foreign country may be excludable from income under section 911 of the Code.

Rev. Rul. 72-423, 1972-2 CB 446.

251. Where petitioner performed only services in bringing about sales of debentures of a German concern, and all of the services in bringing out the purchase and the sale were performed in Germany, the compensation received for the services shall not be included in income for the year 1940 under section 116(a) of the Internal Revenue Code, which was in effect in 1940 and which was not amended until thereafter.

Kollmar, 4 TC 727, Dec. 14,371 (Acq.).

252. Petitioner is a US citizen who was, for the year 1958 and a number of years prior thereto, a bona fide resident of Italy. Income received by petitioner in 1958 from an estate of her deceased husband, which estate was being administered in New Jersey, is taxable to petitioner and is not excluded from US income taxes under the provisions of the Tax Convention between the US and Italy. Executrix and trustee commissions received by petitioner in 1958 pursuant to order of the Probate Court of Bergen County, New Jersey, for serving as an executrix of her husband's estate and trustee of a trust established under his will were from sources outside the US under the provisions of sec. 911(a), I. R. C. 1954, since the services rendered by petitioner, for which these commissions were compensation, were rendered in Italy.
I.V.E. Perkins, 40 TC 330, Dec. 26, 126 (Acq.).

253. Petitioner was a resident of the Republic of Panama whose earned income was from sources outside the US. On January 15, 1962, the company executed a contract with offering the petitioner a special reimbursement for services he performed during the period from January 1, 1949, to December 31, 1961, inclusive, to be paid in installments over a period of years. The amounts due to the petitioner from the special reimbursement were not paid in cash but were credited to him against a loan account he had with the company. In 1968,

dissident shareholders took over the company and terminated petitioner's employment there. At that time, the company still owed the petitioner $330,000 from the special reimbursement. A dispute arose concerning the balance in petitioner's loan account with the company. In fact, the balance due from the loan account was less than the amount owed to him by the company in 1968. In 1973, petitioner and the company entered into a settlement agreement dropping all claims against each other. Held: the amounts credited to petitioner's loan account pursuant to the 1973 settlement were exempt income under sec. 911, I.R.C. 1954.

E.C. McGrath, 53 TCM 363, Dec. 43,771(M), TC Memo. 1987-139.

254. Income derived from taxpayer's manipulation of slot machines located abroad constituted "earned income" within the meaning of Code Sec. 911(b) and was excludible from gross income and exempt from taxation under Code Sec. 911(a)(2) since the other facts necessary to qualify this income for exclusion were shown.

D.A. Robida, CA-9, 72-1 USTC 9450, 460 F2d 1172.

255. A US citizen living in Israel who owned a 66 percent share of a US accounting firm and a US management firm but performed services for those firms while in Israel was entitled to a foreign earned income exclusion. Amounts he received from the firms were for the performance of personal services rather than a distribution of earnings and profits.

J.D. Davis, 60 TCM 1256, Dec. 46,983(M), TC Memo. 1990-588.

Severance pay

256. A US citizen employed in a foreign country from 1955 through 1975 was entitled to exclude as foreign source earned income severance pay received by him in 1975 that was attributable to services performed in 1974 and 1975 where the sole basis for the payment was a 1974 amendment to the source country's law. However, the portion of the severance pay that was attributable to services performed in the years 1955 through 1973 did not qualify for the exclusion.
Rev. Rul. 79-6, 1979-1 CB 244.

Sick leave pay

257. Decedent fulfilled the statutory requirements as to foreign service, having been employed outside the US continuously since 1929. In November, 1944, he returned to the US on furlough until the end of February, 1945. On March 1, 1945, he changed his residence to the US, and as of that date, was granted sick leave subsequently extended through 1946. Salary for the entire period up to his death on December 30, 1945, was charged to the foreign office where he had last held an active status. It was held that such salary payments while on sick leave were attributable to his foreign residence and excludable from gross income under Code Sec. 116(a)(2). Excludability was not dependent upon payment of foreign income taxes for the taxable year.

Chidester, Admr., CtCls, 49-1 USTC 9153, 82 FSupp 322.

State income taxes

258. Where earned income received by a nonresident citizen from sources outside the US was excluded from his gross

income, New York State taxes paid upon such income are "properly allocable to or chargeable against" such foreign earnings, and not deductible.

Carstairs, Exr., DC Pa., 36-1 USTC 9075, 75 FSupp 683.

Stock options

259. Taxpayer was granted an option that qualified as an option granted pursuant to an employee stock purchase plan. This option was attributable to services performed by him during the period he was a bona fide resident of a foreign country. If the stock is disposed of in a qualifying disposition, the taxpayer will realize capital gain, which does not qualify as foreign earned income. But if he makes a disqualifying disposition, the resulting gain characterized as compensation is foreign earned income to the extent it is attributable to personal services performed during the period of foreign residence and the special rules of Code Sec. 911(c) on the receipt of deferred compensation are met.

Rev. Rul. 69-118, 1969-1 CB 135.

Tax home test

260. In the following cases, taxpayers were oilrig workers on rigs off the coasts of different countries and were not entitled to foreign earned income exclusions because they did not establish that they were residents of such countries. In each of these cases, the taxpayers' tax homes were in Louisiana, where each returned for 28-day rest periods following 28-day work periods on the rigs.

L.F. Darden, 53 TCM 498, Dec. 43, 814(M), TC Memo. 1987-

174.

261. Mr. Bujol was employed on an oil rig off the coast of the United Arab Emirates. Mr. Bujol's work schedule consisted of a 28-day work period followed by a 28-day rest period. The work period was spent entirely on the rig, and the rest period was spent either at his residence in Louisiana or in transit to or from the rig. Mr. Bujol was required to maintain a residence in the United States, wherein his wife and daughter resided throughout the year at issue. Held: Mr. Bujol's "abode" remained at his residence in Louisiana; consequently, Mr. Bujol did not have a "tax home" in a foreign country for purposes of sec. 911.

R.C. Bujol, 53 TCM 762, Dec. 43, 895(M), TC Memo. 1987-230.

J.T. Leman, CA-5, 88-1 USTC 9182, 837 F2d 681.

262. Petitioner was employed on offshore oil rigs located in foreign waters. As a result of his employment on the rigs, petitioner spent a total of 157 days outside the United States during 1983. Held, petitioner was not physically present in a foreign country for 330 full days during a period of 12 consecutive months and is therefore ineligible for the foreign earned income exclusion pursuant to sec. 911(a)(1).

J.R. Sparks, Sr., 53 TCM 818, Dec. 43, 913(M), TC Memo. 1987-244.

P.E. Whitesell, 55 TCM 1720, Dec. 45, 011(M), TC Memo. 1988-398.

R.E. Bassett, 55 TCM 867, Dec. 44, 786(M), TC Memo. 1988-218.

T.W. Miller, 55 TCM 1717, Dec. 45, 010(M), TC Memo. 1988-3.

Similarly, with respect to oilrigs in different locations:

J.R. Hummer, 56 TCM 657, Dec. 45, 168(M), TC Memo. 1988-528.

W.H. Bosarge, 56 TCM 1043, Dec. 45, 418(M), TC Memo. 1989-15.

D.A. Benham, 57 TCM 323, Dec. 45, 670(M), TC Memo. 1989-215.

J.R. Moudy, 57 TCM 327, Dec. 45, 671(M), TC Memo. 1989-216.
J.B. Harrington, 93 TC 297, Dec. 45, 989.

J.B. Evans, 109 TCM 1052, Dec. 60, 214(M), TC Memo. 2015-12.

263. An individual who, for the tax years at issue, was required to spend time working Iraq and Afghanistan as part of his job, was not entitled to the foreign earned income tax exclusion for the tax years at issue because he was not a qualified individual for purposes of the exclusion. He did not meet the requirement that his tax home be in a forcign country. His tax home was in the US rather than in a foreign country because he lived on US Air Force bases when he was in Iraq and Afghanistan, he was not allowed to leave the bases, his family did not go with him, he did not travel and he did not open a bank account in either country. Neither country could be considered his primary place of business because he did not establish a residence there in either a real or substantial sense. Also, he spent less than half of his time working in these countries and, for each of the tax years at issue, he earned less than half of his income from services performed in these countries. Further, he did not meet either the bona fide resident

or 330-day physical presence test for purposes of being a qualified individual. He also did not meet the requirements for a waiver of the 330-day requirement because he failed to show that he was required to leave either or both countries because of war, civil unrest or similar adverse conditions.

J.F. Daly, 105 TCM 1850, Dec. 59,562(M), TC Memo. 2013-147.

On the other hand:

264. An Arabic/English linguist who worked in Iraq was entitled to foreign earned income exclusion. His tax home was in Iraq; therefore, he was a qualified individual for purposes of Code Sec. 911(d)(1). The taxpayer credibly testified with respect to his strong ties to Iraq during the relevant period. He was a native of Iraq, a native speaker of Iraqi Arabic and familiar with Iraqi culture. He had ties to family and friends with whom he had stayed in touch long after emigrating to the US. The individual planned to stay in Iraq indefinitely with the expectation that his contract with his employer would be extended. The facts of this case differed from other Code Sec. 911 cases where taxpayers' foreign ties were limited and transitory.

A.Z. Eram, 107 TCM 1320, Dec. 59, 872(M), TC Memo. 2014-60.

265. In an IRS Advice Memorandum, the Chief Counsel's Office has provided guidance on the application of the foreign earned income exclusion under Code Sec. 911 and the combat zone exclusion under Code Sec. 112 to civilian contractors and civilian employees who are not employees of the US or a US agency

Advice Memorandum 2009-003.

Tax return preparation

266. The value of income tax return preparation services provided to expatriate employees was includible in gross income because the benefits were not excludable as a working condition fringe. Moreover, the value of the income tax preparation services constituted wages subject to FICA and FUTA tax. However, for withholding purposes, Chief Counsel determined that the value of the benefit may have been excludable if the employer reasonably believed that the benefit was excludable from the recipient-employee's gross income under Code Sec. 911 and the regulations thereunder.

Field Service Advice Memorandum 200137039, June 19, 2001.

Tax years

267. The benefits of section 116(a) of the Revenue Act of 1928 are limited to " a bona fide nonresident of the United States for more than six months during the taxable year," the "taxable year" being determined by the method of accounting employed rather than by the period in which the services were performed and not only must all of the requirements of that section be satisfied, but the income in question must meet the provisions of section 31 of that act.

Stryker, 29 BTA 1025, Dec. 8407.

268. Plaintiff's husband resided in Venezuela from April 27, 1952, until his death there on January 3, 1953. In seeking in income tax refund under 1939 Code Sec. 116(a)(1), she contended that he had been a bona fide foreign resident “for an uninterrupted period of time which includes an entire taxable year” because as to the deceased, an entire taxable year

extended from January 1, 1953, to January 3, 1953, death shortening the taxable year. Held: "An entire taxable year" means a full 12-months period and not a fraction of a calendar year such as would constitute under some circumstances the taxable year of a taxpayer in event of death.

E. Witt, DC Ga., 56-2 USTC 10,002.

On the other hand:

269. Held: the period from Jan. 1, 1971, through June 25, 1971, the date of the death of the deceased taxpayer, was his "entire taxable year" within the meaning of sec. 911(a)(1), I.R.C. 1954.

T. Roodner Est., 64 TC 680, Dec. 33,353.

270. A US citizen employed by a US corporation and residing in the US was notified that he would be transferred to Australia, and was placed on the payroll of his employer's Australian subsidiary on December 30, 1965. In anticipation of the transfer, he and his family left the US (Hawaii) on December 27, 1965. However, as a result of several personal stopovers, he did not arrive in Australia until January 3, 1966. He reported for work on that day. December 31, 1965, and January 1 and 2, 1966, were holidays in Australia. He and his family intended to make their home in Australia for at least 15 months plus an additional indefinite period. They became integrated members of their community. However, as a result of unexpected events, they returned to the US early in 1967. Held: although petitioner became a "bona fide resident" of Australia, his 1966 earnings were not exempt from taxation under section 911(a)(1) of the 1954 Code because his Australian residence did not span "an uninterrupted period which includes an entire taxable year."

D.F. Dawson, 59 TC 264, Dec. 31,606.

271. A motion picture actor rendered services abroad in 1952 and received compensation of $73,998.97 in 1954. His 18-month limitation period ended February 27, 1954 so it did not include the entire taxable year. The trial court properly held the taxpayer was limited to his claimed exclusion on his return ($3,178.08 being 58/365ths of $20,000) on other foreign income received in that year, and he was not entitled to any additional exclusion by reason of the $73,998.97 compensation payment received. "Taxable year" means the calendar year of receipt and it is immaterial that the income might be attributable to services rendered in a prior taxable year.

Ladd, CA-9, 62-2 USTC 9787, 309 F2d 51.

272. As used in Code Sec. 911(a)(2), the words "taxable year" mean the year in which income attributable to foreign service was received, rather than the year in which services were performed. Domicile in a community property state does not entitle a married couple to a double foreign income exclusion.

J. Renoir, CA-9, 63-2 USTC 9665, 321 F2d 605.

E. Handcock-Ferguson, 21 TCM 1267, Dec. 25, 695(M), TC Memo. 1962-237.

273. Husband and wife were employed abroad under a joint employment contract, which provided a stock option for petitioner-husband alone. Held: petitoners were free to structure the provisions of their joint employment contract as they wished, and abiding by the contract as they made it, must accept the tax consequences of their structural choice.

Commissioner v. National Alfalfa Dehydrating & Milling Co. [74 1 ustc 9456], 417 US 134, 149 (1974). Therefore, they may not allocate any of the gain from petitioner-husband's 1978 disposition of the stock to petitioner-wife for the purpose of computing her foreign earned income exclusion under section 911 IRC 1954. Held further: they may attribute petitioner-husband's stock upon proceeds to their 1977 gross income under the attribution rule of section 911(c)(2) for the limited purpose of computing the foreign earned income exclusion for 1977 under section 911(a)(1) and (c)(1)(B).

R.S. Groetzinger, 87 TC 533, Dec. 43, 307.

Terminal pay

274. Petitioner, a US citizen, worked in China for UNRRA from March 1946 to September 1947. He had worked in Honduras from 1942 to September 1945 for The Institute of Inter-American Affairs and received terminal pay from that organization until March 1946, but his work in Honduras had ceased in September 1945 and he had returned to the US with his family, had found employment with UNRRA and was on its payroll from November 1945. Held: he was not a resident of Honduras in 1946, therefore was not a resident of a foreign country or countries during the entire year 1946, under section 116(a) IRS Code.

Lovald, 16 TC 909, Dec. 18,249.

Time of receipt

275. The time of receipt limitation under section 911(c)(4) of the Code applies to the furlough allowance received in the US by a US citizen church missionary, who earned a 1-year furlough in the US with pay for each four years served overseas and was

required to perform some services in the US while on furlough, and only the portion of the allowance attributable to services performed overseas in the year preceding the furlough year, reduced by the amount attributable to services performed in the US, is excludable from gross income, Rev. Rul. 55-464 superseded.

276. Rev. Rul. 76-191, 1976-1 CB 201.

Travel in restricted countries

277. Tax benefits generally available to US taxpayers living or doing business in a foreign country are limited for some countries. This ruling lists the countries for which Code Sec. 911(d)(8) limits the income exclusions otherwise available under Code Sec. 911 to individuals living abroad. The sole country currently subject to the limitations of Code Sec. 911(d)(8) is Cuba.

Rev. Rul. 2005-3, 2005-1 CB 334.

278. The IRS has issued guidance stating that US citizens and residents who earn income by performing services at the US Naval Base at Guantanamo Bay, Cuba, may elect to exclude such income and housing cost amounts from gross income under Code Sec. 911, provided that they meet the other requirements of the section. The Cuban Assets Control Regulations (31 C.F.R. part 515) do not prohibit transactions related to travel to, from, or within the base.
Notice 2006-84, I.R.B. 2006-41, 677.

Treaty rights

279. Civilian workers of a company operating under a contract with the US Air Force for the operation of missile tracking stations on British islands in the Atlantic Ocean established by treaties between the US and the United Kingdom did not establish bona fide residence abroad since the extraterritorial rights, privileges, and immunities granted by the treaties prevented the physical presence of the workers from ripening into actual residence in a foreign country. Tax Court reversed.

L.T. Matthew, CA-5, 64-2 USTC 9669, 335 F2d 231. Cert. denied, 380 US 943, 85 SCt 1024.

280. Similarly as to a civilian technician at a missile tracking site in the Bahamas.

R.E. Baden, DC Ohio, 64-2 USTC 9740, 233 FSupp 185.

G.O. Boyd, 46 TC 252, Dec. 27, 951.

281. Held: under the unique facts and circumstances of this case, petitioner was a bona fide resident of a foreign country and the income earned without the US during the taxable year is exempt from taxation under the provisions of section 911(a)(1) IRC 1954.
R.W. Benfer, 45 TC 277, Dec. 27,661 (Acq.).

282. The IRS no longer contends that income tax exemption provided in a treaty or other international agreement is in itself the equivalent of a statement by a US citizen that he or she is a nonresident of the foreign country. The question of whether a treaty prevents a citizen from becoming a bona fide resident will

be determined under all the provisions of the treaty, including specific provisions concerning residence or the extent of the total privileges and immunities given to the citizen under the treaty.

Rev. Rul. 72-497, 1972-2 CB 448.

283. The income tax exemption provided under Article V of the UN-Swiss agreement will not in itself prevent a US citizen employed by the United Nations from being a resident of Switzerland for purposes of section 911(a)(1) of the Code.

Rev. Rul. 72-496, 1972-2 CB 447.

284. Prior to the issuance of Rev. Rul. 72-497, the IRS position in Rev. Ruls. 68-553 and 69-449 was rejected.

Scott, Jr., CtCls, 70-2 USTC 9652, 432 F2d 1388.

Trust Territory of Pacific Islands

285. Compensation paid to a US citizen employed by the Government of the Trust Territory of the Pacific Islands for services performed in the Trust Territory qualifies for the foreign earned income exclusion.

Rev. Rul. 68-608, 1968-2 CB 327, modified by Rev. Rul. 80-78, 1980-1 CB 171, and Rev. Rul. 80-167, 1980-1 CB 176.
J.D. McComish, CA-9, 78-2 USTC 9677, 580 F2d 1323.

K.R. Groves, CA-5, 76-2 USTC 9509, 533 F2d 1376. Cert. denied, 429 US 1000, 97 SCt 529.

R.J. Toothman, 37 TCM 603, Dec. 35,095(M), TC Memo. 1978-

140.

286. US citizens who are contract employees of the Government of the Trust Territory of the Pacific Islands and who are not US Civil Service employees are not considered paid by the US or any agency thereof for purposes of the Code Sec. 911 exclusion (both before and after the Foreign Earned Income Act of 1978) and the Code Sec. 913 deduction for excess foreign living costs.

Rev. Rul. 80-78, 1980-1 CB 171, modifying Rev. Rul. 68-608, 1968-2 CB 327, modified by Rev. Rul. 80-167, 1980-1 CB 176, and clarified by Rev. Rul. 85-29, 1985-1 CB 223.

287. Rev. Rul. 80-78, as modified, is clarified to indicate that, for tax years beginning after December 31, 1981, the position of the Service is that the exception to the section 911(a) exclusion in section 911(b)(1)(B)(ii) applies only to amounts paid by the US or an agency thereof to an employee of the US or an agency thereof.
Rev. Rul. 85-29, 1985-1 CB 223, clarifying Rev. Rul. 80-78, 1980-1 CB 171.

288. Pursuant to the Covenant to Establish a Commonwealth of the Northern Mariana Islands in Political Union with the US, for purposes of Code Sec. 931, the Marianas are not considered a possession of the US. Further, for years beginning after 1978, the Government of the Marianas is not a foreign government for purposes of Code Sec. 892 and the Marianas are not a foreign country for purposes of Code Secs. 911 and 913.

Rev. Rul. 80-167, 1980-1 CB 176, modifying Rev. Rul. 68-608, 1968-2 CB 327 and Rev. Rul. 80-78, 1980-1 CB 171, above.

289. Although $95,000 compensation for personal services rendered in Germany by the taxpayer was paid into taxpayer's account with a New York bank, the compensation was from a source "without (outside) the United States".

Kollmar, 4 TC 727, Dec. 14,371 (Acq.).

US possessions

290. Individuals were not entitled to exclude from gross income compensation that they earned as employees of a demilitarization contractor on Johnston Island, a US insular possession. The Code Sec. 911 foreign income exclusion was unavailable because Johnston Island is not a foreign country. Accordingly, the compensation did not constitute foreign earned income, nor did the taxpayers have a foreign country tax home for purposes of the exclusion.

E.N. Umbach, CA-10, 2004-1 USTC 50,148.

291. Individuals were not entitled to exclude from gross income the compensation that they earned as employees of a demilitarization contractor on Johnston Island, a US insular possession located in the central Pacific Ocean. The foreign income exclusion under Code Sec. 911 was unavailable because Johnston Island is a US possession rather than a foreign country. Accordingly, the compensation did not constitute foreign earned income, nor was their tax home in a foreign country for purposes of the exclusion.

J.D. Specking, 117 TC 95, Dec. 54,470.

Vacations in US

292. A terminal vacation is not a temporary absence but a final absence from the foreign country.

Seely, CA-2, 51-1 USTC 9114, 186 F2d 541.

293. In 1947 taxpayer went to Saudi Arabia to work for an oil company. His employment contract terminated in the fall of 1948 and he returned to the United States, where he remained until after December 31, 1948. He seeks to recover income taxes paid for the year 1948 on the ground that he was a bona fide resident of Saudi Arabia and had returned to the US only on a vacation. The jury returned a verdict in favor of the taxpayer on his suit for refund.
J.D. Carter, DC Tex., 58-2 USTC 9570.

Voting in US elections

294. The exercise by a US citizen, a bona fide resident of a foreign country, of his right to vote in elections in the US by absentee ballot will not, generally, jeopardize the right to exclude foreign income under Code Sec. 911(a)(1).

Rev. Rul. 71-101, 1971-1 CB 214.

Waiver of residency requirements due to civil unrest

295. The IRS has announced a waiver for any individual who failed to meet the eligibility requirements of Code Sec. 911(d)(1) because adverse conditions in a foreign country precluded the individual from meeting the requirements for the 2015 tax year. The country for which the eligibility requirements were waived for 2015 was Burundi. An individual

who left Burundi on or after May 14, 2015, will be treated as a qualified individual with respect to the period during which that individual was present in, or was a bona fide resident of, such foreign country if the individual established a reasonable expectation of meeting the requirements of Code Sec. 911(d) but for those adverse conditions.

Rev. Proc. 2016-21, I.R.B. 2016-14, 533.

296. The IRS has released a list of countries[39] for which the existence of adverse conditions during specified periods may excuse failure by a taxpayer to meet the foreign presence or residency requirements for 2013. Those countries are: Libya for departures on or after July 26, 2014; Yemen, for departures on or after September 24, 2014.
Rev. Proc. 2015-25, I.R.B. 2015-14, 848.

297. The IRS has released a list of countries for which the existence of adverse conditions during specified periods may excuse failure by a taxpayer to meet the foreign presence or residency requirements for 2013. Those countries are: Egypt, for departures on or after July 3, 2013; Lebanon, for departures on or after September 5, 2013; Pakistan, for departures on or after August 9, 2013; and Yemen, for departures on or after August 6, 2013.

Rev. Proc. 2014-25, I.R.B. 2012-14, 927.

298. The waiver rules of Code Sec. 911(d)(4) do not apply to a person who begins employment in an already unstable foreign country and who then fails to satisfy the "qualified individual" rules while the unrest continues.

---

[39] This list of countries with adverse conditions is updated every year. This list is kept shorter than you might think.

H.J. Billeaud, 58 TCM 1348, Dec. 46, 364(M), TC Memo. 1990-59.

299. An engineer was unable to exclude from his gross income the income he earned in Saudi Arabia because he was neither a bona fide resident of that country for an uninterrupted period of one tax year nor was he present there for at least 330 full days in a 12-consecutive-month period. He did not qualify for a waiver of the period-of-stay requirements because Saudi Arabia was not included on the list of countries eligible for waiver treatment with respect to the period at issue.

J.C. Branch, 67 TCM 2822, Dec. 49,820(M), TC Memo. 1994-191.

300. An individual who, for the tax years at issue, was required to spend time working Iraq and Afghanistan as part of his job, was not entitled to foreign earned income exclusion for the tax years at issue because he was not a qualified individual for purposes of the exclusion. He did not meet the requirement that his tax home be in a foreign country. Further, he did not meet either the bona fide resident or 330-day physical presence test for purposes of being a qualified individual. He also did not meet the requirements for a waiver of the 330-day requirement because he failed to show that he was required to leave either or both countries because of war, civil unrest or similar adverse conditions.

J.F. Daly, 105 TCM 1850, Dec. 59, 562(M), TC Memo. 2013-147.

Withholding from wages

301. Separate monthly payments by a domestic corporation to its US citizen-employees working overseas, one made in the US and the other in a foreign country and subject to that country's income tax withholding, are wages for purposes of income tax withholding only with respect to those payments made in the US that exceed the amounts excludable under section 911 of the Code.

Rev. Rul. 75-485, 1975-2 CB 414.

CHAPTER 16

The Internal Revenue Code

The code is the actual law. Sometimes it is called the tax code or IRC (Internal Revenue Code). The code is also called title 26 of the US Code. (Title 26 USC).

This chapter contains section 911 of the IRC (IRC 911) which covers foreign earned income and the exclusions. The section is organized in an outline fashion. Each paragraph has a number. These numberings have been spelled out completely to facilitate the lay reader.

The Code is subject to change, although not too often. The most current version should be checked for basing a decision on the wording.

911(a) Exclusion from Gross Income

At the election of a qualified individual (made separately with respect to paragraphs (1) and (2)), there shall be excluded from the gross income of such individual, and exempt from taxation under this subtitle, for any taxable year—

911(a)(1) The foreign earned income of such individual, and

911(a)(2) The housing cost amount of such individual.

911(b) Foreign Earned Income

911(b)(1) Definition

For purposes of this section—

911(b)(1)(A) In General

The term "foreign earned income" with respect to any individual means the amount received by such individual from sources within a foreign country or countries which constitute earned income attributable to services performed by such individual during the period described in subparagraph (A) or (B) of subsection (d)(1), whichever is applicable.

911(b)(1)(B) Certain Amounts Not Included in Foreign Earned Income

The foreign earned income for an individual shall not include amounts—

911(b)(1)(B)(i) Received as a pension or annuity,

911(b)(1)(B)(ii) Paid by the United States or an agency thereof to an employee of the United States or an agency thereof,

911(b)(1)(B)(iii) Included in gross income by reason of section 402(b) (relating to taxability of beneficiary of nonexempt trust) or section 403(c) (relating to taxability of beneficiary under a nonqualified annuity), or

911(b)(1)(B)(iv) Received after the close of the taxable year following the taxable year in which the services to which the amounts are attributable are performed.

911(b)(2) Limitation on Foreign Earned Income

911(b)(2)(A) In General

The foreign earned income of an individual which may be excluded under subsection (a)(1) for any taxable year shall not exceed the amount of foreign earned income computed on a daily basis at an annual rate equal to the exclusion amount for the calendar year in which such taxable year begins.

911(b)(2)(B) Attribution to Year in Which Services Are Performed

For purposes of applying subparagraph (A), amounts received shall be considered received in the taxable year in which the services to which the amounts are attributable are performed.

911(b)(2)(C) Treatment of Community Income

In applying subparagraph (A) with respect to amounts received from services performed by a husband or wife which are community income under community property laws applicable to such income, the aggregate amount which may be excludable from the gross income of such husband and wife under subsection (a)(1) for any taxable year shall equal the amount which would be so excludable if such amounts did not constitute community income.

911(b)(2)(D) Exclusion Amount

911(b)(2)(D)(i) In General

The exclusion amount for any calendar year is $80,000.

911(b)(2)(D)(ii) Inflation Adjustment

In the case of any taxable year beginning in a calendar year after 2005, the $80,000 amount in clause (i) shall be increased by an amount equal to the product of—

911(b)(2)(D)(ii)(I) Such dollar amount, and

911(b)(2)(D)(ii)(II) The cost-of-living adjustment determined under section 1(f)(3) for the calendar year in which the taxable year begins, determined by substituting "2004" for "1992" in subparagraph (B) thereof.

If any increase determined under the preceding sentence is not a multiple of $100, such increase shall be rounded to the next lowest multiple of $100.

911(c) Housing Cost Amount

For purposes of this section—

911(c)(1) In General

The term "housing cost amount" means an amount equal to the excess of—

911(c)(1)(A) The housing expenses of an individual for the taxable year to the extent such expenses do not exceed the amount determined under paragraph (2), over

911(c)(1)(B) An amount equal to the product of—

911(c)(1)(B)(i) 16 percent of the amount (computed on a daily basis) in effect under subsection (b)(2)(D) for the calendar year in which such taxable year begins, multiplied by

911(c)(1)(B)(ii) The number of days of such taxable year within the applicable period described in subparagraph (A) or (B) of subsection (d)(1).

911(c)(2) Limitation

911(c)(2)(A) In General

The amount determined under this paragraph is an amount equal to the product of—

911(c)(2)(A)(i) 30 percent (adjusted as may be provided under subparagraph (B)) of the amount (computed on a daily basis) in effect under subsection (b)(2)(D) for the calendar year in which the taxable year of the individual begins, multiplied by

911(c)(2)(A)(ii) The number of days of such taxable year within the applicable period described in subparagraph (A) or (B) of subsection (d)(1).

911(c)(2)(B) Regulations

The Secretary may issue regulations or other guidance providing for the adjustment of the percentage under subparagraph (A)(i) on the basis of geographic differences in housing costs relative to housing costs in the United States.

911(c)(3) Housing Expenses
911(c)(3)(A) In General

The term "housing expenses" means the reasonable expenses paid or incurred during the taxable year by or on behalf of an individual for housing for the individual (and, if they reside with him, for his spouse and dependents) in a foreign country. The term—

911(c)(3)(A)(i) Includes expenses attributable to the housing (such as utilities and insurance), but

911(c)(3)(A)(ii) Does not include interest and taxes of the kind deductible under section 163 or 164 or any amount allowable as a deduction under section 216(a).

Housing expenses shall not be treated as reasonable to the extent such expenses are lavish or extravagant under the circumstances.

911(c)(3)(B) Second Foreign Household

911(c)(3)(B)(i) In General

Except as provided in clause (ii), only housing expenses incurred with respect to that abode which bears the closest relationship to the tax home of the individual shall be taken into account under paragraph (1).

911(c)(3)(B)(ii) Separate Household for Spouse and Dependents

If an individual maintains a separate abode outside the United States for his spouse and dependents and they do not reside with him because of living conditions which are dangerous, unhealthful, or otherwise adverse, then—

911(c)(3)(B)(ii)(I) The words "if they reside with him" in subparagraph (A) shall be disregarded, and

911(c)(3)(B)(ii)(II) The housing expenses incurred with respect to such abode shall be taken into account under paragraph (1).

911(c)(4) Special Rules Where Housing Expenses Not Provided by Employer
911(c)(4)(A) In General

To the extent the housing cost amount of any individual for any taxable year is not attributable to employer provided amounts, such amount shall be treated as a deduction allowable in computing adjusted gross income to the extent of the limitation of subparagraph (B).

911(c)(4)(B) Limitation

For purposes of subparagraph (A), the limitation of this subparagraph is the excess of—

911(c)(4)(B)(i) The foreign earned income of the individual for the taxable year, over

911(c)(4)(B)(ii) The amount of such income excluded from gross income under subsection (a) for the taxable year.

911(c)(4)(C) 1- Year Carryover of Housing Amounts Not Allowed by Reason of Subparagraph (B)

911(c)(4)(C)(i) In General

The amount not allowable as a deduction for any taxable year under subparagraph (A) by reason of the limitation of subparagraph (B) shall be treated as a deduction allowable in computing adjusted gross income for the succeeding taxable year (and only for the succeeding taxable year) to the extent of the limitation of clause (ii) for such succeeding taxable year.

911(c)(4)(C)(ii) Limitation

For purposes of clause (i), the limitation of this clause for any taxable year is the excess of—

911(c)(4)(C)(ii)(I) The limitation of subparagraph (B) for such taxable year, over

911(c)(4)(C)(ii)(II) Amounts treated as a deduction under subparagraph (A) for such taxable year.

911(c)(4)(D)Employer Provided Amounts

For purposes of this paragraph, the term "employer provided amounts" means any amount paid or incurred on behalf of the individual by the individual's employer which is foreign earned income included in the individual's gross income for the taxable year (without regard to this section).

911(c)(4)(E) Foreign Earned Income

For purposes of this paragraph, an individual's foreign earned income for any taxable year shall be determined without regard to the limitation of subparagraph (A) of subsection (b)(2).

911(d) Definitions and Special Rules

For purposes of this section—

911(d)(1) Qualified Individual

The term "qualified individual" means an individual whose tax home is in a foreign country and who is—

911(d)(1)(A) A citizen of the United States and establishes to the satisfaction of the Secretary that he has been a bona fide resident of a foreign country or countries for an uninterrupted period which includes an entire taxable year, or

911(d)(1)(B) A citizen or resident of the United States and who, during any period of 12 consecutive months, is present in a foreign country or countries during at least 330 full days in such period.

911(d)(2) Earned Income

911(d)(2)(A) In General

The term "earned income" means wages, salaries, or professional fees, and other amounts received as compensation for personal services actually rendered, but does not include that part of the compensation derived by the taxpayer for personal services rendered by him to a corporation which represents a distribution of earnings or profits rather than a reasonable allowance as compensation for the personal services actually rendered.

911(d)(2)(B) Taxpayer Engaged in Trade or Business

In the case of a taxpayer engaged in a trade or business in which both personal services and capital are material income-producing factors, under regulations prescribed by the Secretary, a reasonable allowance as compensation for the personal services rendered by the taxpayer, not in excess of 30 percent of his share of the net profits of such trade or business, shall be considered as earned income.

911(d)(3) Tax Home

The term "tax home" means, with respect to any individual, such individual's home for purposes of section 162(a)(2) (relating to traveling expenses while away from home). An individual shall not be treated as having a tax home in a foreign country for any period for which his abode is within the United States.

911(d)(4) Waiver of Period of Stay in Foreign Country

Notwithstanding paragraph (1), an individual who—

911(d)(4)(A) Is a bona fide resident of, or is present in, a foreign country for any period,

911(d)(4)(B) Leaves such foreign country after August 31, 1978—

911(d)(4)(B)(i) During any period during which the Secretary determines, after consultation with the Secretary of State or his delegate, that individuals were required to leave such foreign country because of war, civil unrest, or similar adverse conditions in such foreign country which precluded the normal conduct of business by such individuals, and

911(d)(4)(B)(ii) Before meeting the requirements of such paragraph (1), and

911(d)(4)(C) Establishes to the satisfaction of the Secretary that such individual could reasonably have been expected to have met such requirements but for the conditions referred to in clause (i) of subparagraph (B),

shall be treated as a qualified individual with respect to the period described in subparagraph (A) during which he was a bona fide resident of, or was present in, the foreign country, and in applying subsections (b)(2)(A), (c)(1)(B)(ii), and (c)(2)(A)(ii) with respect to such individual, only the days within such period shall be taken into account.

911(d)(5) Test of Bona Fide Residence

If—

911(d)(5)(A) An individual who has earned income from sources within a foreign country submits a statement to the authorities of that country that he is not a resident of that country, and

911(d)(5)(B) Such individual is held not subject as a resident of that country to the income tax of that country by its authorities with respect to such earnings,

then such individual shall not be considered a bona fide resident of that country for purposes of paragraph (1)(A).

911(d)(6) Denial of Double Benefits

No deduction or exclusion from gross income under this subtitle or credit against the tax imposed by this chapter (including any credit or deduction for the amount of taxes paid or accrued to a foreign country or possession of the United States) shall be allowed to the extent such deduction, exclusion, or credit is properly allocable to or chargeable against amounts excluded from gross income under subsection (a).

911(d)(7) Aggregate Benefit Cannot Exceed Foreign Earned Income

The sum of the amount excluded under subsection (a) and the amount deducted under subsection (c)(4)(A) for the taxable year shall not exceed the individual's foreign earned income for such year.

911(d)(8) Limitation on Income Earned in Restricted Country

911(d)(8)(A) In General

If travel (or any transaction in connection with such travel) with respect to any foreign country is subject to the regulations described in subparagraph (B) during any period—

911(d)(8)(A)(i) The term "foreign earned income" shall not include any income from sources within such country attributable to services performed during such period,

911(d)(8)(A)(ii) The term "housing expenses" shall not include any expenses allocable to such period for housing in such country or for housing of the spouse or dependents of the taxpayer in another country while the taxpayer is present in such country, and

911(d)(8)(A)(iii) An individual shall not be treated as a bona fide resident of, or as present in, a foreign country for any day during which such individual was present in such country during such period.

911(d)(8)(B) Regulations

For purposes of this paragraph, regulations are described in this subparagraph if such regulations—

911(d)(8)(B)(i) Have been adopted pursuant to thc Trading With the Enemy Act (50 U.S.C. App. 1 et seq.), or the International Emergency Economic Powers Act (50 U.S.C. 1701 et seq.), and

911(d)(8)(B)(ii) Include provisions generally prohibiting citizens and residents of the United States from engaging in transactions related to travel to, from, or within a foreign country.

911(d)(8)(C) Exception

Subparagraph (A) shall not apply to any individual during any period in which such individual's activities are not in violation of the regulations described in subparagraph (B).

911(d)(9) Regulations

The Secretary shall prescribe such regulations as may be necessary or appropriate to carry out the purposes of this section, including regulations providing rules—

911(d)(9)(A) For cases where a husband and wife each have earned income from sources outside the United States, and

911(d)(9)(B) For married individuals filing separate returns.

911(e)Election

911(e)(1) In General

An election under subsection (a) shall apply to the taxable year for which made and to all subsequent taxable years unless revoked under paragraph (2).

911(e)(2) Revocation

A taxpayer may revoke an election made under paragraph (1) for any taxable year after the taxable year for which such election was made. Except with the consent of the Secretary, any taxpayer who makes such a revocation for any taxable year may not make another election under this section for any subsequent taxable year before the 6th taxable year after the taxable year for which such revocation was made.

911(f) Determination of Tax Liability

911(f)(1) In General

If, for any taxable year, any amount is excluded from gross income of a taxpayer under subsection (a), then, notwithstanding sections 1 and 55—

911(f)(1)(A) If such taxpayer has taxable income for such taxable year, the tax imposed by section 1 for such taxable year shall be equal to the excess (if any) of—

911(f)(1)(A)(i) The tax which would be imposed by section 1 for such taxable year if the taxpayer's taxable income were increased by the amount excluded under subsection (a) for such taxable year, over

911(f)(1)(A)(ii) The tax which would be imposed by section 1 for such taxable year if the taxpayer's taxable income were equal to the amount excluded under subsection (a) for such taxable year, and

911(f)(1)(B) If such taxpayer has a taxable excess (as defined in section 55(b)(1)(A)(ii)) for such taxable year, the amount determined under the first sentence of section 55(b)(1)(A)(i) for such taxable year shall be equal to the excess (if any) of—

911(f)(1)(B)(i) The amount which would be determined under such sentence for such taxable year (subject to the limitation of section 55(b)(3)) if the taxpayer's taxable excess (as so defined) were increased by the amount excluded under subsection (a) for such taxable year, over

911(f)(1)(B)(ii) The amount which would be determined under such sentence for such taxable year if the taxpayer's taxable excess (as so defined) were equal to the amount excluded under subsection (a) for such taxable year.

For purposes of this paragraph, the amount excluded under subsection (a) shall be reduced by the aggregate amount of any deductions or exclusions disallowed under subsection (d)(6) with respect to such excluded amount.

911(f)(2) Special Rules
911(f)(2)(A) Regular Tax

In applying section 1(h) for purposes of determining the tax under paragraph (1)(A)(i) for any taxable year in which, without regard to this subsection, the taxpayer's net capital gain exceeds taxable income (hereafter in this subparagraph referred to as the capital gain excess)—

911(f)(2)(A)(i) The taxpayer's net capital gain (determined without regard to section 1(h)(11)) shall be reduced (but not below zero) by such capital gain excess,

911(f)(2)(A)(ii) The taxpayer's qualified dividend income shall be reduced by so much of such capital gain excess as exceeds the taxpayer's net capital gain (determined without regard to section 1(h)(11) and the reduction under clause (i)), and

911(f)(2)(A)(iii) Adjusted net capital gain, unrecaptured section 1250 gain, and 28-percent rate gain shall each be determined after increasing the amount described in section 1(h)(4)(B) by such capital gain excess.

911(f)(2)(B) Alternative Minimum Tax

In applying section 55(b)(3) for purposes of determining the tax under paragraph (1)(B)(i) for any taxable year in which, without regard to this subsection, the taxpayer's net capital gain exceeds the taxable excess (as defined in section 55(b)(1)(A)(ii))—

911(f)(2)(B)(i) The rules of subparagraph (A) shall apply, except that such subparagraph shall be applied by substituting "the taxable excess (as defined in section 55(b)(1)(A)(ii))" for "taxable income", and

911(f)(2)(B)(ii) The reference in section 55(b)(3)(B) to the excess described in section 1(h)(1)(B), and the reference in section 55(b)(3)(C)(ii) to the excess described in section 1(h)(1)(C)(ii), shall each be treated as a reference to each such excess as determined under the rules of subparagraph (A) for purposes of determining the tax under paragraph (1)(A)(i).

911(f)(2)(C) Definitions

Terms used in this paragraph which are also used in section 1(h) shall have the respective meanings given such terms by section 1(h), except that in applying subparagraph (B) the adjustments under part VI of subchapter A shall be taken into account.

911(g) Cross References

For administrative and penal provisions relating to the exclusions provided for in this section, see sections 6001, 6011, 6012(c), and the other provisions of subtitle F.

CHAPTER 17

The Internal Revenue Regulations

The regulations are considered secondary law. They are written by the IRS, not the Congress, based on the authority delegated to the IRS to write necessary regulations to facilitate the implementation of the law (IRC). Regulations can change more frequently than laws. Regulations are not to be confused with IRS Rulings, Procedures, Notices and other publications which carry a descending level of importance in interpreting and applying the law.

The regulations are also known as the treasury regulations or as title 26 of the Code of Federal Regulations (CFR). There is a parallel numbering scheme to the IRC, so, the parallel regulations that support IRC section 911 are found in Regulations 1.911.

This chapter contains Treasury Regulations section 1.911, which covers foreign earned income and the exclusions. The section is organized in an outline fashion.

These regulations are subject to change, although not too often. The most current version should be checked for basing a decision on the wording.

§1.911-1, Partial exclusion for earned income from sources within a foreign country and foreign housing costs

(a)In general

Section 911 provides that a qualified individual may elect to exclude the individual's foreign earned income and the housing cost amount from the individual's gross income for the taxable year. Foreign earned income is excludable to the extent of the applicable limitation for the taxable year. The housing cost amount for the taxable year is excludable to the extent attributable to employer provided amounts. If a portion of the housing cost amount for the taxable year is attributable to non-employer provided amounts, such amount may be deductible by the qualified individual subject to a limitation. The amounts excluded under section 911(a) and the amount deducted under section 911(c)(3)(A) for the taxable year shall not exceed the individual's foreign earned income for such taxable year. Foreign earned income must be earned during a period for which the individual qualifies to make an election under section 911(d)(1). A housing cost amount that would be deductible except for the application of this limitation may be carried over to the next taxable year and is deductible to the extent of the limitation for that year. Except as otherwise provided, §§ 1.911-1 through 1.911-7 apply to taxable years beginning after December 31, 1981. These sections do not apply to any item of income, expense, deduction, or credit arising before January 1, 1982, even if such item is attributable to services performed after December 31, 1981.

(b)Scope

Section 1.911-2 provides rules for determining whether an individual qualifies to make an election under section 911. Section 1.911-3 provides rules for determining the amount of foreign earned income that is excludable under section 911(a)(1). Section 1.911-4 provides rules for determining the housing cost amount and the portions excludable under section 911(a)(2) or deductible under section 911(c)(3). Section 1.911-5 provides special rules applicable to married couples. Section 1.911-6 provides for the disallowance of deductions, exclusions, and credits attributable to amounts excluded under section 911. Section 1.911-7 provides procedural rules for making or revoking an election under section 911. Section 1.911-8 provides a reference to rules applicable to taxable years beginning before January 1, 1982. [Reg. §1.911-1.]

§1.911-2, Qualified individuals

(a)In general

An individual is a qualified individual if:

(1)

The individual's tax home is in a foreign country or countries throughout—

(i)

The period of bona fide residence described in paragraph (a)(2)(i) of this section, or

(ii)

The 330 full days of presence described in paragraph (a)(2)(ii) of this section; and

(2)

The individual is either—

(i)

A citizen of the United States who establishes to the satisfaction of the Commissioner or his delegate that the individual has been a bona fide resident of a foreign country or countries for an uninterrupted period which includes an entire taxable year, or

(ii)

A citizen or resident of the United States who has been physically present in a foreign country or countries for at least 330 full days during any period of twelve consecutive months.

(b)Tax home

For purposes of paragraph (a)(1) of this section, the term "tax home" has the same meaning which it has for purposes of section 162 (a)(2) (relating to travel expenses away from home). Thus, under section 911, an individual's tax home is considered to be located at his regular or principal (if more than one regular) place of business or, if the individual has no regular or principal place of business because of the nature of the business, then at his regular place of abode in a real and substantial sense. An individual shall not, however, be considered to have a tax home in a foreign country for any period for which the individual's abode is in the United States. Temporary presence of the individual in the United States does not necessarily mean that the individual's abode is in the United States during that time. Maintenance of a dwelling in the United States by an individual, whether or not that dwelling is used by the individual's spouse and dependents, does not necessarily mean that the individual's abode is in the United States.

(c)Determination of bona fide residence

For purposes of paragraph (a)(2)(i) of this section, whether an individual is a bona fide resident of a foreign country shall be determined by applying, to the extent practical, the principles of section 871 and the regulations thereunder, relating to the determination of the residence of aliens. Bona fide residence in a foreign country or countries for an uninterrupted period may be established, even if temporary visits are made during the period to the United States or elsewhere on vacation or business. An individual with earned income from sources within a foreign country is not a bona fide resident of that country if:

(1)

The individual claims to be a nonresident of that foreign country in a statement submitted to the authorities of that country, and

(2)

The earned income of the individual is not subject, by reason of nonresidency in the foreign country, to the income tax of that country.

If an individual has submitted a statement of nonresidence to the authorities of a foreign country the accuracy of which has not been resolved as of any date when a determination of the individual's bona fide residence is being made, then the individual will not be considered a bona fide resident of the foreign country as of that date.

(d)Determination of physical presence

For purposes of paragraph (a)(2)(ii) of this section, the following rules apply.

(1)**Twelve-month test**

A period of twelve consecutive months may begin with any day but must end on the day before the corresponding day in the twelfth succeeding month. The twelve month period may begin before or after arrival in a foreign country and may end before or after departure.

(2)**330-day test**

The 330 full days need not be consecutive but may be interrupted by periods during which the individual is not present in a foreign country. In computing the minimum 330 full days of presence in a foreign country or countries, all separate periods of such presence during the period of twelve consecutive months are aggregated. A full day is a continuous period of twenty-four hours beginning with midnight and ending with the following midnight. An individual who has been present in a foreign country and then travels over areas not within any foreign country for less than twenty-four hours shall not be deemed outside a foreign country during the period of travel. If an individual who is in transit between two points outside the United States is physically present in the United States for less than twenty-four hours, such individual shall not be treated as present in the United States during such transit but shall be treated as travelling over areas not within any foreign country. For purposes of this paragraph (d)(2), the term "transit between two points outside the United States" has the same meaning that it has when used in section 7701(b)(6)(C).

(3)**Illustrations of the physical presence requirement**

The physical presence requirement of paragraph (a)(2)(ii) of this section is illustrated by the following examples:

Example (1). B, a U.S. citizen, arrives in Venezuela from New York at 12 noon on April 24, 1982. B remains in Venezuela until 2 p.m. on March 21, 1983, at which time B departs for the United States. Among other possible twelve month periods, B is present in a foreign country an aggregate of 330 full days during each of the following twelve month periods: March 21, 1982 through March 20, 1983; and April 25, 1982 through April 24, 1983.

Example (2). C, a U.S. citizen, travels extensively from the time C leaves the United States on March 5, 1982, until the time C departs the United Kingdom on January 1, 1984, to return to the United States permanently. The schedule of C's travel and the number of full days at each location are listed below:

Country	Time and date of arrival	Time and date of departure	Full days in foreign country
United States		10 p.m. (by air) Mar. 5, 1982	
United Kingdom	9 a.m. Mar. 6, 1982	10 p.m. (by ship) June 25, 1982	110
United States	11 a.m. June 30, 1982	1 p.m. (by ship) July 19, 1982	0
France	3 p.m. July 24, 1982	11 a.m. (by air) Aug. 22, 1983	393
United States	4 p.m. Aug. 22, 1983	9 a.m. (by air) Sept. 4, 1983	0
United Kingdom	9 a.m. Sept. 5, 1983	9 a.m. (by air) Jan. 1, 1984	117
United States	1 p.m. Jan. 1, 1984		

Among other possible twelve month periods, C is present in a foreign country or countries an aggregate of 330 full days during the following twelve month periods: March 2, 1982 through March 1, 1983; and January 21, 1983 through January 20, 1984. The computation of days with respect to each twelve month period may be illustrated as follows:

First twelve month period (March 2, 1982 through March 1, 1983):

	Full days in foreign country
Mar. 2, 1982 through Mar. 6, 1982	0
Mar. 7, 1982 through June 24, 1982	110
June 25, 1982 through July 24, 1982	0
July 25, 1982 through Mar. 1, 1983	220
Total full days	330

Second twelve month period (January 21, 1983 through January 20, 1984):

	Full days in foreign country
Jan. 21, 1983 through Aug. 21, 1983	213
Aug. 22, 1983 through Sept. 5, 1983	0
Sept. 6, 1983 through Dec. 31, 1983	117
Jan. 1, 1984 through Jan. 20, 1984	0
Total full days	330

(e)Special rules

For purposes only of establishing that an individual is a qualified individual under paragraph (a) of this section, residence or presence in a foreign country while there employed by the U.S. government or any agency or instrumentality of the U.S. government counts towards satisfaction of the requirements of § 1.911-2(a). (But see section 911(b)(1)(B)(ii) and § 1.911-3(c)(3) for the rule excluding amounts paid by the U.S. government to an employee from the definition of foreign earned income.) Time spent in a foreign country prior to January 1, 1982, counts toward satisfaction of the bona fide residence and physical presence requirements, even though no exclusion or deduction may be allowed under section 911 for income attributable to services performed during that time. For purposes of paragraph (a)(2)(ii) of this section, the term "resident of the United States" includes an individual for whom a valid election is in effect under section 6013(g) or (h) for the taxable year or years during which the physical presence requirement is satisfied.

(f)Waiver of period of stay in foreign country due to war or civil unrest

Notwithstanding the requirements of paragraph (a) of this section, an individual whose tax home is in a foreign country, and who is a bona fide resident of, or present in, a foreign country for any period, who leaves the foreign country after August 31, 1978, before meeting the requirements of paragraph (a) of this section, may, as provided in this paragraph, qualify to make an election under section 911(a) and § 1.911-7(a). If the Secretary determines, after consultation with the Secretary of State or his delegate, that war, civil unrest, or similar adverse conditions existed in a foreign country, then the Secretary shall publish the name of the foreign country and the dates between which such conditions were deemed to exist. In order to qualify to make an election under this paragraph, the individual must establish to the satisfaction of the Secretary that the individual left a foreign country, the name of which has been published by the Secretary, during the period when adverse conditions existed and that the individual could reasonably have expected to meet the requirements of paragraph (a) of this section but for the adverse conditions. The individual shall attach to his return for the taxable year a statement that the individual expected to meet the requirements of paragraph (a) of this section but for the conditions in the foreign country which precluded the normal conduct of business by the individual. Such individual shall be treated as a qualified individual, but only for the actual period of residence or presence. Thus, in determining the number of the individual's qualifying days, only days within the period of actual residence or presence shall be counted.

(g)United States

The term "United States" when used in a geographical sense includes any territory under the sovereignty of the United States. It includes the states, the District of Columbia, the possessions and territories of the United States, the territorial waters of the United States, the air space over the United States, and the seabed and subsoil of those submarine areas which are adjacent to the territorial waters of the United States and over which the United States has exclusive rights, in accordance with international law, with respect to the exploration and exploitation of natural resources.

(h)Foreign country

The term "foreign country" when used in a geographical sense includes any territory under the sovereignty of a government other than that of the United States. It includes the territorial waters of the foreign country (determined in accordance with the laws of the United States), the air space over the foreign country, and the seabed and subsoil of those submarine areas which are adjacent to the territorial waters of the foreign country and over which the foreign country has exclusive rights, in accordance with international law, with respect to the exploration and exploitation of natural resources. [Reg. §1.911-2.]

§1.911-3, Determination of amount of foreign earned income to be excluded

(a)Definition of foreign earned income

For purposes of section 911 and the regulations thereunder, the term "foreign earned income" means earned income (as defined in paragraph (b) of this section) from sources within a foreign country (as defined in § 1.911-2(h)) that is earned during a period for which the individual qualifies under § 1.911-2(a) to make an election. Earned income is from sources within a foreign country if it is attributable to services performed by an individual in a foreign country or countries. The place of receipt of earned income is immaterial in determining whether earned income is attributable to services performed in a foreign country or countries.

(b)Definition of earned income

(1)In general

The term "earned income" means wages, salaries, professional fees, and other amounts received as compensation for personal services actually rendered including the fair market value of all remuneration paid in any medium other than cash. Earned income does not include any portion of an amount paid by a corporation which represents a distribution of earnings and profits rather than a reasonable allowance as compensation for personal services actually rendered to the corporation.

(2)Earned income from business in which capital is material

In the case of an individual engaged in a trade or business (other than in corporate form) in which both personal services and capital are material income producing factors, a reasonable allowance as compensation for the personal services actually rendered by the individual shall be considered earned income, but the total amount which shall be treated as the earned income of the individual from such trade or business shall in no case exceed thirty percent of the individual's share of the net profits of such trade or business.

(3)Professional fees

Earned income includes all fees received by an individual engaged in a professional occupation (such as doctor or lawyer) in the performance of professional activities. Professional fees constitute earned income even though the individual employs assistants to perform part or all of the services, provided the patients or clients are those of the individual and look to the individual as the person responsible for the services rendered.

(c)Amounts not included in foreign earned income

Foreign earned income does not include an amount:

(1)

Excluded from gross income under section 119;

(2)

Received as a pension or annuity (including social security benefits);

(3)

Paid to an employee by an employer which is the U.S. government or any U.S. government agency or instrumentality;

(4)

Included in the individual's gross income by reason of section 402(b) (relating to the taxability of a beneficiary of a nonexempt trust) or section 403(c) (relating to the taxability of a beneficiary under a nonqualified annuity or under annuities purchased by exempt organizations);

(5)

Included in gross income by reason of § 1.911-6(b)(4)(ii); or

(6)

Received after the close of the first taxable year following the taxable year in which the services giving rise to the amounts were performed. For treatment of amounts received after December 31, 1962, which are attributable to services performed on or before December 31, 1962, and with respect to which there existed on March 12, 1962, a right (whether forfeitable or nonforfeitable) to receive such amounts, see § 1.72-8.

(d)Determination of the amount of foreign earned income that may be excluded under section 911(a)(1)

(1)**In general**

Foreign earned income described in this section may be excluded under section 911(a)(1) and this paragraph only to the extent of the limitation specified in paragraph (d)(2) of this section. Income is considered to be earned in the taxable year in which the services giving rise to the income are performed. The determination of the amount of excluded earned income in this manner does not affect the time for reporting any amounts included in gross income.

(2)**Limitation**

(i)**In general**

The term "section 911(a)(1) limitation" means the amount of foreign earned income for a taxable year which may be excluded under section 911(a)(1). The section 911(a)(1) limitation shall be equal to the lesser of the qualified individual's foreign earned income for the taxable year in excess of amounts that the individual elected to exclude from gross income under section 911(a)(2) or the product of the annual rate for the taxable year (as specified in paragraph (d)(2)(ii) of this section) multiplied by the following fraction:

$$\frac{\text{The number of qualifying days in the taxable year}}{\text{The number of days in the taxable year}}$$

(ii)**Annual rate for the taxable year**

The annual rate for the taxable year is the rate set forth in section 911(b)(2)(A).

(3)**Number of qualifying days**

For purposes of section 911 and the regulations thereunder, the number of qualifying days is the number of days in the taxable year within the period during which the individual met the tax home requirement and either the bona fide residence requirement or the physical presence requirement of § 1.911-2(a). Although the period of bona fide residence must include an entire taxable year, the entire uninterrupted period of residence may include fractional parts of a taxable year. For instance, if an individual who was a calendar year taxpayer established a tax home and a residence in a foreign country as of November 1, 1982, and maintained the tax home and the residence through March 31, 1984, then the uninterrupted period of bona fide residence includes fractional parts of the years 1982 and 1984, and all of 1983. The number of qualifying days in 1982 is sixty-one. The number of qualifying days in 1983 is 365. The number of qualifying days in 1984 is ninety-one. The period during which the physical presence requirement of § 1.911-2(a)(2)(ii) is met is any twelve consecutive month period during which the individual is physically present in one or more foreign countries for 330 days and the individual's tax home is in a foreign country during each day of such physical presence. Such period may include days when the individual is not physically present in a foreign country, and days when the individual does not maintain a tax home in a foreign country.

Such period may include fractional parts of a taxable year. Thus, if an individual's period of physical presence is the twelve-month period beginning June 1, 1982, and ending May 31, 1983, the number of qualifying days in 1982 is 214 and the number of qualifying days in 1983 is 151.

(e)Attribution rules

(1)In general

Foreign earned income is considered to be earned in the taxable year in which the individual performed the services giving rise to the income. If income is earned in one taxable year and received in another taxable year, then, for purposes of determining the amount of foreign earned income that the individual may exclude under section 911(a), the individual must attribute the income to the taxable year in which the services giving rise to the income were performed. Thus, any reimbursement would be attributable to the taxable year in which the services giving rise to the obligation to pay the reimbursement were performed, not the taxable year in which the reimbursement was received. For example, tax equalization payments are normally received in the year after the year in which the services giving rise to the obligation to pay the tax equalization payment were performed. Therefore, such payments will almost always have to be attributed to the prior year. Foreign earned income attributable to services performed in a preceding taxable year shall be excludable from gross income in the year of receipt only to the extent such amount could have been excluded under paragraph (d)(1) in the preceding taxable year, had such amount been received in the preceding taxable year. The taxable year to which income is attributable will be determined on the basis of all the facts and circumstances.

(2)Priority of use of the section 911(a)(1) limitation

Foreign earned income received in the year in which it is earned shall be applied to the section 911(a)(1) limitation for that year before applying income earned in that year that is received in any other year. Foreign earned income that is earned in one year and received in another year shall be applied to the section 911(a)(1) limitation for the year in which it was earned, on a year by year basis, in any order that the individual chooses. (But see section 911(b)(1)(B)(iv)). An individual may not amend his return to change the treatment of income with respect to the section 911(a)(1) exclusion after the period provided by section 6511(a). The special period of limitation provided by section 6511(d)(3) does not apply for this purpose. For example, C, a qualified individual, receives an advance bonus of $10,000 in 1982, salary of $70,000 in 1983, and a performance bonus of $10,000 in 1984, all of which are foreign earned income for 1983. C has a section 911(a)(1) limitation for 1983 of $80,000, and has no housing cost amount exclusion. On his income tax return for 1983, C elects to exclude foreign earned income of $70,000 received in 1983. C may also exclude his $10,000 advance bonus received in 1982 (by filing an amended return for 1982), or he may exclude the $10,000 performance bonus received in 1984 on his 1984 income tax return. However, C may not exclude part of the 1982 bonus and part of the 1984 bonus.

(3)**Exception for year-end payroll period**

Notwithstanding paragraph (e)(1) of this section, salary or wage payments of a cash basis taxpayer shall be attributed entirely to the year of receipt under the following circumstances:

(i)

The period for which the payment is made is a normal payroll period of the employer which regularly applies to the employee;

(ii)

The payroll period includes the last day of the employee's taxable year;

(iii)

The payroll period does not exceed 16 days; and

(iv)

The payment is part of a normal payroll of the employer that is distributed at the same time, in relation to the payroll period, that such payroll would normally be distributed, and is distributed before the end of the next succeeding payroll period.

(4)**Attribution of bonuses and substantially nonvested property to periods in which services were performed**

(i)**In general**

Bonuses and substantially nonvested property are attributable to all of the services giving rise to the income on the basis of all the facts and circumstances. If an individual receives a bonus or substantially nonvested property (as defined in § 1.83-3(b)) and it is determined to be attributable to services performed in more than one taxable year, then, for purposes of determining the amount eligible for exclusion from gross income in the year the bonus is received or the property vests, a portion of such amount shall be treated as attributable to services performed in each taxable year (or portion thereof) during the period when services giving rise to the bonus or the substantially nonvested property were performed. Such portion shall be determined by dividing the amount of the bonus or the excess of the fair market value of the vested property over the amount paid, if any, for the vested property, by the number of months in the period when services giving rise to such amount were performed, and multiplying the quotient by the number of months in such period in the taxable year. For purposes of this section, the term "month" means a calendar month. A fraction of a calendar month shall be deemed a month if it includes fifteen or more days.

(ii)**Examples**

The following examples illustrate the application of this paragraph (e)(4).

Example (1). A, an employee of M Corporation during all of 1983 and 1984, worked in the United States from January 1 through April 30, 1983, and received $12,000 of salary for that period. A worked in country F from May 1, 1983 through the end of 1984, and is a qualified individual under § 1.911-2(a) for that period. For the period from May 1 through December 31, 1983, A received $32,000 of salary. M pays a bonus on December 20, 1983 to each of M's employees in an amount equal to 10 percent of the employee's regular wages or salary for the 1983 calendar year. The amount of A's bonus is $4,400 for 1983. The portion of A's bonus that is attributable to services performed in country F and is foreign earned income for 1983 is $3,200, or $32,000 × 10 percent. The remaining $1,200 of A's bonus is attributable to services performed in the United States, and is not foreign earned income.

Example (2). The facts are the same as in example (1), except that M determines bonuses separately for each country based on the productivity of the employees in that country. M pays a bonus to employees in country F, in the amount of 15 percent of each employee's wages or salary earned in country F. A's country F bonus is $4,800 for 1983 ($32,000 × 15 percent), and is foreign earned income for 1983. If A also receives a bonus (or if A's bonus is increased) for working in the United States during 1983, that amount is not foreign earned income.

Example (3). X corporation offers its employees a bonus of $40,000 if the employee accepts employment in a foreign country and remains in a foreign country for a period of at least four years. A, an employee of X, is a calendar year and cash basis taxpayer. A accepts employment with X in foreign country F. A begins work in F on July 1, 1983 and continues to work in F for X until June 30, 1987. In 1987 X pays A a $40,000 bonus. The bonus is attributable to services A performed from July 1, 1983 through June 30, 1987. The amount of the bonus attributable to 1987 is $5,000 (($40,000 ÷ 48) × 6). The amount of the bonus attributable to 1986 is $10,000 (($40,000 ÷ 48) × 12). A may exclude the $10,000 attributable to 1986 only to the extent that amount could have been excluded under section 911(a)(1) had A received it in 1986. The remaining $25,000 is attributable to services performed in taxable years before 1986. Such amounts may not be excluded under section 911 because they are received after the close of the taxable year following the taxable year in which the services giving rise to the income were performed.

(iii)**Special rule for elections under section 83(b)**

If an individual receives substantially nonvested property and makes an election under section 83(b) and § 1.83-2(a) to include in his gross income the amount determined under section 83(b)(1)(A) and (B) and § 1.83-2(a) for the taxable year in which the property is transferred (as defined in § 1.83-3(a)), then, for the purpose of determining the amount eligible for exclusion in the year of receipt, the individual may elect either of the following options:

(A)

Substantially nonvested property may be treated as attributable entirely to services performed in the taxable year in which an election to include it in income is made. If so treated, then the amount otherwise included in gross income as determined under § 1.83-2(a) will be excludable under section 911(a) for such year subject to the limitation provided in § 1.911-3(d)(2) for such year.

(B)

A portion of the substantially nonvested property may be treated as attributable to services performed or to be performed in each taxable year during which the substantial risk of forfeiture (as defined in section 83(c) and § 1.83-3(c)) exists. The portion treated as attributable to services performed or to be performed in each taxable year is determined by dividing the amount of the substantially nonvested property included in gross income as determined under § 1.83-2(a) by the number of months during the period when a substantial risk of forfeiture exists. The quotient is multiplied by the total number of months in the taxable year during which a substantial risk of forfeiture exists. The amount determined to be attributable to services performed in the year the election is made shall be excluded from gross income for such year as provided in paragraph (d)(2) of this section. Amounts treated as attributable to services performed in subsequent taxable years shall be excludable in the year of receipt only to the extent such amounts could be excluded under paragraph (d)(2) of this section in such subsequent year. An individual may obtain such additional exclusion by filing an amended return for the taxable year in which the property was transferred. The individual may only amend his or her return within the period provided by section 6511(a) and the regulations thereunder.

(5)**Moving expense reimbursements**

(i)**Source of reimbursements**

For the purpose of determining whether a moving expense reimbursement is attributable to services performed within a foreign country or within the United States, in the absence of evidence to the contrary, the reimbursement shall be attributable to future services to be performed at the new principal place of work. Thus, a reimbursement received by an employee from his employer for the expenses of a move to a foreign country will generally be attributable to services performed in the foreign country. A reimbursement received by an employee from his employer for the expenses of a move from a foreign country to the United States will generally be attributable to services performed in the United States. For purposes of this paragraph (e)(5), evidence to the contrary includes, but is not limited to, an agreement, between the employer and the employee, or a statement of company policy, which is reduced to writing before the move to the foreign country and which is entered into or established to induce the employee or employees to move to a foreign country. The writing must state that the employer will reimburse the employee for moving expenses incurred in returning to the United States regardless of whether the employee continues to work for the employer after the employee returns to the United States. The writing may contain conditions upon which the right to reimbursement is determined as long as the conditions set forth standards that are definitely ascertainable and the conditions can only be fulfilled prior to, or through completion of, the employee's return move to the United States that is the subject of the writing. In no case will an oral agreement or statement of company policy concerning moving expenses be considered evidence to the contrary. For the purpose of determining whether a storage expense reimbursement is attributable to services performed within a foreign country, in the case of storage expenses incurred after December 31, 1983, the reimbursement shall be attributable to services performed during the period of time for which the storage expenses are incurred.

(ii)Attribution of foreign source reimbursements to taxable years in which services are performed

(A)In general

If a reimbursement for moving expenses is determined to be from foreign sources under paragraph (e)(5)(i) of this section, then for the purpose of determining the amount eligible for exclusion in accordance with paragraphs (d)(2) and (e)(2) of this section, the reimbursement shall be considered attributable to services performed in the year of the move as long as the individual is a qualified individual for a period that includes 120 days in the year of the move. The period that is used in determining the number of qualifying days for purposes of the individual's section 911(a)(1) limitation (under paragraph (d)(2) of this section) must also be used in determining whether the individual is a qualified individual for a period that includes 120 days in the year of the move. If the individual is not a qualified individual for such period, then the individual shall treat a portion of the reimbursement as attributable to services performed in the year of the move, and a portion as attributable to services performed in the succeeding taxable year, if the move is from the United States to a foreign country, or to the prior taxable year, if the move is from a foreign country to the United States. The portion of the reimbursement treated as attributable to services performed in the year of the move shall be determined by multiplying the total reimbursement by the following fraction:

$$\frac{\text{The number of qualifying days (as defined in paragraph (d)(3) of this section) in the year of the move}}{\text{The number of days in the taxable year of the move.}}$$

The remaining portion of the reimbursement shall be treated as attributable to services performed in the year succeeding or preceding the year of the move. Amounts treated as attributable to services performed in a year succeeding or preceding the year of the move shall be excludable in the year of receipt only to the extent such amounts could be excluded under paragraph (d)(2) of this section in such succeeding or preceding year.

(B)**Moves beginning before January 1, 1984**

Notwithstanding paragraph (e)(5)(ii)(A) of this section, this paragraph (e)(5)(ii)(B) shall apply for moves begun before January 1, 1984. If a reimbursement for moving expenses is determined to be from foreign sources under paragraph (e)(5)(i) of this section, then for the purpose of determining the amount eligible for exclusion in accordance with paragraphs (d)(2) and (e)(2) of this section, the reimbursement shall be considered attributable to services performed in the year of the move. However, if the individual does not qualify under section 911(d)(1) and § 1.911-2(a) for the entire taxable year of the move, then the individual shall treat a portion of the reimbursement as attributable to services performed in the succeeding taxable year, if the move is from the United States to a foreign country, or to the prior taxable year, if the move is from a foreign country to the United States. The portion of the reimbursement treated as attributable to services performed in the year succeeding or preceding the move shall be determined by multiplying the total reimbursement by the following fraction:

$$\frac{\text{The number of qualifying days (as defined in paragraph (d)(3) of this section) in the year of the move}}{\text{The number of days in the taxable year of the move.}}$$

and subtracting the product from the total reimbursement. Amounts treated as attributable to services performed in a year succeeding or preceding the year of the move shall be excludable in the year of receipt only to the extent such amounts could be excluded under paragraph (d)(2) of this section in such succeeding or preceding year.

(f)Examples

The following examples illustrate the application of this section.

Example (1). A is a U.S. citizen and calendar year taxpayer. A's tax home was in foreign country F and A was physically present in F for 330 days during the period from July 4, 1982 through July 3, 1983. The number of A's qualifying days in 1982 as determined under paragraph (d)(2) of this section is 181. In 1982 A receives $40,000 attributable to services performed in foreign country F in 1982. Under paragraph (d)(2) of this section A's section 911(a)(1) limitation is $37,192, that is the lesser of $40,000 (foreign earned income) or

$$\$75{,}000 \text{ (annual rate)} \times \frac{181 \text{ (qualifying days)}}{365 \text{ (days in taxable year)}}.$$

Example (2). The facts are the same as in example (1) except that in 1982 A receives $30,000 attributable to services performed in foreign country F. A excludes this amount from gross income under paragraph (d) of this section. In addition, in 1983 A receives $10,000 attributable to services performed in F in 1982 and $35,000 attributable to services performed in F in 1983. On his return for 1983, A must report $45,000 of income. A's section 911(a)(1) limitation for 1983 is the lesser of $35,000 (foreign earned income) or $40,329, the annual rate for the taxable year multiplied by a fraction the numerator of which is A's qualifying days in the taxable year and the denominator of which is the number of days in the taxable year ($80,000 × 184/365). On his tax return for 1983 A may exclude $35,000 attributable to services performed in 1983. A may only exclude $7,192 of the $10,000 received in 1983 attributable to services performed in 1982 because such amount is only excludable in 1983 to the extent such amount could have been excluded in 1982 subject to the section 911(a)(1) limitation for 1982 which is $37,192 ($75,000 × 181/365). No portion of amounts attributable to services performed in 1982 may be used in calculating A's section 911(a)(1) limitation for 1983. Thus, even though A could have excluded an additional $6,329 in 1983 if A had had more foreign earned income attributable to 1983, A may not exclude the $2,808 of remaining foreign earned income attributable to 1982.

Example (3). C is a U.S. citizen and calendar year taxpayer. C establishes a bona fide residence and a tax home in foreign country J on March 1, 1982, and maintains a tax home and a residence in J until December 31, 1986. In March of 1982 C's employer, Y corporation, transfers stock in Y to C. The stock is subject to forfeiture if C returns to the U.S. before January 1, 1985. C elects under section 83(b) to include $15,000, the amount determined with respect to such stock under section 83(b)(1), in gross income in 1982. C's other foreign earned income in 1982 is

$58,000. C elects under paragraph (e)(4)(iii)(B) of this section to treat the stock as if earned over the period of the substantial risk of forfeiture. The number of months in the period of the substantial risk of forfeiture is thirty-four. The number of months in the taxable year 1982 within the period of foreign employment is ten. For purposes of determining C's section 911(a)(1) limitation, $4,412 (($15,000/34) × 10) of the amount included in gross income under section 83(b) is treated as attributable to services performed in 1982, $5,294 is treated as attributable to services to be performed in 1983, and $5,294 is treated as attributable to services to be performed in 1984. In 1982, C excludes $62,412 under section 911(a)(1). That is the lesser of foreign earned income for 1982 ($56,000 + $4,412) or the annual rate for the taxable year multiplied by a fraction the numerator of which is C's qualifying days in the taxable year and the denominator of which is the number of days in the taxable year ($75,000 × 306/365). C continues to perform services in foreign country J throughout 1983 and 1984. C would be able to exclude the remaining $5,294 attributable to services performed in 1983 and $5,294 attributable to services performed in 1984 if those amounts would be excludable if they had been received in 1983 or 1984 respectively. If C is entitled to exclude the additional amounts, C must claim the exclusion by filing an amended return for 1982.

Example (4). D is a U.S. citizen and calendar year taxpayer. In September, 1984 D moves to foreign country K. D is physically present in K, and D's tax home is in K, from September 15, 1984 through December 31, 1985. D receives $6,000 in April, 1985 from his employer, as a reimbursement for expenses of moving to K, pursuant to a written agreement that such moving expenses would be reimbursed to D upon successful completion of 6 months employment in K. Under paragraph (e)(5)(i) of this section, the reimbursement is attributable to services performed in K. Under the physical presence test of § 1.911-2(a)(2)(ii), among other periods D is a qualified individual for the period of August 10, 1984 through August 9, 1985, which includes 144 days in 1984. Under paragraph (e)(5)(ii)(A) of this section, for the purpose of determining the amount eligible for exclusion, the reimbursement is considered attributable to services performed in 1984 (the year of the move) because D is a qualified individual under § 1.911-2(a) for a period that includes 120 days in 1984. The reimbursement may be excluded under paragraphs (d)(2) and (c)(2) of this section, to the extent that D's foreign earned income for 1984 that was earned and received in 1984 was less than the annual rate for the taxable year multiplied by the number of D's qualifying days in the taxable year over the number of days in D's taxable year ($80,000 × 144/366), or $31,475.

Example (5). The facts are the same as in example (4) except that D is not a qualified individual under the physical presence test, but is a qualified individual under the bona fide residence test for the period of September 15, 1984 through December 31, 1985. Under paragraph (e)(5)(ii)(A) of this section, for the purpose of determining the amount eligible for exclusion, the reimbursement is considered attributable to services performed in 1984 and 1985 because D is not a qualified individual for a period that includes 120 days in 1984 (the year of the move). The portion of the reimbursement treated as attributable to services performed in 1984 is $6,000 × 108/366, or $1,770, and may be excluded, subject to D's 1984 section 911(a)(1) limitation. The balance of the reimbursement, $4,230, is treated as attributable to services performed in 1985, and may be excluded to the extent provided in paragraphs (d)(2) and (e)(2) of this section.

Example (6). The facts are the same as in Example (4), with the following additions. Before D moved to K, D and his employer signed a written agreement that D would perform services for the employer for at least one year, primarily in country K, and, if D did not voluntarily cease to work for the employer primarily in country K before one year had elapsed, the employer would reimburse D for one-half of D's expenses, up to a maximum of $4,000, of moving back to the United States. The agreement also stated that, if D did not voluntarily leave the employment in K before two years had elapsed, the employer would reimburse D for all of D's reasonable expenses of moving back to the United States. The agreement further stated that D's right to reimbursement would not be conditioned upon the performance of services after D ceased to work in K. D worked in country K for all of 1985. On January 1, 1986, D left K and moved to the United States. In February, 1986 the employer paid D $3,500 as reimbursement for one-half of D's expenses of moving to the United States. Although D did not fulfill the condition in the agreement to receive full reimbursement, all of the conditions in the agreement set forth definitely ascertainable standards and no condition could be fulfilled after D moved back to the United States. The agreement fulfills the requirements of paragraph (e)(5)(i) of this section, and therefore is evidence that the reimbursement should not be attributable to future services to be performed at D's new principal place of work. Under the facts and circumstances, the reimbursement is attributable to services performed in K. Under paragraph (e)(5)(ii)(A) of this section, the entire reimbursement is attributable to services performed in 1985. The amount attributable in 1985 may be excluded to the extent provided in paragraphs (d)(2) and (e)(2) of this section. [Reg. §1.911-3.]

§1.911-4, Determination of housing cost amount eligible for exclusion or deduction

(a)Definition of housing cost amount

The term "housing cost amount" means an amount equal to the reasonable expenses paid or incurred (as defined in section 7701(a)(25)) during the taxable year by or on behalf of the individual attributable to housing in a foreign country for the individual and any spouse or dependents who reside with the individual (or live in a second foreign household described in paragraph (b)(5) of this section) less the base housing amount as defined in paragraph (c) of this section. The housing cost amount must be reduced by the amount of any military or section 912 allowance or similar allowance excludable from gross income that is intended to compensate the individual or the individual's spouse in whole or in part for the expenses of housing during the same period for which the individual claims a housing cost amount exclusion or deduction.

(b)Housing expenses

(1)Included expenses

For purposes of paragraph (a) of this section, housing expenses include rent, the fair rental value of housing provided in kind by the employer, utilities (other than telephone charges), real and personal property insurance, occupancy taxes not described in paragraph (b)(2)(v) of this section, nonrefundable fees paid for securing a leasehold, rental of furniture and accessories, household repairs, and residential parking.

(2)Excluded expenses

Housing expenses do not include:

(i)

The cost of house purchase, improvements, and other costs that are capital expenditures;

(ii)

The cost of purchased furniture or accessories or domestic labor (maids, gardeners, etc.);

(iii)

Amortized payments of principal with respect to an evidence of indebtedness secured by a mortgage on the taxpayers housing;

(iv)

Depreciation of housing owned by the taxpayer, or amortization or depreciation of capital improvements made to housing leased by the taxpayer;

(v)

Interest and taxes deductible under section 163 or 164 or other amounts deductible under section 216(a) (relating to deduction of interest and taxes by cooperative housing corporation tenant);

(vi)

The expenses of more than one foreign household except as provided in paragraph (b)(5) of this section;

(vii)

Expenses excluded from gross income under section 119;

(viii)

Expenses claimed as deductible moving expenses under section 217; or

(ix)

The cost of a pay television subscription.

(3)**Limitation**

Housing expenses are taken into account for purposes of this section only to the extent attributable to housing for portions of the taxable year within the period during which the individual satisfies the requirements of § 1.911-2(a). Housing expenses are not taken into account for the period during which the value of the individual's housing is excluded from gross income under section 119, unless the individual maintains a second foreign household described in paragraph (b)(5) of this section. If an individual maintains two foreign households, only expenses incurred with respect to the abode which bears the closest relationship, not necessarily geographic, with respect to the individual's tax home shall be taken into account, unless one of the households is a second foreign household.

(4)**Reasonableness**

An amount paid for housing shall not be treated as reasonable, for purposes of paragraph (a) of this section, to the extent that the expense is lavish or extravagant under the circumstances.

(5)**Expenses of a second foreign household**

(i)**In general**

The term "second foreign household" means a separate abode maintained by an individual outside of the U.S. for his or her spouse or dependents (who, if minors, are in the individual's legal custody or the joint custody of the individual and the individual's spouse) at a place other than the tax home of the individual because of adverse living conditions at the individual's tax home. If an individual maintains a second foreign household the expenses of the second foreign household may be included in the individual's housing expenses under paragraph (b)(1) of this section. Under no circumstances shall an individual be considered to maintain more than one second foreign household at the same time.

(ii)**Adverse living conditions**

Solely for purposes of paragraph (b)(5)(i) of this section, adverse living conditions are living conditions which are dangerous, unhealthful, or otherwise adverse. Adverse living conditions include a state of warfare or civil insurrection in the general area of the individual's tax home. Adverse living conditions exist if the individual resides on the business premises of the employer for the convenience of the employer and, because of the nature of the business (for example, a construction site or drilling rig), it is not feasible for the employer to provide housing for the individual's spouse or dependents. The criteria used by the Department of State in granting a separate maintenance allowance are relevant, but not determinative, for purposes of determining whether a separate household is provided because of adverse living conditions.

(c)Base housing amount

(1)In general

The base housing amount is equal to the product of 16 percent of the annual salary of an employee of the United States who is compensated at a rate equal to the annual salary rate paid for step 1 of grade GS-14, multiplied by the following fraction:

$$\frac{\text{The number of qualifying days}}{\text{The number of days in the taxable year}}$$

For purposes of the above fraction, the number of qualifying days is determined in accordance with § 1.911-3(d)(3).

(2)Annual salary of step 1 of grade GS-14

The annual salary rate for a step 1 of grade GS-14 is determined on January first of the calendar year in which the individual's taxable year begins.

(d)Housing costs amount exclusion

(1)Limitation

A qualified individual who has elected to exclude his or her housing cost amount may only exclude the lesser of the full amount of either the individual's housing cost amount attributable to employer provided amounts or the individual's foreign earned income for the taxable year. A qualified individual who elects to exclude his or her housing cost amount may not claim less than the full amount of the housing cost exclusion determined under this paragraph.

(2)Employer provided amounts

For purposes of this section, the term "employer provided amounts" means any amounts paid or incurred on behalf of the individual by the individual's employer which are foreign earned income included in the individual's gross income for the taxable year (without regard to section 911). Employer provided amounts include, but are not limited to, the following amounts: any salary paid by the employer to the employee; any reimbursement paid by the employer to the employee for housing expenses, educational expenses for the individual's dependents, or as part of a tax equalization plan; the fair market value of compensation provided in kind (including lodging, unless excluded under section 119, relating to meals and lodging furnished for the convenience of the employer); and any amount paid by the employer to any third party on behalf of the employee. An individual will only have earnings that are not employer provided amounts if the individual has earnings from self-employment.

(3)Housing cost amount attributable to employer provided amounts

For the purpose of determining what portion of the housing cost amount is excludable and what portion is deductible the following rules apply. If the individual has no income from self-employment, then the entire housing cost amount is attributable to employer provided amounts and is, therefore, excludable to the extent of the limitation provided in paragraph (d)(1) of this section. If the individual only has income from self-employment, then the entire housing cost amount is attributable to non-employer provided amounts and is, therefore, deductible to the extent of the limitation provided in paragraph (e) of this section. In all other instances, the housing cost amount attributable to employer provided amounts shall be determined by multiplying the housing cost amount by the following fraction: employer provided amounts over foreign earned income for the taxable year. The housing cost amount attributable to non-employer provided amounts shall be determined by subtracting the portion of the housing cost amount attributable to employer provided amounts from the total housing cost amount.

(e)Housing cost amount deduction

(1)In general

If a portion of the individual's housing cost amount is determined under paragraph (d)(3) of this section to be attributable to non-employer provided amounts, the individual may deduct that amount from gross income for the taxable year but only to the extent of the individual's foreign earned income (as defined in § 1.911-3) for the taxable year in excess of foreign earned income excluded and the housing cost amount excluded from gross income for the taxable year under § 1.911-3 and this section.

(2)Carryover

If any portion of the individual's housing cost amount deduction is disallowed for the taxable year under paragraph (e)(1) of this section, such portion shall be carried over and treated as a deduction from gross income for the succeeding taxable year (but only for the succeeding taxable year) to the extent of the excess, if any, of:

(i)

The amount of foreign earned income for the succeeding taxable year less the foreign earned income and the housing cost amount excluded from gross income under § 1.911-3 and this section for the succeeding taxable year over,

(ii)

The portion, if any, of the housing cost amount that is deductible under paragraph (e)(1) of this section for the succeeding taxable year.

(f)Examples

The following examples illustrate the application of this section. In all examples the annual rate for a step 1 of GS-14 as of January first of the calendar year in which the individual's taxable year begins is $39,689.

Example (1). B, a U.S. citizen, is a calendar year taxpayer who was a bona fide resident of and whose tax home was located in foreign country G for the entire taxable year 1982. B receives an $80,000 salary from B's employer for services performed in G. B incurs no business expenses. B receives housing provided by B's employer with a fair rental value of $15,000. The value of the housing furnished by B's employer is not excluded from gross income under section 119. B pays $10,000 for housing expenses. B's gross income and foreign earned income for 1982 is $95,000. B elects the foreign earned income exclusion of section 911(a)(1) and the housing cost amount exclusion of section 911(a)(2). B must first compute his housing cost amount exclusion. B's housing cost amount is $18,650 determined by reducing B's housing expenses, $25,000 ($15,000 fair rental value of housing and $10,000 of other expenses), by the base housing amount of $6,350 (($39,689 × .16) × 365/365). Because B has no income from self-employment, the entire amount is attributable to employer provided amounts and, therefore, is excludable. B's section 911(a)(1) limitation is over $75,000. That is the lesser of $75,000 × 365/365 or $95,000 − 18,650. B's total exclusion for 1982 under section 911(a)(1) and (2) is $93,650.

Example (2). The facts are the same as in example (1) except that B's salary for 1982 is $70,000. B's foreign earned income for 1982 is

$85,000. B's housing cost amount is $18,650, all of which is attributable to employer provided amounts. B's housing cost amount is excludable to the extent of the lesser of B's housing cost amount attributable to employer provided amounts, $18,650, or the foreign earned income for the taxable year, $85,000. Thus, B excludes $18,650 under section 911(a)(2). B's section 911(a)(1) limitation for 1982 is $66,350 (the lesser of $75,000 × 365/365 or $85,000 – 18,650). B's total exclusion for 1982 under section 911(a)(1) and (2) is $85,000.

Example (3). The facts are the same as in example (2) except that in 1983, B receives $5,000 attributable to services performed in 1982. B may exclude the entire $5,000 in 1983 because such amount would have been excludable under § 1.911-3(d)(1) had it been received in 1982.

Example (4). C is a U.S. citizen, self-employed, and a calendar year and cash basis taxpayer. C arrived in foreign country H on October 3, 1982, and departed from H on March 8, 1984. C's tax home was located in H throughout that period. C was physically present for 330 full days during the twelve consecutive month period August 30, 1982 through August 29, 1983. The number of C's qualifying days in 1982 is 124. During 1982 C had $35,000 of foreign earned income, none of which was attributable to employer provided amounts, and $8,000 of reasonable housing expenses. C's housing cost amount is $5,843 ($8,000 – ((39,689 × .16) × 124/365)). C elects to exclude her foreign earned income under § 1.911-3(d)(1). C's section 911(a)(1) limitation for 1982 is $25,479 (the lesser of C's foreign earned income for the taxable year ($35,000) or the annual rate for the taxable year multiplied by the number of C's qualifying days over the number of days in the taxable year ($75,000 × 124/365 = $25,479)). C may not claim the housing cost amount exclusion under section 911(a)(2) because no portion of the housing cost amount is attributable to employer provided amounts. C may deduct the lesser of her housing cost amount ($5,843) or her foreign earned income in excess of amounts excluded under section 911(a) ($35,000 – 25,479 = $9,521). Thus, C's housing cost amount deduction is $5,843.

Example (5). The facts are the same as in example (4) except that C had $30,000 of foreign earned income for 1982, none of which was attributable to employer provided amounts. C elects to exclude $25,479 under § 1.911-3(d)(1). C may only deduct $4,521 of her housing cost amount under paragraph (e)(1) of this section because her foreign earned income in excess of amounts excluded under section 911(a) is $4,521 ($30,000 – 25,479). The $1322 of unused housing cost amount deduction may be carried over to the subsequent taxable year.

Example (6). The facts are the same as in example (4) except that C had $15,000 of foreign earned income for 1982, none of which was attributable to employer provided amounts. C elects to exclude the entire $15,000 under § 1.911-3(d)(1). C is not entitled to a housing cost amount deduction for 1982 since she has no foreign earned income in excess of amounts excluded under section 911(a). C may carryover her entire housing cost amount deduction to 1983.

Example (7). The facts are the same as in example (6). In addition, during taxable year 1983 C had $115,000 of foreign earned income, none of which was attributable to employer provided amounts, and $40,000 of reasonable housing expenses. C elects to exclude her foreign earned income under § 1.911-3(d)(1). C's section 911(a)(1) limitation is the lesser of $115,000 or $80,000 ($80,000 × 365/365). C's housing cost amount for 1983 is $33,650 (40,000 – ($39,689 × .16) × 365/365). Since no portion of that amount is attributable to employer provided amounts, C may not claim a housing cost amount exclusion. C may deduct the lesser of her housing cost amount ($33,650) or her foreign earned income in excess of amounts excluded under section 911(a) ($115,000 – 80,000 = 35,000). Thus, C may deduct her $33,650 housing cost amount in 1983. In addition, C may deduct $1,350 of the housing cost amount deduction carried over from taxable year 1982 (($115,000 – 80,000) – 33,650 = $1,350). The remaining $4,493 ($5,843 – 1,350) of the housing cost amount deduction carried over from taxable year 1982 may not be deducted in 1983 or carried over to 1984.

Example (8). D is a U.S. citizen and a calendar year and cash basis taxpayer. D is a bona fide resident of and maintains his tax home in foreign country J for all of taxable year 1984. In 1984, D earns $80,000 of foreign earned income, $60,000 of which is an employer provided amount and $20,000 of which is a non-employer provided amount. D's total housing cost amount for 1984 is $25,000. D elects to exclude, under section 911(a)(2), the portion of his housing cost amount that is attributable to employer provided amounts. D's excludable housing cost amount is $18,750; that is the total housing cost amount ($25,000) multiplied by employer provided amounts for the taxable year ($60,000) over foreign earned income for the taxable year ($80,000). D also elects to exclude his foreign earned income under § 1.911-3(d)(1). D's section 911(a)(1) limitation for 1984 is $61,250 (the lesser of $80,000 – $18,750 or $80,000 × 366/366). D's total exclusion for 1984 under section 911(a)(1) and (2) is $80,000. D cannot claim a housing cost amount deduction in 1984 because D has no foreign earned income in excess of his foreign earned income and housing cost amount excluded from gross income for the taxable year under § 1.911-3 and this section. D may carry over his housing cost amount deduction of $6,250, the total housing cost amount less the portion attributable to employer provided amounts ($25,000 – 18,750), to taxable year 1985. [Reg. §1.911-4.]

§1.911-5, Special rules for married couples

(a)Married couples with two qualified individuals

(1)In general

In the case in which a husband and wife both are qualified individuals under § 1.911-2(a), each individual may make one or more elections under § 1.911-7 and exclude from gross income foreign earned income and exclude or deduct housing cost amounts subject to the rules of paragraph (a)(2) and (3) of this section.

(2)Computation of excluded foreign earned income

The amount of excludable foreign earned income is determined separately for each spouse under the rules of § 1.911-3 on the basis of the income attributable to the services of that spouse. If the spouses file separate returns each may exclude the amount of his or her foreign earned income attributable to his or her services subject to the limitations of § 1.911-3(d)(2). If the spouses file a joint return, the sum of these foreign earned income amounts so determined for each spouse may be excluded. For example, H and W both qualify under § 1.911-2(a)(2)(i) for the entire 1983 taxable year. During 1983 W earns $100,000 of foreign earned income and H earns $45,000 of foreign earned income. H and W file a joint return for 1983. On their joint return H and W may exclude from gross income a total of $125,000. That amount is determined by adding W's section 911(a)(1) limitation, $80,000 (the lesser of $80,000 × 365/365 or $100,000), and H's section 911(a)(1) limitation, $45,000 (the lesser of $80,000 × 365/365 or $45,000).

(3)Computation of housing cost amount

(i)Spouses residing together

If the spouses reside together, and file a joint return, they may compute their housing cost amount either jointly or separately. If the spouses reside together and file separate returns, they must compute their housing cost amounts separately. If the spouses compute their housing cost amounts separately, they may allocate the housing expenses to either of them or between them for the purpose of calculating separate housing cost amounts, but each spouse claiming a housing cost amount exclusion or deduction must use his or her full base housing amount in such computation. If the spouses compute their housing cost amount jointly, then only one of the spouses may claim the housing cost amount exclusion or deduction. Either spouse may claim the housing cost amount exclusion or deduction; however, if the spouses have different periods of residence or presence and the spouse with the shorter period of residence or presence claims the exclusion or deduction, then only the expenses incurred in that shorter period may be claimed as housing expenses. The spouse claiming the exclusion or deduction may aggregate the couple's housing expenses, and subtract his or her base housing amount. For example, H and W reside together and file a joint return. H was a bona fide resident of and maintained his tax home in foreign country M from August 17, 1982 through December 31, 1983. W was a bona fide resident of and maintained her tax home in foreign country M from September 15, 1982 through December 31, 1983. During 1982, H and W earn and receive, respectively, $25,000 and $10,000 of foreign earned income. H paid $10,000 for qualified housing expenses in 1982, $7,500 of that was for qualified housing expenses incurred from September 15, 1982 through December 31, 1982. W paid $3,000 for qualified housing expenses in 1982 all of which were incurred during her period of residence. H and W may choose to compute their housing cost amount jointly. If they do so and H claims the housing cost amount exclusion his exclusion would be $10,617. H's housing expenses would be $13,000 ($10,000 + $3,000) and his base housing amount would be $2,383 (($39,689 × .16) × 137/365 = $2,383). If instead W claims the housing cost amount exclusion her exclusion would be $8,621. W's housing expenses would be $10,500 ($7,500 + 3,000) and her base housing amount would be $1,879 (($39,689 × .16) × 108/365 = $1,879). If H and W file jointly and both claim a housing cost amount exclusion, then H's and W's housing cost amounts would be, respectively, $7,617 ($10,000 – 2,383) and $1,121 ($3,000 – 1,879).

(ii)**Spouses residing apart**

If the spouses reside apart, both spouses may exclude or deduct their housing cost amount if the spouses have different tax homes that are not within reasonable commuting distance (as defined in § 1.119-(d)(4)) of each other and neither spouse's residence is within a reasonable commuting distance of the other spouse's tax home. If the spouses' tax homes, or one spouse's residence and the other spouse's tax home, are within a reasonable commuting distance of each other, only one spouse may exclude or deduct his or her housing cost amount. Regardless of whether the spouses file joint or separate returns, the amount of the housing cost amount exclusion or deduction must be determined separately for each spouse under the rules of § 1.911-4. If both spouses claim a housing cost amount exclusion or deduction directly as qualified individuals, neither may claim any such exclusion or deduction under section 911(c)(2)(B)(ii), relating to a second foreign household maintained for the other spouse. If one spouse fails to claim a housing cost amount exclusion or deduction which that spouse could claim directly, the other spouse may claim such exclusion or deduction under section 911(c)(2)(B)(ii), relating to a second foreign household maintained for the first spouse, provided that all the requirements of that section are met. Spouses may not claim more than one second foreign household and the expenses of such household may only be claimed by one spouse. For example, if both H and W are qualified individuals and H's tax home is in London and W's tax home is in Paris, then both H and W may exclude or deduct their housing cost amounts; however, H and W must compute these amounts separately regardless of whether they file joint or separate returns. If instead of living in Paris, W lives in an area where there are adverse living conditions and W maintains H's home in London, then W may add those housing expenses to her housing expenses and compute one base housing amount. In that case H may not claim a housing cost amount exclusion or deduction.

(iii)**Housing cost amount attributable to employer provided amounts**

Each spouse claiming a housing cost amount exclusion or deduction shall compute the portion of the housing cost amount that is attributable to employer provided amounts separately, based on his or her separate foreign earned incomc, in accordance with § 1.911-4(d)(3).

(b)Married couples with community income

The amount of excludable foreign earned income of a husband and wife with community income is determined separately for each spouse in accordance with paragraph (a) of this section on the basis of income attributable to that spouse's services without regard to community property laws. See sections 879 and 6013(g) and (h) for special rules regarding treatment of community income of a nonresident alien individual married to a U.S. citizen or resident. [Reg. §1.911-5.]

§1.911-6, Disallowance of deductions, exclusions, and credits

(a)In general

No deduction or exclusion from gross income under Subtitle A of the Code or credit against the tax imposed by chapter 1 of the Code shall be allowed to the extent the deduction, exclusion, or credit is properly allocable to or chargeable against amounts excluded from gross income under section 911(a). For purposes of the preceding sentence, deductions, exclusions, and credits which are definitely related (as provided in § 1.861-8), in whole or in part, to earned income shall be allocated and apportioned to foreign earned income and U.S. source earned income in accordance with the rules contained in § 1.861-8. Deductions, exclusions, and credits which are definitely related to all gross income under § 1.861-8, including deductions for interest described in § 1.861-8(e)(2)(ii), are definitely related, in whole or in part, to earned income. In the case of interest expense allocable, in whole or in part, to foreign earned income under § 1.861-8(e)(2)(ii), the expense shall normally be apportioned under option one of the optional gross income methods of apportionment (§1.861-8(e)(2)(vi)(A)), but without regard to conditions *(1)* and *(2)* of subdivision (vi)(A) (the fifty percent conditions). Such interest expense shall not normally be apportioned under the asset method of § 1.861-8(e)(2)(v). This is because, where section 911 is the operative section, the expense normally relates more closely to gross income generated from activities than to the amount of capital utilized or invested in activities or property. Deductions that are allocated and apportioned to foreign earned income must then be allocated and apportioned to foreign earned income that is excluded under section 911(a). If an individual has foreign earned income from both self-employment and other employment, the amount excluded under section 911(a)(1) shall be deemed to include a pro rata amount of the self-employment income and the income from other employment; thus, a pro rata portion of deductible expenses attributable to self-employment income must be disallowed. For purposes of section 911(d)(6) and this section only, deductions, exclusions, or credits which are not definitely related to any class of gross income shall not be allocable or chargeable to excluded amounts and are, therefore, deductible to the extent allowed by chapter 1 of the Code. Examples of deductions that are not definitely related to a class of gross income are personal and family medical expenses, qualified retirement contributions (but see section 219(b)(1)), real estate taxes and mortgage interest on a personal residence, charitable contributions, alimony payments, and deductions for personal exemptions. In addition, for purposes of this section, amounts excludable or deductible under section 911 or 119 shall not be allocable or chargeable to other amounts excluded under section 911(a). Thus, an individual's housing cost amount which is excludable or deductible under § 1.911-4(d) for a taxable year is not apportioned in part to the individual's foreign earned income which is excluded for such year under § 1.911-3(d). Therefore, the entire amount of such exclusion or deduction is allowed to the extent provided in § 1.911-4. This section does not affect the time for claiming any deduction, exclusion, or credit that is not allocated or apportioned to excluded amounts.

(b)Moving expenses

(1)In general

No deduction shall be allowed for moving expenses under section 217 to the extent the deduction is properly allocable to or chargeable against amounts of foreign earned income excluded from gross income under section 911(a). If an individual's new principal place of work is in a foreign country, deductible moving expenses will be allocable to foreign earned income. If an individual treats a reimbursement from his employer for the expenses of a move from a foreign country to the United States as attributable to services performed in a foreign country under § 1.911-3(e)(5)(i), then deductible moving expenses attributable to that move will be allocable to foreign earned income. If the individual is a qualified individual who elects to exclude foreign earned income under section 911(a), then some or all of such moving expenses must be disallowed as a deduction.

(2)Attribution of moving expense deduction to taxable years in which services are performed

If a moving expense deduction is properly allocable to foreign earned income, the deduction shall be considered attributable to services performed in the year of the move as long as the individual is a qualified individual under § 1.911-2(a) for a period that includes 120 days in the year of the move. If the individual is not a qualified individual for such period, then the individual shall treat the deduction as attributable to services performed in both the year of the move and the succeeding taxable year, if the move is from the United States to the foreign country, or the prior taxable year, if the move is from a foreign country to the United States. Notwithstanding the preceding two sentences, storage expenses incurred after December 31, 1983 shall be treated as attributable to services performed in the year in which the expenses are incurred.

(3)**Formula for disallowance of moving expense deduction**

The portion of the moving expense deduction that is disallowed shall be determined by multiplying the moving expense deduction by a fraction the numerator of which is all amounts excluded under section 911(a) for the year or years to which the deduction is attributable (under paragraph (b)(2) of this section) and the denominator of which is foreign earned income (as defined in § 1.911-3(a)) for that year or years.

(4)**Effect of disallowance based on attribution of deduction to subsequent year's income**

An individual may claim a moving expense deduction in the taxable year in which the amount of the expense is paid or incurred even if attributable, in part, to the succeeding year. However, at such time as the individual excludes income under section 911(a) for the year or years to which the deduction is attributable, the individual shall either—

(i)

file an amended return for the year in which the deduction was claimed that does not claim the portion of the deduction that is disallowed because it is chargeable against excluded income, or

(ii)

include in income for the year following the year in which the deduction was claimed an amount equal to the amount of the deduction that is disallowed.

Any amount included in income under paragraph (b)(4)(ii) of this section is not foreign earned income.

(5)**Moves beginning before January 1, 1984**

Notwithstanding paragraph (b)(1) through (3) of this section, the rules of this paragraph (b)(5) shall apply for moves beginning before January 1, 1984.

(i)**Individual qualifies for the entire taxable year of the move**

If the individual is a qualified individual for the entire taxable year of the move, then the amount of moving expenses disallowed shall be determined by multiplying the moving expense deduction otherwise allowable by a fraction the numerator of which is the foreign earned income excluded under section 911(a) for the taxable year of the move and the denominator of which is the foreign earned income for the same taxable year.

(ii)Individual qualifies for less than the entire taxable year of the move

If the individual is a qualified individual for less than the entire taxable year of the move, then, for the purpose of determining the portion of the otherwise allowable moving expense deduction that is disallowed, the individual must attribute a portion of the otherwise allowable moving expense deduction either to the succeeding taxable year, if the move is from the United States to a foreign country, or to the prior taxable year, if the move is from a foreign country to the United States. The portion of the moving expense deduction treated as attributable to services performed in the year of the move shall be determined by multiplying the otherwise allowable moving expense deduction by the following fraction:

$$\frac{\text{The number of qualifying days (as defined in § 1.911-3(d)(3)) in the year of the move}}{\text{The number of days in the taxable year of the move.}}$$

The portion of the moving expense deduction treated as attributable to the year succeeding or preceding the move shall be determined by subtracting the portion of the moving expense deduction that is attributable to the year of the move from the total moving expense deduction. The allocation of a portion of the moving expense deduction to a succeeding or preceding taxable year does not affect the time for claiming the allowable moving expense deduction. The portion of the moving expense deduction that is disallowed shall be determined by multiplying the moving expense deduction attributable to the year of the move or the succeeding or preceding year, as the case may be, by a fraction the numerator of which is amounts excluded under section 911(a) for that year and the denominator of which is foreign earned income for that year.

(c)Foreign taxes

(1)**Amount disallowed**

No deduction or credit is allowed for foreign income, war profits, or excess profits taxes paid or accrued with respect to amounts excluded from gross income under section 911. To determine the amount of disallowed foreign taxes, multiply the foreign tax imposed on foreign earned income (as defined in § 1.911-3(a)) received or accrued during the taxable year by a fraction, the numerator of which is amounts excluded under section 911(a) in such taxable year less deductible expenses properly allocated to such amounts (see paragraphs (a) and (b) of this section), and the denominator of which is foreign earned income (as defined in § 1.911-3(a)) received or accrued during the taxable year less deductible expenses properly allocated or apportioned thereto. For the purpose of determining the extent to which foreign taxes are disallowed, the housing cost amount deduction is treated as definitely related to foreign earned income that is not excluded. If the foreign tax is imposed on foreign earned income and some other income (for example, earned income from sources within the United States or an amount not subject to tax in the United States), and the taxes on the other amount cannot be segregated, then the denominator equals the total of the amounts subject to tax less deductible expenses allocable to all such amounts.

(2)**Definitions and special rules**

(i)**Taxable year**

For purposes of paragraph (c)(1) of this section, the term "taxable year" means the individual's taxable year for U.S. tax purposes. Such term includes the portion of any foreign taxable year within the individual's U.S. taxable year and excludes the portion of any foreign taxable year not within the individual's U.S. taxable year.

(ii)**Apportionment of foreign taxes**

For purposes of this paragraph (c), foreign taxes imposed on foreign earned income shall be deemed to accrue, on a pro rata basis, to income as the income is received or accrued. The taxes so accrued shall be apportioned to the taxable year during which the income is received or accrued. This rule applies for all individuals, regardless of their method of accounting.

(iii)**Effect of disallowance**

The disallowance of foreign taxes under this paragraph (c) shall not affect the time for claiming any deduction or credit for foreign taxes paid. Rather, the disallowance shall only affect the amount of taxes considered paid or accrued to any foreign country.

(iv)**Interest on foreign taxes**

Any interest expense incurred on a liability for foreign taxes is allocated and apportioned not under this paragraph (c) but under paragraph (a) of this section to foreign earned income and then to excluded foreign earned income and to that extent disallowed as a deduction under paragraph (a). In that regard, see also § 1.861-8(e)(2) for the specific rules for allocation and apportionment of interest expense.

(d)Examples

The following examples illustrate the application of this section.

Example (1). In 1982 A, an architect, operates his business as a sole proprietorship in which capital is not a material income producing factor. A receives $1,000,000 in gross receipts, all of which is foreign source earned income, and incurs $500,000 of otherwise deductible business expenses definitely related to the foreign earned income. A elects to exclude $75,000 under section 911(a)(1). The expenses must be apportioned to excluded earned income as follows: $500,000 × $75,000/1,000,000. Thus, $37,500 of the business expenses are not deductible.

Example (2). The facts are the same as in example (1), except that $100,000 of A's gross receipts is U.S. source earned income and $68,000 of A's business expenses are attributable to the U.S. source earned income. Thus, A has $900,000 of foreign earned income and $432,000 of deductions allocated to foreign earned income. The expenses apportioned to excluded earned income are $432,000 × $75,000/$900,000, or $36,000, which are not deductible.

Example (3). B is a U.S. citizen, calendar year and cash basis taxpayer. B moves to foreign country N and maintains a tax home and is physically present there from July 1, 1984 through May 26, 1985. Among other possible periods, B is a qualified individual for 219 days in the year of the move. B pays $6,000 of otherwise deductible moving expenses in 1984. For 1984, B's foreign earned income is $60,000 and B excludes $47,869 ($80,000 × 219/366) under section 911(a). Under paragraph (b)(2) of this section, B's moving expenses are attributable to services performed in 1984. Under paragraph (b)(3) of this section, $6,000 × $47,869/$60,000, or $4,789, of B's moving expense deduction is disallowed. B may deduct $1,211 of moving expenses on his 1984 return.

Example (4). The facts are the same as in example (3) except that B maintains a tax home and is physically present in foreign country N from October 9, 1984 through September 3, 1985. Among other possible periods, B is a qualified individual for no more than 119 days in 1984 and 281 days in 1985. B's foreign earned income for 1984 is $60,000. B's foreign earned income for 1985 is $150,000. Because B is a qualified individual for less than 120 days in the year of the move, under paragraph (b)(2) of this section, B's moving expenses are attributable to services performed in 1984 and 1985. At the close of 1984, B may either seek an extension of time to file under § 1.911-7(c) or may file an income tax return without claiming the exclusions or deduction under section 911. B does not seek an extension and files without excluding foreign earned income; thus B may deduct his moving expenses in full. B later amends his 1984 return and excludes foreign earned income for that year. B excludes foreign earned income for 1985. B must determine the portion of the moving expense deduction that is disallowed. The portion of the moving expense deduction that is disallowed is determined by multiplying the otherwise allowable moving expense deduction by a fraction. The numerator of the fraction is the sum of amounts excluded under section 911(a) for 1984 and 1985, that is, $26,082, or $80,000 × 119/365, plus $61,589, or $80,000 × 281/365, which totals $87,671. The denominator of the fraction is the sum of foreign earned income for 1984 and 1985, that is, $60,000 plus $150,000, or $210,000. B's allowable moving expense deduction is $3,495, or $6,000—($6,000 × $87,671/$210,000). If B does not file an amended 1984 return (and does not exclude foreign earned income for 1984), but excludes foreign earned income under section 911(a) for 1985, a portion of his moving expense deduction is disallowed, based on the same formula. The amount disallowed is $6,000 × $61,589/$210,000, or $1,760. This amount may be recaptured either by filing an amended return for 1984 or by including it in income for 1985 (in which case it is not foreign earned income).

Example (5). C is a U.S. citizen, a self-employed individual, and a cash basis and calendar year taxpayer. For the entire 1982 taxable year C maintained his tax home and his bona fide residence in foreign country P. During 1982 C earned and received $120,000 of foreign earned income, none of which was attributable to employer provided amounts. C paid $40,000 of business expenses. C elected to exclude foreign earned income under section 911(a)(1) and claimed a housing cost amount deduction of $15,000. C received $10,000 of foreign source interest income which was included with C's earned income in a single tax base and taxed at graduated rates. For 1982, C paid $30,000 in income tax to foreign country P. The amount of C's business expenses that is properly apportioned to excluded amounts (and therefore, not deductible) equals $25,000, which is determined by multiplying the otherwise allowable deductions by C's excluded amounts over C's foreign earned income ($40,000 × $75,000/$120,000). The amount of country P tax that is properly apportioned to excluded amounts (and therefore, not deductible or creditable) equals $20,000, which is determined by multiplying the tax of $30,000 by the following fraction:

$50,000 ($75,000 excluded amounts less $25,000 of deductible expenses allocable thereto)

$75,000 (($120,000 foreign earned income less $40,000 of deductible expenses allocable thereto) less $15,000 (housing cost amount deduction allocable thereto) plus $10,000 other taxable income).

Example (6). D is a U.S. citizen and an accrual basis and calendar year taxpayer for U.S. tax purposes. For the entire period from January 1, 1982 through December 31, 1983, D maintains his tax home and his bona fide residence in foreign country R. For purposes of R's income tax, D is a cash basis taxpayer and uses a fiscal year that begins on April 1 and ends on the following March 31. During his entire period of residence in R, D receives foreign earned income of $10,000 each month, all of which is attributable to employer provided amounts. For his foreign taxable year ending March 31, 1982, D pays $10,000 of income tax to R. For his foreign taxable year ending March 31, 1983, D pays $54,000 of income tax to R. Under paragraph (c)(2)(ii) of this section, all of the $10,000 of tax paid for his foreign taxable year ending March 31, 1982 is imposed on foreign earned income received in 1982, as is $40,500 or 9/12 × $54,000, of tax paid for his foreign taxable year ending March 31, 1983. (D received $10,000 per month for the last 3 months of his foreign taxable year ending March 31, 1982, all of which are within his U.S. taxable year ending December 31, 1982 under paragraph (c)(2)(i) of this section, and $10,000 per month for each month of his foreign taxable year ending March 31, 1983, of which the first 9 months are within his U.S. taxable year ending December 31, 1982. Under paragraph (c)(2)(ii) of this section, foreign taxes are deemed to accrue on a pro rata basis to income as it is received or accrued. Thus, all of the $10,000 of foreign taxes imposed on the income received during D's foreign taxable year ending March 31, 1982 accrue to D's 1982 foreign earned income, as do 9/12 (or $90,000/$120,000) of foreign taxes imposed on income received during D's foreign taxable year ending March 31, 1983, for purposes of determining the amount of D's foreign taxes that is disallowed.) For 1982, D has no deductible expenses, and elects to exclude his housing cost amount of $21,000 under section 911(a)(2) and foreign earned income of $75,000 under section 911(a)(1). The amount of D's foreign taxes disallowed for deduction or credit purposes for 1982 is $8,000 (that is, $10,000 × $96,000/$120,000) of the taxes for his foreign taxable year ending March 31, 1982, plus $32,400 (that is, $40,500 × $96,000/$120,000) of the taxes for his foreign taxable year ending March 31, 1983, or $40,400. From 1982, D has $2,000 ($10,000 – $8,000) of deductible or creditable taxes accrued on March 31, 1982, and $8,100 ($40,500 – $32,400) of deductible or creditable taxes accrued on March 31, 1983, after the disallowance based on his 1982 excluded income.

Example (7). E is a United States citizen, calendar year and cash basis taxpayer. E is physically present in and establishes his tax home in foreign country S on May 1, 1981. For purposes of country S, E's taxable year begins on April 1 and ends the following March 31. E receives foreign earned income of $15,000 each month beginning May 1, 1981. At the end of his foreign taxable year ending on March 31, 1982, E pays $70,000 of income tax to S on $165,000 of foreign earned income. Under section 911, as in effect for taxable years beginning before January 1, 1982, E may not exclude any income that is earned or received during 1981. None of E's taxes paid in 1982 that are attributable to income earned or received in 1981 are subject to disallowance because, under paragraph (c)(2)(ii) of this section, the only taxes disallowed are those deemed to accrue on income earned and received after December 31, 1981, and excluded from gross income. The amount of E's taxes paid in 1982 that are attributable to 1981 is $50,909, or $70,000 × $120,000/$165,000. E elects to exclude foreign earned income for 1982. The amount of E's taxes paid to S in 1982 that accrue to 1982 foreign earned income, and are therefore subject to disallowance based on excluded income, is $19,091, or $70,000 × $45,000/$165,000. [Reg. §1.911-6.]

§1.911-7, Procedural rules

(a)Elections of a qualified individual

(1)In general

In order to receive either exclusion provided by section 911(a), a qualified individual must elect, separately with respect to each exclusion, to exclude foreign earned income under section 911(a)(1) and the housing cost amount under section 911(a)(2). Any such elections may be made on Form 2555 or on a comparable form. Each election must be filed either with the income tax return, or with an amended return, for the first taxable year of the individual for which the election is to be effective. An election once made remains in effect for that year and all subsequent years unless revoked under paragraph (b) of this section. Each election shall contain information sufficient to determine whether the individual is a qualified individual as provided in § 1.911-2. The statement shall include the following information:

(i)

The individual's name, address, and social security number;

(ii)

The name of the individual's employer;

(iii)

Whether the individual claimed exclusions under section 911 for earlier years after 1981 and within the five preceding taxable years;

(iv)

Whether the individual has revoked a previously made election and the taxable year for which such revocation was effective;

(v)

The exclusion or exclusions the individual is electing;

(vi)

The foreign country or countries in which the individual's tax home is located and the date when such tax home was established;

(vii)

The status (either bona fide residence or physical presence) under which the individual claims the exclusion;

(viii)

The individual's qualifying period of residence or presence;

(ix)

The individual's foreign earned income for the taxable year including the fair market value of all noncash remuneration; and,

(x)

If the individual elects to exclude the housing cost amount, the individual's housing expenses.

(2)Requirement of a return

(i)**In general**

In order to make a valid election under this paragraph (a), the election must be made:

(A)

With an income tax return that is timely filed (including any extensions of time to file),

(B)

With a later return filed within the period prescribed in section 6511(a) amending the foregoing timely filed income tax return,

(C)

With an original income tax return that is filed within one year after the due date of the return (determined without regard to any extension of time to file); this one year period does not constitute an extension of time for any purpose—it is merely a period during which a valid election may be made on a late return, or

(D)

With an income tax return filed after the period described in paragraphs (a)(2)(i)(A), (B), or (C) of this section provided—

(1)

The taxpayer owes no federal income tax after taking into account the exclusion and files Form 1040 with Form 2555 or a comparable form attached either before or after the Internal Revenue Service discovers that the taxpayer failed to elect the exclusion; or

(2)

The taxpayer owes federal income tax after taking into account the exclusion and files Form 1040 with Form 2555 or a comparable form attached before the Internal Revenue Service discovers that the taxpayer failed to elect the exclusion.

(3)

A taxpayer filing an income tax return pursuant to paragraph (a)(2)(i)(D)(*1*) or (*2*) of this section must type or legibly print the following statement at the top of the first page of the Form 1040: "Filed Pursuant to Section 1.911-7(a)(2)(i)(D)."

(ii)**Election for 1982 and 1983 taxable years**

Solely for purposes of paragraph (a)(2)(i)(A) of this section, an income tax return for any taxable year beginning before January 1, 1984 shall be considered timely filed if it is filed on or before July 23, 1985.

(3)Housing cost amount deduction

An individual does not have to make an election in order to claim the housing cost amount deduction. However, such individual must provide the Commissioner with information sufficient to determine the individual's correct amount of tax. Such information shall include the following: the individual's name, address, and social security number; the name of the individual's employer; the foreign country in which the individual's tax home was established; the status under which the individual claims the deduction; the individual's qualifying period of residence or presence; the individual's foreign earned income for the taxable year; and the individual's housing expenses.

(4)Effect of immaterial error or omission

An inadvertent error or omission of information required to be provided to make an election under this paragraph (a) shall not render the election invalid if the error or omission is not material in determining whether the individual is a qualified individual or whether the individual intends to make the election.

(b)Revocation of election

(1)**In general**

An individual may revoke any election made under paragraph (a) of this section for any taxable year. A revocation must be made separately with respect to each election. The individual may revoke an election for any taxable year, including the first taxable year for which an election was effective, by filing a statement that the individual is revoking one or more of the previously made elections. The statement must be filed with the income tax return, or with an amended return, for the first taxable year of individual for which the revocation is to be effective. A revocation once made is effective for that year and all subsequent years. If an election is revoked for any taxable year, including the first taxable year for which the election was effective, the individual may not, without the consent of the Commissioner, again make the same election until the sixth taxable year following the taxable year for which the revocation was first effective. For example, a qualified individual makes an election to exclude foreign earned income under section 911(a)(1) and files it with his 1982 income tax return. The individual files 1983 and 1984 income tax returns on which he excludes his foreign earned income. Then, within 3 years after filing his 1982 income tax return, the individual files an amended 1982 income tax return with a statement revoking his election to exclude foreign earned income under section 911(a)(1). The revocation of the election is effective for taxable years 1982, 1983, and 1984. The individual may not elect to exclude income under section 911(a)(1) for any taxable year before 1988, unless he obtains consent to reelect under paragraph (b)(2) of this section.

(2)**Reelection before sixth taxable year after revocation**

If an individual revoked an election under paragraph (b)(1) of this section and within five taxable years the individual wishes to reelect the same exclusion, then the individual may apply for consent to the reelection. The application for consent shall be made by requesting a ruling from the Associate Chief Counsel (Technical), National Office, Internal Revenue Service, 1111 Constitution Avenue NW., Washington, D.C. 20224. In determining whether to consent to a reelection the Associate Chief Counsel or his delegate shall consider any facts and circumstances that may be relevant to the determination. Relevant facts and circumstances may include the following: a period of United States residence, a move from one foreign country to another foreign country with differing tax rates, a substantial change in the tax laws of the foreign country of residence or physical presence, and a change of employer.

(c)Returns and extensions

(1)**In general**

Any return filed before completion of the period necessary to qualify an individual for any exclusion or deduction provided by section 911 shall be filed without regard to any exclusion or deduction provided by that section. A claim for a credit or refund of any overpayment of tax may be filed, however, if the taxpayer subsequently qualifies for any exclusion or deduction under section 911. See section 6012(c) and § 1.6012-1(a)(3), relating to returns to be filed and information to be furnished by individuals who qualify for any exclusion or deduction under section 911.

(2)Extensions

An individual desiring an extension of time (in addition to the automatic extension of time granted by § 1.6081-4) for filing a return until after the completion of the qualifying period described in paragraph (c)(1) of this section for claiming any exclusion or deduction under section 911 may apply for an extension. An individual whose moving expense deduction is attributable to services performed in two years may apply for an extension of time for filing a return until after the end of the second year. The individual may make such application on Form 2350, "Application for Extension of Time to File U.S. Income Tax Return" or in any other manner prescribed by the Commissioner. The application must be filed in accordance with the instructions to the form or as prescribed by the Commissioner. The application must set forth the facts relied on to justify the extension of time requested and must include a statement as to the earliest date the individual expects to become entitled to any exclusion or deduction by reason of completion of the qualifying period.

(d)Declaration of estimated tax

In estimating gross income for the purpose of determining whether a declaration of estimated tax must be made for any taxable year, an individual is not required to take into account income which the individual reasonably believes will be excluded from gross income under the provisions of section 911. In computing estimated tax, however, the individual must take into account, among other things, the denial of the foreign tax credit for foreign taxes allocable to the excluded income (see § 1.911-6(c)).

(e)Effective/applicability date

This section applies to applications for extension of time to file returns filed after July 1, 2008. [Reg. §1.911-7.]

§1.911-8, Former deduction for certain expenses of living abroad

For rules relating to the deduction for certain expenses of living abroad applicable to taxable years beginning before January 1, 1982, see 26 CFR §§ 1.913-1 through 1.913-13 as they appeared in the Code of Federal Regulations revised as of April 1, 1982. [Reg. §1.911-8.]

Bibliography

Treaties

OECD, *Convention on Mutual Administrative Assistance in Tax Matters* (2011) <www.oecd.org/ctp/exchange-of-tax-information/Amended_Convention_June2011_EN.pdf> accessed 22 May 2013.

OECD, *Status of the Convention on Mutual Administrative Assistance in Tax Matters and Amending Protocol-22 May 2013* (2013) <www.oecd.org/ctp/exchange-of-tax-information/Status_of_convention.pdf> accessed 22 May 2013.

United Nations Convention on the Law of the Sea, <www.un.org/depts/los/convention_agreements/convention_overview_convention.htm> accessed 23 December 2016.

United Nations, *Vienna Convention on the Law of Treaties* (1969) <www.untreaty.un.org/ilc/texts/instruments/english/conventions/1_1_1969.pdf> accessed 17 May 2013.

US Treasury, *The U.S. Model Income Tax Convention of November 15, 2006* (2006) <www.treasury.gov/press-center/press-releases/Documents/hp16801.pdf> accessed 12 June 2013.

US Treasury, *United States Model Technical Explanation Accompanying the U.S. Model Income Tax Convention of November 15, 2006* (2006) <www.treasury.gov/press-center/press-releases/Documents/hp16802.pdf> accessed 12 June 2013.

Laws

Internal Revenue Code (tax code), 26 U.S. Code

Regulations

IRS Regulations section, 26 CFR

Cases – US Tax Court

A. Joyce Payne, Appellant v. United States, Appellee (1992) 92-2 USTC 50,609

Alan W. Ladd and Sue Carol Ladd, Appellants v. Robert A. Riddell, District Director of Internal Revenue, Los Angeles, California, etc., Appellee (1962) 62-2 USTC 9787

Arnold A. Morse, Sr., and Hellen V. Morse v. The United States (1971) 71-1 USTC 9482

Augustus B. Chidester, Administrator of the Estate of Lewis M. Mallery, Deceased, v. The United States (1949) 49-1 USTC 9153

Commissioner of Internal Revenue, Petitioner v. Eldon E. Wolfe and Sara A. Wolfe, Respondents (1966) 66-1 USTC 9375

Commissioner of Internal Revenue, Petitioner v. Lyon Tyler Matthew, et al., Respondents 64-2 USTC 9669

Daniel A. Robida, Petitioner-Appellee v. Commissioner of Internal Revenue, Respondent-Appellant (1972) 72-1 USTC 9450

David W. Matthews and Christa Matthews, Ronald Davis and Marie Davis, Appellants v. Commissioner of Internal Revenue, Appellee (1990) 90-2 USTC 50,363

Earl O. Bergersen and Evelyn K. Bergersen, Petitioners v. Commissioner of Internal Revenue, Respondent (1997) 97-1 USTC 50,295

Edward R. Fink and Joan O. Fink v. the United States (1972) 72-1 USTC 9254

Ellsworth M. Dunn, Petitioner v. Commissioner of Internal Revenue, Respondent (1955) 55-1 USTC 9297

Ertan Eren, Susan Eren, Petitioners-Appellants v. Commissioner of Internal Revenue, Respondent-Appellee (1999) 99-1 USTC 50,599

Eugene M. Brueck, Plaintiff v. United States of America, Defendant (1963) 63-2 USTC 9786

F. A. Moore and wife Julia F. Moore, Appellants v. United States of America, Appellee (1961) 61-1 USTC 9441

Frank Morris and Cynthia D. Morris v. The United States (1967) 1967 CCH 8182

Frank S. Scott, Jr. v. The United States. Alvin C. Warnick and Barbara W. Warnick v. The United States, (1970) 70-2 USTC 9652

Frederick H. Vogt v. The United States (1976) 76-2 USTC 9482

George Y. Erlandson, Petitioner v. Commissioner of Internal Revenue, Respondent (1960) 60-1 USTC 9364

Glenn Weible and Patricia Weible, Appellants v. United States of America, Appellee (1957) 57-1 USTC 9589

Howard J. Sochurek, Petitioner v. Commissioner of Internal Revenue, Respondent (1962) 62-1 USTC 9293

Hunter B. Davidson et al., Plaintiffs v. United States of America et al., Defendants (1987) 87-2 USTC 9473

In the District Court of the United States for the District of Connecticut., Peter Yaross v. Frank W. Kraemer, Collector of Internal Revenue for the District of Connecticut. (1949) 49-1 USTC 9207

In the District Court of the United States for the District of Hawaii, Masao Seki, Plaintiff v. The United States of America, Defendant (1954) 54-2 USTC 9563

In the District Court of the United States for the Western District of Kentucky, at Louisville, Clinton H. Wood, Plaintiff v. Seldon R. Glenn, etc., Defendant (1950) 50-2 USTC 9351

In the United States District Court for the District of Idaho., Southern Division, Sotero Meso, Plaintiff v. John R. Viley, former Collector of Internal Revenue, Defendant (1952) 52-1 USTC 9159

In the United States District Court for the District of Maryland, George E. Ditman v. George Hofferbert, Collector of Internal Revenue (1955) 56-1 USTC 9186

In the United States District Court for the District of Maryland, Francis White v. George Hofferbert, Collector of Internal Revenue for the District of Maryland (1950) 50-1 USTC 9197

In the United States District Court for the Eastern District of Tennessee, Northern Division, Edward P. Krichbaum v. United States of America (1956) 56-1 USTC 9362

In the United States District Court for the Southern District of Illinois, Northern Division, Glenn A. Glackin, Plaintiff v. United States of America, Defendant (1952) 53-1 USTC 9103

In the United States District Court, for the Northern District of California, Southern Division, Winsor Boyden Meals, Plaintiff v. United States of America, Defendant (1953) 53-1 USTC 9225

J. Haseltine Carstairs, Executor of the Estate of Charles S. Carstairs, deceased, Plaintiff, v. The United States of America, Defendant (1936) 36-1 USTC 9075

Jean Renoir and Dido Freire Renoir, Petitioners v. Commissioner of Internal Revenue, Respondent (1963) 63-2 USTC 9665

John Balestreri, Petitioner, v. Commissioner of Internal Revenue, Respondent (1942) 47 B.T.A. 241

John D. Carter v. The United States of America (1958) 58-2 USTC 9570

Jon F. and Constance M. Hartung, Petitioners-Appellees v. Commissioner of Internal Revenue, Respondent-Appellant (1973) 73-2 USTC 9616

Joseph T. Smith and Marie A. Smith, Petitioners-Appellants v. Commissioner of Internal Revenue, Respondent-Appellee (1983) 83-1 USTC 9255

Julius B. Stryker Petitioner, V. Commissioner of Internal Revenue, Respondent (1934) 29 B.T.A. 1025

Kenneth R. Groves and Peggy L. Groves, Plaintiffs-Appellants v. United States of America, Defendant-Appellee (1976) 76-2 USTC 9509

Lawrence L. Tweedy and Grace V. Tweedy, Petitioners, v. Commissioner of Internal Revenue, Respondent (1942) 47 B.T.A. 341

LeRoy D. Brummitt and Mary A. Brummitt v. The United States (1964) 64-1 USTC 9310

Louis D. Beaumont, Petitioner, v. Guy T. Helvering, Commissioner of Internal Revenue (1934) 4 USTC 1320

Meade A. Carpenter, Jr., Plaintiff-Appellee v. United States of America, Defendant-Appellant (1974) 74-1 USTC 9473

Norman C. Fuller, Appellant v. George Hofferbert, Collector of Internal Revenue, District of Maryland, Appellee (1953) 53-1 USTC 9405

O'Kelly W. Myers, Petitioner v. Commissioner of Internal Revenue, Respondent (1950) 50-1 USTC 9253

Paul Edward Swenson, Appellant, v. Kate Thomas, Community Survivor of W. A. Thomas, Deceased, Appellee (1947) 47-2 USTC 9404

Reuel J. Foreman and Evelyn M. Foreman, Plaintiffs-Appellants v. The United States, Defendant-Appellee (1995) 95-2 USTC 50,386

Richard C. DeFir, Plaintiff v. United States of America, Defendant (1957) 57-1 USTC 9403

Robert A. Henningsen, Petitioner and Cross-Respondent, and R. A. and Margaret Henningsen, Petitioners v. Commissioner of Internal Revenue, Respondent and Cross-Petitioner (1957) 57-1 USTC 9637

Robert H. Cook and Joan M. Cook v. The United States, Sources without the U. S (1979) 79-1 USTC 9335

Robert W. Seeley and Glen McD. Seeley, Petitioners v. Commissioner of Internal Revenue, Respondent (1951) 51-1 USTC 9114

Thomas Browne Foster, Plaintiff-Appellant v. United States of America, Defendant-Appellee (1964) 64-1 USTC 9362

U. S. Court of Appeals, 1st Circuit, Boleslaw D. Kalinski and Dorothy M. Kalinski, Petitioners, Appellants v. Commissioner of Internal Revenue, Respondent, Appellee (1976) 76-1 USTC 9177

U. S. District Court, Dist. N. J., Renato J. Supino and Muriel Supino, Plaintiffs v. United States of America, Defendant (1961) 61-1 USTC 9375

U. S. District Court, Dist. Puerto Rico, United States of America, Plaintiff v. Felix Benitez Rexach et al., Defendants (1971) 71-1 USTC 9340

U. S. District Court, East. Dist. La., Lester A. Plaisance v. United States of America (1977) 77-2 USTC 9485

U. S. District Court, No. Dist. Ga., Gainesville Div., Esther Witt v. United States of America (1956) 56-2 USTC 10,002

U. S. District Court, So. Dist. Fla., Miami Div., George L. Fly and Myrthel M. Fly, Plaintiffs v. United States of America, Defendant (1967) 67-2 USTC 9601

U.S. District Court, Dist. Colo., Alois T. Wagner and Adeline E. Wagner, Plaintiffs v. United States of America, Defendant (1985) 86-1 USTC 9186

United States of America, Appellant v. John C. Johnson and Lillian F. Johnson, Appellees (1967) 68-1 USTC 9106

William Chin, Cecily Chin, Plaintiffs-Appellees v. United States of America, Defendant-Appellant (1995) 95-1 USTC 50,302

Cases – Tax Court Memoranda

Patrick J. Abrams and Paula R. Abrams v. Commissioner, CCH Dec. 46,901(M),60 T.C.M. 915,T.C. Memo. 1990-517, (Sept. 26, 1990).

William H. Adair and Patricia Adair v. Commissioner, CCH Dec. 50,946(M),70 T.C.M. 998,T.C. Memo. 1995-493, (Oct. 11, 1995).

A. Eugene Adams and Ruth C. H. Adams v. Commissioner, CCH Dec. 26,295(M),22 T.C.M. 1215,T.C. Memo. 1963-241, (Sept. 9, 1963).

William M. Adams, Jr. and Sharon Kay Adams v. Commissioner, CCH Dec. 45,518(M), 56 T.C.M. 1394,T.C. Memo. 1989-91, (Mar. 6, 1989).

William D. Alexander v. Commissioner, CCH Dec. 35,571(M),37 T.C.M. 1849-75,T.C. Memo. 1978-487, (Dec. 6, 1978).

James D. Allen v. Commissioner, CCH Dec. 29,157(M),27 T.C.M. 1082,T.C. Memo. 1968-218, (Sept. 25, 1968).

Herman Frederick Baehre v. Commissioner, CCH Dec. 17,841,15 T.C. No. 236,15 T.C. No. 36, (Sept. 19, 1950).

Abraham Barocas and Muriel J. Barocas v. Commissioner, CCH Dec. 33,243(M),34 T.C.M. 755,T.C. Memo. 1975-172, (May. 28, 1975).

Everett Benbow v. Commissioner, CCH Dec. 19,570(M),12 T.C.M. 380, (Apr. 8, 1953).

Richard W. Benfer and Elaine P. Benfer v. C.ommissioner, CCH Dec. 27,661,45 T.C. No. 277,45 T.C. No. 25, (Dec. 19, 1965)

Dean A. Benham and Estate of Ruth R. Benham, Deceased, Dean A. Benham, Executor v. Commissioner, CCH Dec. 45,670(M),57 T.C.M. 323,T.C. Memo. 1989-215, (May. 3, 1989).

William Henry Bosarge and Marilyn J. Bosarge v. Commissioner, CCH Dec. 45,418(M),56 T.C.M. 1043,T.C. Memo. 1989-15, (Jan. 9, 1989).

Charles F. Bouldin v. Commissioner, CCH Dec. 15,765,8 T.C. No. 959,8 T.C. No. 110, (May. 5, 1947).

John C. Branch v. Commissioner, CCH Dec. 49,820(M),67 T.C.M. 2822,T.C. Memo. 1994-191, (Apr. 27, 1994).

Anne Moen Bullitt Brewster v. Commissioner, CCH Dec. 30,402,55 T.C. No. 251,55 T.C. No. 24, (Oct. 28, 1970).

Floyd Dean Brobst v. Commissioner, CCH Dec. 45,082(M),56 T.C.M. 282,T.C. Memo. 1988-456, (Sept. 21, 1988).

Carl K. Brooke and Mary E. Brooke v. Commissioner, CCH Dec. 44,114(M),54 T.C.M. 132,T.C. Memo. 1987-400, (Aug. 11, 1987).

David J. Butka and Sabine I. Butka v. Commissioner, CCH Dec. 44,913,91 T.C. No. 110,91 T.C. No. 13, (July 25, 1988).

James H. Cameron and Theresa D. Cameron v. Commissioner, CCH Dec. 45,129(M),56 T.C.M. 496,T.C. Memo. 1988-496, (Oct. 12, 1988).

Paul J. Charpentier v. Commissioner, CCH Dec. 57,143(M),T.C. Memo. 2007-314,94 T.C.M. 399, (Oct. 14, 2007).

Antoine L. Cini, Petitioner v. Commissioner of Internal Revenue, Respondent, Gertrud Cini, Petitioner v. Commissioner of Internal Revenue, Respondent, CCH Dec. 34,272,67 T.C. No. 857,67 T.C. No. 68, (Feb. 27, 1977).

Edward D. Clark v. Commissioner, CCH Dec. 57,376(M),T.C. Memo. 2008-71,95 T.C.M. 1265, (Mar. 18, 2008).

Joe S. Cobb and Joyce H. Cobb v. Commissioner, CCH Dec. 47,535(M),62 T.C.M. 408,T.C. Memo. 1991-376, (Aug. 7, 1991).

William T. Coffey v. Commissioner, CCH Dec. 31,339(M),31 T.C.M. 344,T.C. Memo. 1972-87, (Apr. 12, 1972).

Joe Buck Coker v. Commissioner, CCH Dec. 49,747(M),67 T.C.M. 2515,T.C. Memo. 1994-129, (Mar. 28, 1994).

Ivor Cornman, Petitioner v. Commissioner of Internal Revenue, Respondent, CCH Dec. 33,085,63 T.C. No. 653,63 T.C. No. 63, (Mar. 17, 1975).

Dudley Y. Coyle v. Commissioner, CCH Dec. 29,497(M),28 T.C.M. 299,T.C. Memo. 1969-53, (Mar. 16, 1969).

Raymond A. Craig and Norma F. Craig, Petitioners v. Commissioner of Internal Revenue, Respondent, CCH Dec. 26, 811,73 T.C. No. 1034, 73 T.C. No. 883. (Mar. 5, 1980).

Len Sampson Crane v. Commissioner, CCH Dec. 18,992(M),11 T.C.M. 516, (May 20, 1952).

Samuel B. Croyle v. Commissioner, CCH Dec. 37,388(M),41 T.C.M. 339,T.C. Memo. 1980-501, (Nov. 5, 1980).

James F. Daly and Candace H. Daly v. Commissioner, CCH Dec. 59,562(M),T.C. Memo. 2013-147,105 T.C.M. 1850, (June 5, 2013).

Clifford R. Dammers and Robin A. Dammers, Petitioners v. Commissioner of Internal Revenue, Respondent, CCH Dec. 37,919,76 T.C. No. 835,76 T.C. No. 71, (May 20, 1981).

Joel D. Davis and Evelyn Davis v. Commissioner, CCH Dec. 46,983(M),60 T.C.M. 1256,T.C. Memo. 1990-588, (Nov. 18, 1990).

Donald F. and Eleanore A. Dawson v. Commissioner, CCH Dec. 31,606,59 T.C. No. 264,59 T.C. No. 27, (Nov. 19, 1972).

Juan R. deTorres and Jacquelyn S. deTorres v. Commissioner, CCH Dec. 48,983(M),65 T.C.M. 2381,T.C. Memo. 1993-161, (Apr. 13, 1993).

Henry Warren Dickinson v. Commissioner, CCH Dec. 20,851(M),14 T.C.M. 82,T.C. Memo. 1955-24, (Jan. 30, 1955).

Hermine Dinger v. Commissioner, CCH Dec. 60,367(M),T.C. Memo. 2015-145,110 T.C.M. 130, (Aug. 5, 2015).

Cecil A. Donaldson and Liselotte Donaldson v. Commissioner, CCH Dec. 29,467,51 T.C. No. 830,51 T.C. No. 82, (Feb. 24, 1969).

Elizabeth T. Dougherty v. Commissioner, CCH Dec. 47,605(M),62 T.C.M. 680,T.C. Memo. 1991-442, (Sept. 9, 1991).

Laurence P. Dowd and Juliet R. Dowd v. Commissioner, CCH Dec. 25,158,37 T.C. No. 399, 37 T.C. No. 43, (Dec. 3, 1961).

James S. Doyle v. Commissioner, CCH Dec. 45,980(M), 57 T.C.M. 1436,T.C. Memo. 1989-463, (Aug. 28, 1989).

Carol Dean Duley v. Commissioner, Orville E. Duley and Dorothy R. Duley v. Commissioner, CCH Dec. 37,915(M), 41 T.C.M. 1521,T.C. Memo. 1981-246, (May 19, 1981).

Jack Ray Dye v. Commissioner, CCH Dec. 46,787(M), 60 T.C.M. 446,T.C. Memo. 1990-420, (Aug. 5, 1990)

Donald R. Dykes and Essie J. Dykes v. Commissioner, CCH Dec. 31,036(M),30 T.C.M. 1141,T.C. Memo. 1971-266, (Oct. 17, 1971).

Amad Zaker Eram v. Commissioner, CCH Dec. 59,872(M),T.C. Memo. 2014-60,107 T.C.M. 1320, (Apr. 6, 2014).

William and Erna Howell v. Commissioner, CCH Dec. 38,387(M),42 T.C.M. 1564,T.C. Memo. 1981-631, (Oct. 26, 1981).

John and Johnnie M. Eubanks v. Commissioner, CCH Dec. 45,696(M),57 T.C.M. 391,T.C. Memo. 1989-233, (May 10, 1989).

William J. Faltesek v. Commissioner, CCH Dec. 45,743,92 T.C. No. 1204,92 T.C. No. 78, (June 5, 1989).

Robert E. Farrell and Frances G. Farrell, Plaintiffs v. United States of America, Defendant, 2001-1 U.S.T.C. 50,279, (Feb. 11, 2001).

Jose V. Ferrer v. Commissioner, CCH Dec. 28,937,50 T.C. No. 177,50 T.C. No. 19, (Apr. 29, 1968).

Grant Foster and Barbara Dunn Foster v. Commissioner, CCH Dec. 27,557(M),24 T.C.M. 1268,T.C. Memo. 1965-246, (Sept. 13, 1965).

Marilyn Fugit, Surviving Spouse of Raymond Fugit, Deceased, and Marilyn Fugit v. Commissioner, CCH Dec. 33,195(M), 34 T.C.M. 646,T.C. Memo. 1975-140, (May 11, 1975).

David R. Galistel v. Commissioner, CCH Dec. 33,974(M),35 T.C.M. 1107,T.C. Memo. 1976-253, (Aug. 15, 1976).

Lynn W. and Eleanor T. Gelhar v. Commissioner, CCH Dec. 48,086(M),63 T.C.M. 2466,T.C. Memo. 1992-162, (Mar. 22, 1992).

Eric Stephen Gerencser v. Commissioner, CCH Dec. 60,671(M),T.C. Memo. 2016-151,112 T.C.M. 218, (Aug. 9, 2016).

William A. Gillis v. Commissioner, CCH Dec. 43,532(M),52 T.C.M. 1128,T.C. Memo. 1986-576, (Dec. 7, 1986).

Robert S. Groetzinger and Beverly L. Groetzinger v. Commissioner, CCH Dec. 43,307,87 T.C. No. 533, (Aug. 25, 1986).

Frederick F. Hack and Eleanore Hack v. Commissioner, CCH Dec. 24,112,33 T.C. No. 1089,33 T.C. No. 124, (Mar. 30, 1960).

Carol Patton Hagerty (Formerly Mrs. Carol Patton) Cases of the following petitioners are consolidated herewith: Carol Patton Hagerty (Formerly Mrs. Carol Patton), docket No. 4792-70, and William J. Hagerty, docket No. 5497-70. v. Commissioner, CCH Dec. 32,060(M),32 T.C.M. 788,T.C. Memo. 1973-162, (July 23, 1973).

Burlin B. Hamer and Marjorie A. Hamer v. Commissioner, CCH Dec. 20,341,22 T.C. No. 343,22 T.C. No. 45, (May 16, 1954).

Lonnie L. and Mildred D. Harper v. Commissioner, CCH Dec. 46,404(M),58 T.C.M. 1509,T.C. Memo. 1990-94, (Feb. 26, 1990).

Jon F. Hartung and Constance M. Hartung v. Commissioner, CCH Dec. 30,357,55 T.C. No. 1, (Sept. 30, 1970).

Audio Gray Harvey v. Commissioner, CCH Dec. 16,231,10 T.C. No. 183,10 T.C. No. 25, (Jan. 29, 1948).

Carman F. Hawkins and Mary Jane Hawkins v. Commissioner, CCH Dec. 49,202(M),66 T.C.M. 332,T.C. Memo. 1993-350, (Aug. 10, 1993).

Richard E. Heinzelman v. Commissioner, CCH Dec. 37,877(M),41 T.C.M. 1423,T.C. Memo. 1981-218, (May. 3, 1981).

Frieda Hempel v. Commissioner, CCH Dec. 15,888(M), 6 T.C.M. 743, (June 22, 1947).

Humberto Hernandez and Ileana Hernandez v. Commissioner, CCH Dec. 36,184(M), 38 T.C.M. 1068,T.C. Memo. 1979-272, (July 22, 1979).

Ernest Rudolf Hertig, CCH Dec. 19,272,19 T.C. No. 109,19 T.C. No. 19, (Oct. 29, 1952).

Liston F. Hills and Catherine F. Hills, Petitioners v. Commissioner of Internal Revenue, Respondent, Edward G. Voss and Dorothy T. Voss,

Petitioners v. Commissioner of Internal Revenue, Respondent CCH Dec. 36,276,72 T.C. No. 958,72 T.C. No. 79, (Aug. 28, 1979).

Douglas L. Hoppes v. Commissioner, CCH Dec. 45,691(M),57 T.C.M. 366,T.C. Memo. 1989-228, (May 10, 1989).

Harold E. Howe and Jean D. Howe v. Commissioner, CCH Dec. 44,860(M),55 T.C.M. 1153,T.C. Memo. 1988-277, (June 26, 1988).

William Hughes and Mary Ann Hughes, Petitioners v. Commissioner of Internal Revenue, Respondent, CCH Dec. 33,547,65 T.C, No. 566,65 T.C. No. 50. (Dec. 15, 1975).

James R. Hummer v. Commissioner, CCH Dec. 45,168(M),56 T.C.M. 657,T.C. Memo. 1988-528, (Nov. 13, 1988).

Domer L. Ishler, Plaintiff v. Commissioner of Internal Revenue, United States of America, et al., Defendants, 2007-1 U.S.T.C. 50,408, (July 4, 2006).

Chesley O. James and Shirley B. James v. Commissioner, CCH Dec. 44,845(M),55 T.C.M. 1112,T.C. Memo. 1988-266, (June 21, 1988).

Harry T. Johnson, Jr., and Jeanne E. Johnson v. Commissioner, CCH Dec. 34,720(M),36 T.C.M. 1531,T.C. Memo. 1977-377, (Oct. 30, 1977).

Harold F. Jones and Rita C. Jones, Husband and Wife v. Commissioner, CCH Dec. 15,018,6 T.C. No. 412,6 T.C. No. 54, (Mar. 10, 1946).

Lynn F. Jones v. Commissioner, CCH Dec. 36,183(M), 38 T.C.M. 1064,T.C. Memo. 1979-271, (July 22, 1979).

Stephen Jones v. Commissioner, CCH Dec. 55,016(M),85 T.C.M. 767,T.C. Memo. 2003-14, (Jan. 13, 2003).

Cristian L. and Nicola M. Juliard v. Commissioner, CCH Dec. 47,363(M),61 T.C.M. 2683,T.C. Memo. 1991-230, (May 22, 1991).

H. Kalicak Construction Co., et al. On October 6, 1981, this Court granted respondent's motion to consolidate the following cases: H. Kalicak Construction Co. v. Commissioner, Docket No. 5030-81; Harold Kalicak v. Commissioner, Docket No. 5098-81; T. Thomas Heeter and Audrey Heeter v. Commissioner, Docket No. 5456-81. By our Order of December 5, 1983, Docket No. 5456-81 was severed from consolidation based upon the statement of the parties that a basis for disposition by settlement had been reached, and respondent's motion to consolidate with the remaining two cases, H. Kalicak Construction Co. v. Commissioner, Docket No. 25040-81, was granted. v. Commissioner, CCH Dec. 41,558(M),48 T.C.M. 1403,T.C. Memo. 1984-552, (Oct. 15, 1984).

Frank L. Kluckhohn and June E. Kluckhohn v. Commissioner, CCH Dec. 19,158,18 T.C. No. 892,18 T.C. No. 113, (Aug. 21, 1952).

Herman A. Kollmar and Emma F. Kollmar, Husband and Wife v. Commissioner, CCH Dec. 14,371,4 T.C. No. 727,4 T.C. No. 85, (Feb. 4, 1945).

Frederick Lambach and Jacqueline Lambach v. Commissioner, CCH Dec. 18,888(M),11 T.C.M. 330, (Apr. 3, 1952).

David P. Lansdown v. Commissioner, CCH Dec. 50,114(M),68 T.C.M. 680,T.C. Memo. 1994-452, (Sept. 7, 1994).

Leonard and Lillian H. Larsen v. Commissioner, CCH Dec. 20,801,23 T.C. No. 599,23 T.C. No. 79, (Jan. 6, 1955).

Anne Laughlin v. Commissioner, CCH Dec. 21,970,27 T.C. No. 23,27 T.C. No. 2, (Oct. 15, 1956).

Marsden R. Leeder and Rose Leeder, his wife v. Commissioner, CCH Dec. 24,125(M),19 T.C.M. 352,T.C. Memo. 1960-69, (Apr. 10, 1960).

Christina Jeannine LeTourneau v. Commissioner, CCH Dec. 58,951(M),T.C. Memo. 2012-45,103 T.C.M. 1229, (Feb. 20, 2012).

Raymond C. Lewis and Edyth F. Lewis v. Commissioner, CCH Dec. 23,856(M),18 T.C.M. 1059,T.C. Memo. 1959-219, (Nov. 26, 1959).

Amy L. Lockhart v. Commissioner, Tex E. Lockhart v. Commissioner, CCH Dec. 18,860(M),11 T.C.M. 254, (Mar. 20, 1952).

Richard H. Lovald v. Commissioner, CCH Dec. 18,249,16 T.C. No. 909,16 T.C. No. 110, (Apr. 25, 1951).

John L. Lovelady v. Commissioner, CCH Dec. 45,173(M),56 T.C.M. 689,T.C. Memo. 1988-533, (Nov. 15, 1988).

Albert McCarroll Marckwardt and Gloria Suarez Marckwardt v. Commissioner, CCH Dec. 47,497(M),62 T.C.M. 262,T.C. Memo. 1991-347, (July 28, 1991).

Richard L. and Rosmarie Markus v. Commissioner, CCH Dec. 31,111(M),30 T.C.M. 1346,T.C. Memo. 1971-313, (Dec. 12, 1971).

Victor G. Marty, Jr. and Georganne S. Marty v. Commissioner, CCH Dec. 31,212(M),31 T.C.M. 26,T.C. Memo. 1971-11,T.C. Memo. 1972-11, (Jan. 11, 1972).

Lisa M. Matt v. Commissioner, CCH Dec. 46,547(M),59 T.C.M. 472,T.C. Memo. 1990-209, (Apr. 24, 1990).

Joseph A. McCurnin v. Commissioner, CCH Dec. 22,953,30 T.C. No. 143,30 T.C. No. 14, (Apr. 28, 1958).

Nancy McDonald v. Commissioner, CCH Dec. 60,391(M),T.C. Memo. 2015-169,110 T.C.M. 239, (Aug. 24, 2015).

Eugene C. McGrath v. Commissioner, CCH Dec. 43,771(M),53 T.C.M. 363,T.C. Memo. 1987-139, (Mar. 15, 1987).

Andrew O. Miller, Jr., and Jeanne W. Miller v. Commissioner, CCH Dec. 29,690,52 T.C. No. 752,52 T.C. No. 79, (Aug. 5, 1969).

James D. Mooney and Ida May Mooney v. Commissioner, CCH Dec. 16,080,9 T.C. No. 713,9 T.C. No. 96, (Oct. 19, 1947).

Eugene K. Morley and Joyce C. Morley v. Commissioner, CCH Dec. 39,408(M),44 T.C.M. 1337,T.C. Memo. 1982-586, (Oct. 4, 1982).

James R. Moudy v. Commissioner, CCH Dec. 45,671(M),57 T.C.M. 327,T.C. Memo. 1989-216, (May 3, 1989).

William D. Mount and Margaret E. Mount, et al. Docket Nos. 2314-86 and 12989-86, both involving Jesse L. Wells and Mary L. Wells, are consolidated herewith. v. Commissioner, CCH Dec. 45,915(M),57 T.C.M. 1188,T.C. Memo. 1989-405, (Aug. 6, 1989).

Anthony and Helen V. Nahacky v. Commissioner, CCH Dec. 28,492(M),26 T.C.M. 572,T.C. Memo. 1967-128, (June 7, 1967).

Donald H. and Edwina C. Nelson v. Commissioner, CCH Dec. 23,145,30 T.C. No. 1151,30 T.C. No. 121, (Aug. 20, 1958).

Ewell K. and Phyllis Nold v. Commissioner, CCH Dec. 28,582(M),26 T.C.M. 802,T.C. Memo. 1967-171, (Aug. 22, 1967).

George A. Page and Judith F. Page, his wife, v. Commissioner, CCH Dec. 20,968,24 T.C. No. 52,24 T.C. No. 8, (Apr. 20, 1955).

Melvin Painter and Alice Painter v. Commissioner, CCH Dec. 33,842(M),35 T.C.M. 731,T.C. Memo. 1976-164, (May. 23, 1976).

Irene Vavasour Elder Perkins v. Commissioner, CCH Dec. 26,126,40 T.C. No. 330,40 T.C. No. 40, (May 16, 1963).

Fred H. Pierce v. Commissioner, CCH Dec. 20,373,22 T.C. No. 493,22 T.C. No. 62, (June 7, 1954).

Theodore F. Pope v. Commissioner, CCH Dec. 37,176(M),40 T.C.M. 1045,T.C. Memo. 1980-332, (Aug. 24, 1980).

Howard E. Powell v. Commissioner, CCH Dec. 18,565(M),10 T.C.M. 928, (Sept. 27, 1951).

Anthony Quinn and Katherine Quinn v. Commissioner, CCH Dec. 32,501(M),33 T.C.M. 310,T.C. Memo. 1974-64, (Mar. 17, 1974).

Frank E. Raffensperger and Mary A. Raffensperger v. Commissioner, CCH Dec. 24,114,33 T.C. No. 1097,33 T.C. No. 126, (Mar. 30, 1960).

Donald R. Redding and Betty F. Redding v. Commissioner, CCH Dec. 38,837(M),43 T.C.M. 719,T.C. Memo. 1982-111, (Mar. 7, 1982).

James R. and Linda L. Richard v. Commissioner, CCH Dec. 44,785(M), 55 T.C.M. 864,T.C. Memo. 1988-217, (May 15, 1988).

Paul V. Riley, Jr., Petitioner v. Commissioner of Internal Revenue, Respondent, CCH Dec. 26,975,74 T.C. No. 414,74 T.C. No. 29. (May 26, 1980).

Clarence R. Ritchie v. Commissioner, CCH Dec. 45,939(M),57 T.C.M. 1282,T.C. Memo. 1989-426, (Aug. 14, 1989).

William D. and Yen-Ling K. Rogers v. Commissioner., CCH Dec. 57,827(M),T.C. Memo. 2009-111,97 T.C.M. 1573, (May 19, 2009).

William D. Rogers and Yen-Ling K. Rogers, Appellants v. Commissioner of Internal Revenue Service, Appellee., 2015-1 U.S.T.C. 50,273, (Apr. 16, 2015).

Estate of Theodore Roodner, Deceased, Ronald Wagner, Administrator, Petitioner v. Commissioner of Internal Revenue, Respondent, CCH Dec. 33,353,64 T.C. No. 680,64 T.C. No. 67, (July 29, 1975).

David E. Rose v. Commissioner, CCH Dec. 18,072,16 T.C. No. 232,16 T.C. No. 30, (Jan. 28, 1951).

Dell Ross v. Commissioner, CCH Dec. 32,740(M),33 T.C.M. 982,T.C. Memo. 1974-221, (Aug. 26, 1974).

George Rousku and Esther Rousku v. Commissioner, CCH Dec. 30,839,56 T.C. No. 548,56 T.C. No. 43, (June 20, 1971).

Ramon R. Santiago v. Commissioner, CCH Dec. 32,177,61 T.C. No. 53,61 T.C. No. 6, (Oct. 16, 1973).

Elliot D. Sass v. Commissioner, CCH Dec. 20,692(M), 13 T.C.M. 1091,T.C. Memo. 1954-212, (Nov. 29, 1954).

John J. Scheuren, Jr., Petitioners' names appear variously in the record of this case as Scheuren or Scheurin. Margaret B. Scheuren v. Commissioner, CCH Dec. 24,684(M),20 T.C.M. 289,T.C. Memo. 1961-52, (Feb. 26, 1961).

Bert J. Schoneberger, Petitioner v. Commissioner of Internal Revenue, Respondent, CCH Dec. 37,138,74 T.C. No. 1016,74 T.C. No. 75, (Aug. 6, 1980).

Leif J. Sverdrup v. Commissioner, CCH Dec. 17,644,14 T.C. No. 859,14 T.C. No. 105, (May 15, 1950).

Henry Joseph Shelonzek, Jr., and Barbara Jolanta Shelonzek v. Commissioner, CCH Dec. 44,673(M),55 T.C.M. 515,T.C. Memo. 1988-137, (Mar. 29, 1988).

Frank J. Sherman and Madeline E. Sherman v. Commissioner, CCH Dec. 27,379(M),24 T.C.M. 650,T.C. Memo. 1965-126, (May 10, 1965)

Ivan Maxim Sislik v. Commissioner, CCH Dec. 46,015(M), 58 T.C.M. 115,T.C. Memo. 1989-495, (Sept. 6, 1989).

Joseph N. and Margaret J. Soboleski v. Commissioner, CCH Dec. 43,860,88 T.C. No. 1024,88 T.C. No. 56, (Apr. 21, 1987).

Helen Robinson Solano v. Commissioner, CCH Dec. 32,705,62 T.C. No. 562,62 T.C. No. 64, (July 30, 1974).

Larry G. Solomon v. Commissioner, CCH Dec. 49,376(M),66 T.C.M. 1201,T.C. Memo. 1993-509, (Nov. 2, 1993).

Frank Souza and Cecelia Souza v. Commissioner, CCH Dec. 24,036,33 T.C. No. 817,33 T.C. No. 93, (Feb. 7, 1960).

Joseph D. Specking, et al. Cases of the following petitioners are consolidated herewith: Eric N. Umbach, Docket No. 12348-99; and Robert J. Haessly, Docket No. 14496-99. v. Commissioner, CCH Dec. 54,470,117 T.C. No. 95,117 T.C. No. 9, (Aug. 27, 2001).

James M. Steel and Theresa B. Steel v. Commissioner, CCH Dec. 45,012(M),55 T.C.M. 1721,T.C. Memo. 1988-399, (Aug. 24, 1988).

Lois Kaiser Stierhout v. Commissioner, CCH Dec. 21,080,24 T.C. No. 483,24 T.C. No. 54, (June 23, 1955).

Tracy M. Stright and Eileen G. Stright v. Commissioner, CCH Dec. 49,451(M),66 T.C.M. 1490,T.C. Memo. 1993-576, (Dec. 6, 1993).

Samuel Striker v. Commissioner, CCH Dec. 60,479(M),T.C. Memo. 2015-248,110 T.C.M. 623, (Dec. 27, 2015).

Myron R. Struck and Thelma C. Struck v. Commissioner, CCH Dec. 56,845(M),T.C. Memo. 2007-42,93 T.C.M. 928, (Feb. 21, 2007).

Ken Miller Supply, Inc. v. Commissioner, Kenneth R. Miller and Lois N. Miller v. Commissioner, CCH Dec. 35,224(M), 37 T.C.M. 974,T.C. Memo. 1978-228, (June 19, 1978).

Billy Lee Swicegood and Carolyn Lowder Swicegood v. Commissioner, CCH Dec. 45,984(M), 57 T.C.M. 1456,T.C. Memo. 1989-467, (Aug. 28, 1989).

Amaro A. Taibo v. Commissioner, CCH Dec. 55,733(M),T.C. Memo. 2004-196,88 T.C.M. 181, (Aug. 30, 2004).

Ronald B. Talmage; Annette C. Talmage, Petitioners-Appellants v. Commissioner of Internal Revenue, Respondent-Appellee., 2010-2 U.S.T.C. 50,550, (Aug. 5, 2010).

Chester D. Taylor, Jr., and Rita K. Taylor v. Commissioner, CCH Dec. 30,700(M), 30 T.C.M. 233,T.C. Memo. 1971-53, (Mar. 28, 1971).

Robert W. Teskey v. Commissioner, CCH Dec. 23,006,30 T.C. No. 456,30 T.C. No. 41, (May 28, 1958).

Mark Tobey v. Commissioner, CCH Dec. 31,971,60 T.C. No. 227,60 T.C. No. 27, (May 16, 1973).

Kurt Van Yost v. Commissioner, CCH Dec. 39,328(M),44 T.C.M. 1071,T.C. Memo. 1982-516, (Sept. 12, 1982).

Johnnie R. and Ethel Vance v. Commissioner, CCH Dec. 19,861(M), 12 T.C.M. 966, (Aug. 26, 1953).

Gerald L. Walker and Mildred McMeans Walker v. Commissioner, CCH Dec. 22,283(M),16 T.C.M. 171,T.C. Memo. 1957-40, (Mar. 11, 1957).

Lyle D. Welsh and Beverly A. Welsh v. Commissioner, CCH Dec. 45,149(M),56 T.C.M. 560,T.C. Memo. 1988-512, (Oct. 30, 1988).

Leigh White v. Commissioner, CCH Dec. 20,398,22 T.C. No. 585,22 T.C. No. 76, (June 16, 1954).

Agnes E. Wilson, Petitioner v. Commissioner, CCH Dec. 30,092(M),29 T.C.M. 481,T.C. Memo. 1970-105, (May 5, 1970).

William R. and Gertrude L. Wilson v. Commissioner, CCH Dec. 47,662(M),62 T.C.M. 900,T.C. Memo. 1991-491, (Sept. 29, 1991).

Michael H. Wojciechowski v. Commissioner, CCH Dec. 47,373(M),61 T.C.M. 2758,T.C. Memo. 1991-239, (May 28, 1991).

Harry A. Woodward v. Commissioner, CCH Dec. 46,308(M),58 T.C.M. 1133,T.C. Memo. 1990-7, (Jan. 3, 1990).

Dennis Ray Wyrick v. Commissioner, CCH Dec. 33,991(M),35 T.C.M. 1176,T.C. Memo. 1976-268, (Aug. 22, 1976).

Daneen L. Young v. Commissioner, John C. Siddall v. Commissioner, CCH Dec. 32,553(M),33 T.C.M. 488,T.C. Memo. 1974-99, (Apr. 21, 1974).

Internal Revenue Rulings

Revenue Ruling 2005-3, (Dec. 27, 2004)

Revenue Ruling 54-483, (Dec. 31, 1953)

Revenue Ruling 54-612, (Dec. 31, 1953)

Revenue Ruling 54-72, (Dec. 31, 1953)

Revenue Ruling 55-246, (Dec. 31, 1954)

Revenue Ruling 55-384, (Dec. 31, 1954)

Revenue Ruling 55-497, 1955-2 CB 292

Revenue Ruling 55-497, (Dec. 31, 1954)

Revenue Ruling 55-6, (Dec. 31, 1954)

Revenue Ruling 58-4, (Dec. 31, 1957)

Revenue Ruling 58-485, (Dec. 31, 1957)

Revenue Ruling 60-36, (Dec. 31, 1959)

Revenue Ruling 63-50, (Dec. 31, 1962)

Revenue Ruling 64-255, (Dec. 31, 1963)

Revenue Ruling 66-326, (Dec. 31, 1965)

Revenue Ruling 66-56, (Dec. 31, 1965)

Revenue Ruling 67-158, (Dec. 31, 1966)

Revenue Ruling 67-52, (Dec. 31, 1966)

Revenue Ruling 67-87, (Dec. 31, 1966)

Revenue Ruling 68-81, (Dec. 31, 1967)

Revenue Ruling 69-118, (Dec. 31, 1968)

Revenue Ruling 69-213, (Dec. 31, 1968)

Revenue Ruling 69-238, (Dec. 31, 1968)

Revenue Ruling 69-448, (Dec. 31, 1968)

Revenue Ruling 70-374, (Dec. 31, 1969)

Revenue Ruling 71-101, (Dec. 31, 1970)

Revenue Ruling 71-199, (Dec. 31, 1970)

Revenue Ruling 72-423, (Dec. 31, 1971)

Revenue Ruling 72-496, (Dec. 31, 1971)

Revenue Ruling 72-497, (Dec. 31, 1971)

Revenue Ruling 73-181, (Dec. 31, 1972)

Revenue Ruling 73-492, (Dec. 31, 1972)

Revenue Ruling 75-485, (Dec. 31, 1974)

Revenue Ruling 75-84, (Dec. 31, 1974)

Revenue Ruling 75-85, (Dec. 31, 1974)

Revenue Ruling 75-86, (Dec. 31, 1974)

Revenue Ruling 75-86, (Dec. 31, 1974)

Revenue Ruling 76-163, (Dec. 31, 1975)

Revenue Ruling 76-191, (Dec. 31, 1975)

Revenue Ruling 77-167, (Dec. 31, 1976)

Revenue Ruling 78-254, (Dec. 31, 1977)

Revenue Ruling 79-199, (Dec. 31, 1978)

Revenue Ruling 79-6, (Dec. 31, 1978)

Revenue Ruling 79-85, (Dec. 31, 1978)

Revenue Ruling 79-85, (Dec. 31, 1978)

Revenue Ruling 80-208, (Dec. 31, 1979)

Revenue Ruling 80-254, (Dec. 31, 1979)

Revenue Ruling 85-29, (Dec. 31, 1984)

Revenue Ruling 87-38, (May. 17, 1987)

Revenue Ruling 90-77, (Dec. 31, 1989)

Revenue Ruling 91-58, (Dec. 31, 1990)

Internal Revenue Procedures, Notices, Private Letter Rulings

Revenue Procedure 2015-25, (Mar. 23, 2015)

Revenue Procedure 2016-21, (Mar. 16, 2016)

Revenue Procedure 64-48, (Dec. 31, 1963)

Revenue Procedure 80-16, (Dec. 31, 1979)

Notice 2007-16, (Feb. 12, 2007)

UIL No. 911.01-00 Earned income from sources without U.S., Bona fide resident, Letter Ruling 8526002, (Feb. 25, 1985), (Feb. 24, 1985).

UIL No. 911.11-03, Letter Ruling 9625060, (Mar. 28, 1996), (Mar. 27, 1996).

IRS Publications

Internal Revenue Service, "Form 673: Statement for Claiming Exemption from Withholding on Foreign Earned Income Eligible for the Exclusion(s) Provided by Section 911" (2016) <www.irs.gov> 23 Dec. 2016

--, "Form 8840: Closer Connection Exception Statement for Aliens" (2016) <www.irs.gov> 23 Dec. 2016.

--, "Instructions for Form 2555" (2016) <www.irs.gov> 23 Dec. 2016.

--, "Form 2555: Foreign Earned Income" (2016) <www.irs.gov> 23 Dec. 2016.

--, "Tax Guide for U.S. Citizens and Residents Aliens Abroad" (2016), IRS Publication 54.

--, "IRS 2015 Data Book" (2016) <www.irs.gov/pub/irs-soi/15databk.pdf> 18 Oct. 2016.

--, "LB&I International Practice Unit-Audit: Calculating Foreign Earned Income Exclusion – Employee" (2015). <www.irs.gov/businesses/corporations/international-practice-units> 23 Dec. 2016.

--, "LB&I International Practice Unit-Audit: Calculating Foreign Earned Income Exclusion - Self Employed Individual" (2015) <www.irs.gov/businesses/corporations/international-practice-units> 23 Dec. 2016.

--, "LB&I International Practice Unit-Audit: Deemed Annual Royalty Income Inclusion Under IRC 367(d)" (2015) <www.irs.gov/businesses/corporations/international-practice-units> 23 Dec. 2016.

--, "LB&I International Practice Unit-Audit: Foreign Housing Deduction" (2016) <www.irs.gov/businesses/corporations/international-practice-units> 23 Dec. 2016.

--, "LB&I International Practice Unit-Audit: IRC 911 Election and Revocation" (2014)

<www.irs.gov/businesses/corporations/international-practice-units> 23 Dec. 2016.

--, "LB&I International Practice Unit-Audit: Non-Services FDAP Income" (2015) <www.irs.gov/businesses/corporations/international-practice-units> 23 Dec. 2016.

--, "LB&I International Practice Unit-Audit: Physical Presence Test for Purposes of Qualifying for IRC 911 Tax Benefits" (2015) www.irs.gov/businesses/corporations/international-practice-units> 23 Dec. 2016.

--, "LB&I International Practice Unit-Audit: Sourcing of Fringe Benefits for FTC Limitation" (2015) <www.irs.gov/businesses/corporations/international-practice-units> 23 Dec. 2016.

--, "LB&I International Practice Unit-Audit: Tax Home for Purposes of IRC 911" (2014) <www.irs.gov/businesses/corporations/international-practice-units> 23 Dec. 2016.

--, "Offshore Voluntary Compliance Efforts Top $10 Billion; More than 100,000 Taxpayers Come Back into Compliance" (2016) IR-2016-137.

--, "Tax Research: Understanding Sources of Tax Law (Why my IRC beats your Rev Proc!)" Wolters Klewer. <www.cchgroup.com/media/wk/taa/pdfs/accounting-firms/tax/understanding-sources-tax-law-fact-sheet.pdf> 18 Oct 2016.

Secondary Sources

Avi-Yonah, R.S., "Double Tax Treaties: An Introduction" (2007) <www.ssrn.com/abstract=1048441> 10 May 2013.

Balnadu, S., "The Foreign Earned Income Exclusion" (2016) 6 *Contemporary Tax Journal* <www.scholarworks.sjsu.edu/cgi/viewcontent.cgi?article=1087&context=sjsumstjournal> 27 Dec. 2016.

Bogenschneider B.N., 'The Professional Ethics of US Tax Treaty Interpretation' (2016) 8 *Southern J Bus Ethics* 237 <www.ssrn.com/abstract=2879884> 5 Jan. 2017.

Brummer C, "Why Soft Law Dominates International Finance--And Not Trade" (2010) 13(3) *J Intl Economic L* 623.

Cluett, R.G., “United States: Sound and Fury, Signifying What? The U.S. Foreign Earned Income Exclusion Debate” (2009) <www.capdale.com/files/Publication/387b38f9-75d2-491f-9028-38e3b594dd90/Presentation/PublicationAttachment/b9cb4dea-8c1d-4690-85f4-420713d407e5/Cluett%20TNI%20Article.pdf>23 Dec. 2016.

Department of the Treasury, “FY2017 U.S. Budget in Brief” (2016) <www.treasury.gov/about/budget-performance/budget-in-brief/Documents/FY17FactSheet.pdf> 27 Sept. 2016.

Elsayyad, M., 'Bargaining Over Tax Information Exchange' (Max Planck Institute, 2012) <www.ssrn.com/abstract=2012593> 22 May 2013.

Feldman, N.E. and Slemrod, J., “Estimating Tax Noncompliance with Evidence from Unaudited Tax Returns” (2007) 117 *Economic Journal* 518 p. 327.

G20 Research Group, “G20 Leaders Statement: The Hangzhou Summit” (2016)<www.g20.utoronto.ca/2016/160905-communique.html> 28 Jan. 2017.

--, 'G20Gottselig, G., “The Role of Tax Policy in the Global Economic Crisis” *IMF Survey Mag.*, 2009 <www.imf.org/external/pubs/ft/survey/so/2009/INT091709A.htm> 28 May 2013.

Gravelle, J.G., “Tax Havens: International Tax Avoidance and Evasion” (2013) <www.fas.org/sgp/crs/misc/R40623.pdf> 3 June 2013.

Greenwald, L.J. and Kaplan, D.H., “The Exceptional Importance of Getting U.S. International Tax Compliance Right” (2011) <www.sandw.com/assets/htmldocuments/The-Exceptional-Importance-of-Getting-US-Tax-Right-B1323415.pdf> 16 Sept. 2016.

Hasenauer, C. and Prinz, J., “Implementation of OECD standard on exchange of information” (2010) 21 Intl Tax Rev 39.

Hollenbeck, S. and Keenan Kahr, M., “Individual Foreign -Earned Income and Foreign Tax Credit, 2011” (2015) Internal Revenue Service <www.irs.gov/pub/irs-soi/14insprbulforearnincome.pdf> 23 Dec. 2016.

Joint Committee on Taxation, “Overview of the Federal Tax System as in Effect for 2016” (2016)<www.jct.gov/publications.html?func=startdown&id=4912> 2 Nov. 2016.

Keen, M. and Ligthart, J,E,, "Incentives and Information Exchange in International Taxation" (2004) <www.ssrn.com/abstract=567081> 22 May 2013.

Kenny, L.W. and Winner, S.L., "Tax Systems in the World: An Empirical Investigation into the Importance of Tax Bases, Collection Costs and Political Regime" (2001) 13 Intl Tax & Pub Fin.

Knight, L.G., "The earned income exclusion for foreign residence" (1989) *CPA Journal,* Feb. 1989 <www.archives.cpajournal.com/old/07133072.htm> 27 Dec. 2016.

Kurlander, G., "Foreign Earned income Exclusion: Redefining the Exception for Amounts Paid by the United States Under I.R.C. 911" (1983) 68 *Cornell Law Review* 4 <www.scholarship.law.cornell.edu/cgi/viewcontent.cgi?article=4316&context=clr> 27 Dec. 2016.

Lennard, M., "The UN Model Tax Convention as compared with the OECD Model Tax Convention-Current Points of Difference and Recent Developments" *Asia-Pacific Tax Bulletin,* 2009 <www.taxjustice.net/cms/upload/pdf/Lennard_0902_UN_Vs_OECD.pdf> 22 May 2013.

McKenzie, R., "Afraid to file your return because you owe IRS? Here's how IRS collects delinquencies" (2016) *Forbes* 10 Apr 2016 <www.forbes.com/sites/irswatch/2016/04/10/afraid-to-file-your-return-because-you-owe-irs-heres-how-collection-works/#644343cd7ddb> 18 Oct. 2016.

Miller, A. and Oats, L., "Principles of International Taxation" 3rd ed. (2012) Bloomsbury Professional Ltd., West Sussex. UK.

OECD Secretary-General, "OECD Secretary General Repoty to G20 Finance Ministers: Chengdu People's Republic of China 23-24 July 2016" (2016) <www.oecd.org/ctp/oecd-secretary-general-tax-report-g20-finance-ministers-july-2016.pdf?utm_campaign=FATCA+News_26_20160810&utm_source=newsletter&utm_medium=newsletter> 11 Oct. 2016.

Postlewaite, P.F. and Stern, G.E., "Innocents Abroad? The 1978 Foreign Earned Income Act and the Case for Its Repeal" (1979) 65 *Virginia Law Review* 6, p. 1093.

Rettig, C., "IRS New Release: Foreign Account Filings Top 1 Million; Taxpayers Need to Know Their Filing Requirements" (2016) IRS News

Release IR-2016-42, 1 Mar 2016 <https://www.irs.gov/pub/irs-news/IR-16-042.pdf>17 Oct. 2016.

Rosenzweig, A.H., “Thinking Outside the (Tax) Treaty” (2012) 2012(3) *Wisconsin L Rev* 717.

Sapirie, M., “The Personal Impact of Offshore Enforcement” (2013) TaxAnalysts, 16 July 2013. <www.taxanalysts.org/content/news-analysis-personal-impact-offshore-enforcement>13 July 2016.

Shaviro, D., “The 2008 Financial Crisis: Implications or Income Tax Reform” (2011) *NYU L and Econ Research Paper* No. 09-35 <www.ssrn.com/abstract=1442089> 4 May 2013.

Sundberg, A., “History of US Taxes Abroad from 1787 to 2001” <www.americansabroad.org/history-of-us-taxes-abroad-from-1787-to-2001>27 Dec. 2016.

Atwood, T.J., et al., “Home Country Tax System Characteristics and Corporate Tax Avoidance: International Evidence” (2012) 87(6) *Acctg Rev* p. 1831.

U.S. Competant Authority at OECD, “Global Awareness Training for International Tax Examiners” <www.irs.gov/pub/irs-utl/Global_Awareness_Training_for_IEs.pdf> 13 Oct. 2016.

United States Government Accountability Office, “Tax Policy: Economic Benefits of Income Exclusion for U.S. Citizens Working Abroad are Uncertain” (2014) GAO-14-387.

VanderWolk, J.P., “The New World of Tax Information Exchange” (2010) 13(2) Asia-Pacific J Taxation <www.ssrn.com/abstract=1582452> 22 May 2013.

Vogel, K., “Double Tax Treaties and Their Interpretation” (1986) 4 *Intl Tax & Bus Law* 1.

Woods, R.W., “FATCA, IRS Global Tax Law, Is Everywhere -- Even Russia & China” (2014) <www.forbes.com/sites/robertwood/2014/07/01/fatca-is-finally-here-even-in-russia-china/#41395cc02299> 27 Sept. 2016.

Woods, R.W., “IRS Power To Revoke Passports Signed Into Law” (2015) <www.forbes.com/sites/robertwood/2015/12/04/irs-power-over-passports-signed-into-law/#3a35522a2030> 27 Sept. 2016.

Zucman, G., "Taxing across Borders: Tracking Personal Wealth and Corporate Profits" (2014) 28 *Journal of Economic Perspectives* 4, 121.

Index

About the Author

Clinton Donnelly manages Donnelly Tax Law (donnellytaxlaw.com), which specializes in income taxes compliance for US citizens living abroad and foreigners with US filing needs. He has saved his clients millions of dollars in IRS penalties. His firm does tax returns, tax amnesty, and tax debt resolution. He has CPAs, Enrolled Agents, and lawyers working for him.

He is an Enrolled Agent licensed by the IRS and authorized to represent US taxpayers worldwide. To be an Enrolled Agent, he had to pass three days of intensive examinations. (He does NOT work for the IRS.)

His law degree is in international laws of finance and banking from the University of Liverpool. He has an undergraduate degree Computer Science. He has been a very successful businessman all his life. Presently, he lives in the Republic of Panama.

www.ingramcontent.com/pod-product-compliance
Lightning Source LLC
LaVergne TN
LVHW052250200926
848481LV00002B/322
9780998672502